Good footpath — — — —
(sufficiently distinct to b____

Intermittent footpath
(difficult to follow in mist)

Route recommended
    but no path
(if recommended one way only, arrow indicates direction)

Wall ◦◦◦◦◦◦◦◦◦◦◦◦◦   Broken wall • • • • • • • • • • •

Fence —+—+—+—+—   Broken fence ııııııııııııııııı

Marshy ground ⋎⋎⋎⋎⋎   Trees ⚭⚭⚭⚭⚭⚭

Crags ⛰⛰⛰⛰   Boulders ⬡⬡⬡⬡⬡

Stream or River
        (arrow indicates direction of flow)

Waterfall ⌇⌇⌇   Bridge

Buildings ▪▪▪   Unenclosed road ∷∷∷∷∷∷∷∷∷

Contours (at 100' intervals) ⋯⋯⋯ 1900
                                    1800
                                    1700

Summit-cairn ▲   Other (prominent) cairns △

THE
SOUTHERN
FELLS

A PICTORIAL GUIDE

TO THE

LAKELAND FELLS

being an illustrated account
of a study and exploration
of the mountains in the
English Lake District

by

A Wainwright

BOOK FOUR
THE SOUTHERN FELLS

MICHAEL JOSEPH LTD

Published by the Penguin Group
27 Wrights Lane, London W8, England

Penguin Books Ltd Registered Offices:
Harmondsworth, Middlesex, England

First published by Michael Joseph
1992
Originally published by the Westmorland Gazette, 1960

Printed by Titus Wilson and Son, Kendal

ISBN 0 7181 4003 6

PUBLISHED

by

MICHAEL JOSEPH

LONDON

This book was previously published by

WESTMORLAND GAZETTE

Publishers in Kendal

Gladstone's Finger,
Gladstone Knott,
Crinkle Crags

Publisher's Note

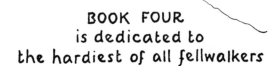

BOOK FOUR
is dedicated to
the hardiest of all fellwalkers

THE SHEEP OF LAKELAND

the truest lovers of the mountains,
their natural homes
and providers of their food and shelter,

Classification and Definition

Any division of the Lakeland fells into geographical districts must necessarily be arbitrary, just as the location of the outer boundaries of Lakeland must always be a matter of opinion. Any attempt to define internal or external boundaries is certain to invite criticism, and he who takes it upon himself to say where Lakeland starts and finishes, or, for example, where the Central Fells merge into the Southern Fells and *which* fells are the Central Fells and which the Southern and *why* they need be so classified, must not expect his pronouncements to be generally accepted.

Yet for present purposes some plan of classification and definition must be used. County and parochial boundaries are no help, nor is the recently-defined area of the Lakeland National Park, for this book is concerned only with the high ground.

First, the external boundaries.   Straight lines linking the extremities of the outlying lakes enclose all the higher fells very conveniently. There are a few fells of lesser height to the north and east, however, that are typically Lakeland in character and cannot properly be omitted : these are brought in, somewhat untidily, by extending the lines in those areas. Thus:

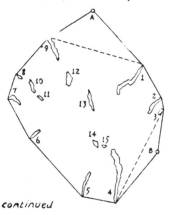

1 : *Ullswater*
2 : *Hawes Water*
3 : proposed *Swindale Rest*
4 : *Windermere*
5 : *Coniston Water*
6 : *Wast Water*
7 : *Ennerdale Water*
8 : *Loweswater*
9 : *Bassenthwaite Lake*
10 : *Crummock Water*
11 : *Buttermere*
12 : *Derwent Water*
13 : *Thirlmere*
14 : *Grasmere*
15 : *Rydal Water*
A : *Caldbeck*
B : *Longsleddale (church)*

continued

Classification and Definition

continued

The complete Guide is planned to include all the fells in the area enclosed by the straight lines of the diagram. This is an undertaking quite beyond the compass of a single volume, and it is necessary, therefore, to divide the area into convenient sections, making the fullest use of natural boundaries (lakes, valleys and low passes) so that each district is, as far as possible, self-contained and independent of the rest.

This division gives seven areas, each with a well-defined group of fells, and each will be the subject of a separate volume

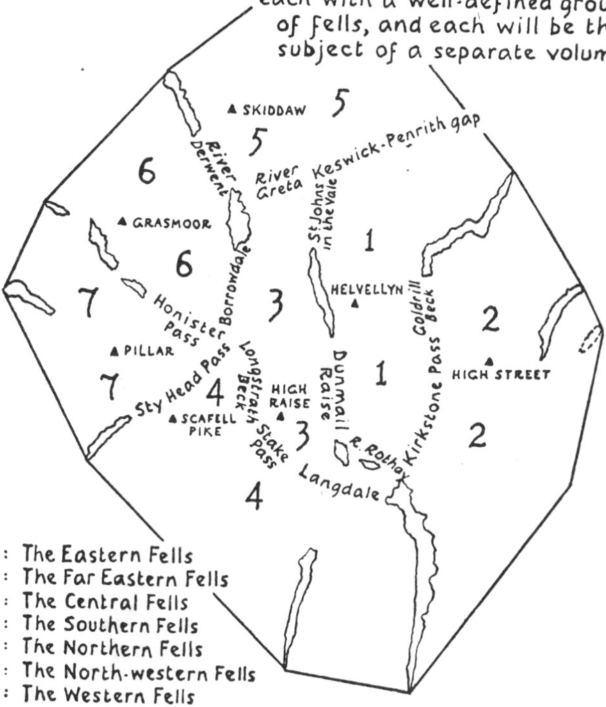

1: The Eastern Fells
2: The Far Eastern Fells
3: The Central Fells
4: The Southern Fells
5: The Northern Fells
6: The North-western Fells
7: The Western Fells

INTRODUCTION

Notes on the Illustrations

THE MAPS.................. Many excellent books have been written
about Lakeland, but the best literature of all for the walker
is that published by the Director General of Ordnance Survey,
the 1" map for companionship and guidance on expeditions, the
2½" map for exploration both on the fells and by the fireside.
These admirable maps are remarkably accurate topographically
but there is a crying need for a revision of the paths on the hills:
several walkers' tracks that have come into use during the past
few decades, some of them now broad highways, are not shown at
all; other paths still shown on the maps have fallen into neglect
and can no longer be traced on the ground.

    The popular Bartholomew 1" map is a
beautiful picture, fit for a frame, but this
too is unreliable for paths; indeed here the
defect is much more serious, for routes are
indicated where no paths ever existed, nor
ever could — the cartographer has preferred
to take precipices in his stride rather than
deflect his graceful curves over easy ground.

    Hence the justification for the maps in this book: they have
the one merit (of importance to walkers) of being dependable as
regards delineation of *paths*. They are intended as supplements
to the Ordnance Survey maps, certainly not as substitutes

THE VIEWS............... Various devices have
been used to illustrate the views from the
summits of the fells. The full panorama
in the form of an outline drawing is most
satisfactory generally, and this method
has been adopted for the main viewpoints.

THE DIAGRAMS OF ASCENTS.................... The routes of ascent
of the higher fells are depicted by diagrams that do not pretend
to strict accuracy: they are neither plans
nor elevations; in fact there is deliberate
distortion in order to show detail clearly:
usually they are represented as viewed
from imaginary 'space-stations.' But it is
hoped they will be useful and interesting.

THE DRAWINGS....... The drawings at least are honest attempts
to reproduce what the eye sees: they illustrate features of
interest and also serve the dual purpose of breaking up the
text and balancing the layout of the pages, and of filling up
awkward blank spaces, like this:

Thirlmere

THE
SOUTHERN
FELLS

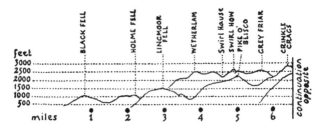

The Southern Fells comprise two well-defined mountain systems.

The larger is the Scafell-Bowfell massif, which forms a great arc around the head of Eskdale; it is bounded by Wasdale in the west, and eastwards by the headwaters of the Duddon and the Brathay, while to the north the high ground descends into Borrowdale and Great Langdale.   Within this area the fells are the highest, the roughest and the grandest in Lakeland: they are of volcanic origin and the naked rock is much in evidence in the form of towering crags and wildernesses of boulders and scree. Progress on foot across these arid wastes is slow and often laborious, but there is an exhilarating feeling of freedom and sense of achievement on the airy ridges poised high above deep valleys. This is magnificent territory for the fellwalker. There is nothing better than this.

The smaller group, the Coniston fells, rises east of the Duddon and west of Yewdale; the Brathay is the northern boundary. Compact, distinctive, with several summits of uniform height just above 2500' the slaty Coniston fells bear many industrial scars which detract little from the general excellence of the scenery and, indeed, provide an added interest. The dry turfy ridges are a joy to tread.

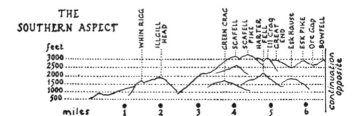

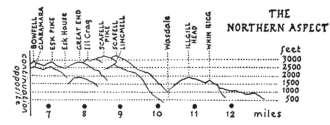

The rugged heights of the Southern Fells are set off to perfection by the lovely valleys leading into them, and much of the pleasure of mountain days spent in this region is contributed by the delightful approaches. The valleys have strongly individual characteristics—— Great Langdale has glorious curves and a simple grandeur; Wasdale is primitive and unspoiled, an emerald amongst sombre hills; Borrowdale has enchanting recesses and side·valleys; the Duddon is newly afforested —yet all are alike in their sparkling radiance, in their verdant freshness. But precedence must be granted to Eskdale, the one valley that gives full allegiance to the Southern Fells and in some ways the most delectable of all. This is a valley where walkers really come into their own, a sanctuary of peace and solitude, a very special preserve for those who travel on foot.

The provision of accommodation is a major industry in Borrowdale and Great Langdale, and at Coniston, but is strictly limited in the remote, less accessible and sparsely populated southern valleys. In summertime, in all the valleys serving the area, the available accommodation is fully taxed, and seekers after beds and breakfasts are advised to arrange each night's lodging in advance.

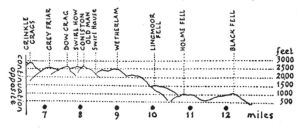

THE SOUTHERN FELLS

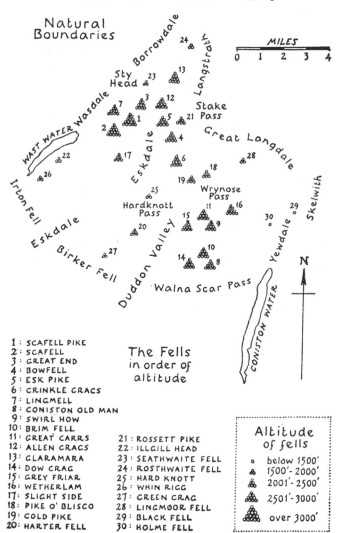

Natural Boundaries

MILES
0 1 2 3 4

The Fells in order of altitude

1 : SCAFELL PIKE
2 : SCAFELL
3 : GREAT END
4 : BOWFELL
5 : ESK PIKE
6 : CRINKLE CRAGS
7 : LINGMELL
8 : CONISTON OLD MAN
9 : SWIRL HOW
10 : BRIM FELL
11 : GREAT CARRS
12 : ALLEN CRAGS
13 : GLARAMARA
14 : DOW CRAG
15 : GREY FRIAR
16 : WETHERLAM
17 : SLIGHT SIDE
18 : PIKE O' BLISCO
19 : COLD PIKE
20 : HARTER FELL

21 : ROSSETT PIKE
22 : ILLGILL HEAD
23 : SEATHWAITE FELL
24 : ROSTHWAITE FELL
25 : HARD KNOTT
26 : WHIN RIGG
27 : GREEN CRAG
28 : LINGMOOR FELL
29 : BLACK FELL
30 : HOLME FELL

Altitude of fells

○ below 1500'
♠ 1500'- 2000'
♠ 2001'- 2500'
♠ 2501'- 3000'
♠ over 3000'

THE SOUTHERN FELLS

in the order of their appearance in this book

Each fell is the subject of a separate chapter

Allen Crags

from Sprinkling Tarn

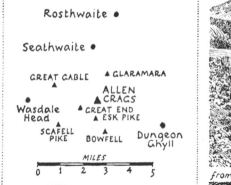

Rosthwaite •

Seathwaite •

GREAT GABLE ▲ ▲ GLARAMARA

▲ ALLEN
CRAGS

• ▲ CREAT END
Wasdale ▲ ESK PIKE
Head

SCAFELL ▲ ▲ • Dungeon
PIKE BOWFELL Ghyll

MILES

0 1 2 3 4 5

from Ruddy Gill

NATURAL FEATURES

Some fells there are, of respectable height, of distinct merit as viewpoints, and often in fine situations, which never seem to attract or challenge walkers and have no place in fireside memories of Lakeland: they are 'left for another day', habitually passed by, and rarely find mention in print or conversation. Such a one is Allen Crags, grandly positioned overlooking Esk Hause; it is really in the heart of things and on intimate terms with Bowfell, the Scafells and Great Gable — old favourites, glorious objectives for a day's walk and climbed many thousands of times every year. But did anyone, apart from an odd guide-book writer or other eccentric, ever set forth from Wasdale or Borrowdale or Langdale with the sole unswerving purpose of climbing Allen Crags?

It is true that the summit is frequently traversed, but only because it lies athwart the fine ridge between Esk Hause and Glaramara and so cannot well be avoided on this journey. The ridge must properly be regarded as the most northerly extremity of the Scafell structure for the Esk Hause-Sty Head path, which is often thought to mark its furthest extension, merely runs along a high shelf, geographically insignificant, across the gradual fall to valley-level. The Scafell massif has its northern roots in Borrowdale.

The two principal summits on the ridge are Allen Crags and Glaramara. The former is slightly the higher, but Glaramara has the greater appeal and is a popular ascent. A low depression between them, occupied by a cluster of miniature tarns, is a convenient common boundary. On the crest of Allen Crags walking is simple, but rocky outcrops occur everywhere. To east and west the fell is clearly defined, with a rough declivity to Allencrags Gill on the east flank and an easier slope, characterised by grey slabs, descending to Grains Gill westwards.

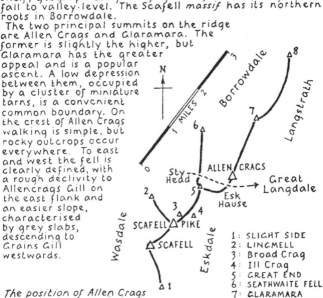

1: SLIGHT SIDE
2: LINGMELL
3: BROAD CRAG
4: ILL CRAG
5: GREAT END
6: SEATHWAITE FELL
7: GLARAMARA
8: ROSTHWAITE FELL

The position of Allen Crags in the Scafell ridge system

MAP

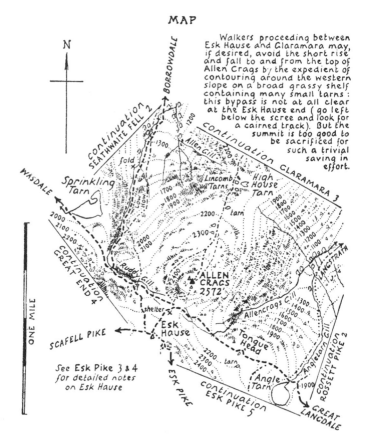

Walkers proceeding between Esk Hause and Glaramara may, if desired, avoid the short rise and fall to and from the top of Allen Crags by the expedient of contouring around the western slope on a broad grassy shelf containing many small tarns: this bypass is not at all clear at the Esk Hause end (go left below the scree and look for a cairned track). But the summit is too good to be sacrificed for such a trivial saving in effort.

See Esk Pike 3 & 4 for detailed notes on Esk Hause

Attention is drawn to a new variation path recently brought into use to cut off the sharp corner of Ruddy Gill. Particularly in ascending from Borrowdale the variation is not easily located although its course will be obvious from the old bridle path above Low How: it starts across marshy ground from the old path, then climbs steeply up a grass bank, with frequent cairns, to easy ground above, Ruddy Gill being met and crossed just at the point where the ravine commences. In descending from Esk Hause it is more likely to be noticed, as a narrow grassy trod.

This variation will probably become popular as the usual well-beaten path alongside Ruddy Gill, already unpleasantly stony, deteriorates still further, and, when its roughnesses are smoothed out by foot-traffic, will save a few minutes for anyone journeying between Borrowdale and Esk Hause. Its scenery and views, however, do not compare favourably with those of Ruddy Gill.

ASCENT FROM BORROWDALE
2250 feet of ascent : 4½ miles from Seatoller
(4 miles via Allen Gill)

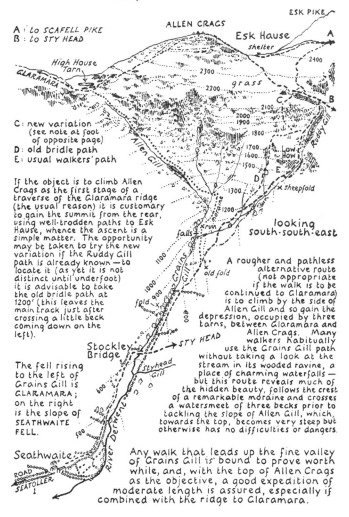

A: to SCAFELL PIKE
B: to STY HEAD

ALLEN CRAGS

ESK PIKE

Esk Hause
shelter

High House Tarn

CLARAMARA

2400

2300

2200

grass

2100

2000
1900

1800

1700
1600
1500

1300

1200

Low How

Ruddy Gill

sheepfold

C: new variation
(see note at foot
of opposite page)
D: old bridle path
E: usual walkers' path

Allen Gill

looking
south-south-east

If the object is to climb Allen
Crags as the first stage of a
traverse of the Glaramara ridge
(the usual reason) it is customary
to gain the summit from the rear,
using well-trodden paths to Esk
Hause, whence the ascent is a
simple matter. The opportunity
may be taken to try the new
variation if the Ruddy Gill
path is already known — to
locate it (as yet it is not
distinct until underfoot)
it is advisable to take
the old bridle path at
1200' (this leaves the
main track just after
crossing a little beck
coming down on the
left).

A rougher and pathless
alternative route
(not appropriate
if the walk is to be
continued to Glaramara)
is to climb by the side of
Allen Gill and so gain the
depression, occupied by three
tarns, between Glaramara and
Allen Crags. Many
walkers habitually
use the Grains Gill path
without taking a look at
the stream in its wooded ravine, a
place of charming waterfalls —
but this route reveals much of
the hidden beauty, follows the crest
of a remarkable moraine and crosses
a watersmeet of three becks prior to
tackling the slope of Allen Gill, which,
towards the top, becomes very steep but
otherwise has no difficulties or dangers.

x ruin
falls
Grains Gill
old fold
fold
1100
1000 900
600

Stockley
Bridge

STY HEAD

Styhead Gill

The fell rising
to the left of
Grains Gill is
CLARAMARA;
on the right
is the slope of
SEATHWAITE FELL.

Seathwaite

ROAD
SEATOLLER
1

River Derwent

500

Any walk that leads up the fine valley
of Grains Gill is bound to prove worth
while, and, with the top of Allen Crags
as the objective, a good expedition of
moderate length is assured, especially if
combined with the ridge to Glaramara.

THE SUMMIT

CLARAMARA
(main summit)

This quiet, attractive top is a pleasant refuge from the busy thoroughfares converging on Esk Hause, only five minutes away. Unexpectedly there are three good cairns on the twenty yards of level summit, that in the middle, set on a rock, being slightly the highest. Patches of stones and low outcrops add an interest to the top of the fell but the distant views will appeal more.

DESCENTS: The quickest and easiest way to anywhere is to go down the short south slope to the Esk Hause shelter and make use of the good paths there found, which bring Great Langdale, Wasdale or Borrowdale within an hour and a half's march. *In mist*, the smallest of the three cairns serves a useful function, as an indicator of the direction of Esk Hause. A small crag to the right of the route makes it desirable to keep to the sketchy path if possible, or, if not, to proceed warily.

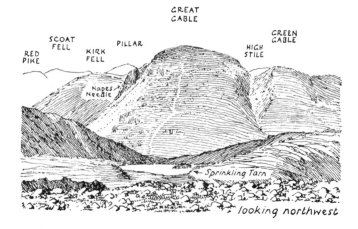

GREAT
GABLE

SCOAT
FELL   PILLAR   GREEN
                                                GABLE
RED   KIRK   HIGH
PIKE   FELL   STILE

Napes
Needle

←Sprinkling Tarn

→ *looking northwest*

THE VIEW

The high shadowed walls of the Bowfell and Scafell groups effectively close the southern horizon at close quarters (although there is a distant view to Black Combe over Esk Hause) and from this viewpoint appear sombre, gloomy and unattractive.

Interest lies mainly in the northern arc, where there is a wealth of detail, all of it pleasant to behold, Borrowdale and its environs making a beautiful picture. It may be noted that from this summit (and no other) the two High Raises are seen, one beyond the other, in a direct line, but this is hardly worth writing home about.

The furrowed precipice of Great End holds the attention, but the finest mountain scene is provided by Great Gable, and keen eyes may detect the black silhouette of Napes Needle on its steep southern slope.

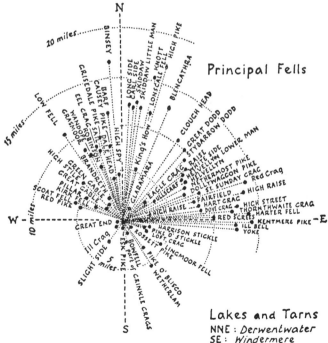

Principal Fells

Lakes and Tarns

NNE : Derwentwater
SE : Windermere
SE : Wise Een Tarn

NW to NE : tarns on Allen Crags
NW : Sprinkling Tarn and other tarns on Seathwaite Fell

RIDGE ROUTE

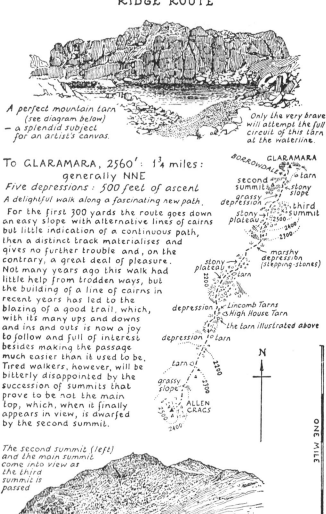

A perfect mountain tarn (see diagram below) – a splendid subject for an artist's canvas.

Only the very brave will attempt the full circuit of this tarn at the waterline.

To GLARAMARA, 2560': 1¼ miles:
generally NNE
Five depressions : 500 feet of ascent
A delightful walk along a fascinating new path.

For the first 300 yards the route goes down an easy slope with alternative lines of cairns but little indication of a continuous path, then a distinct track materialises and gives no further trouble and, on the contrary, a great deal of pleasure. Not many years ago this walk had little help from trodden ways, but the building of a line of cairns in recent years has led to the blazing of a good trail, which, with its many ups and downs and ins and outs is now a joy to follow and full of interest besides making the passage much easier than it used to be. Tired walkers, however, will be bitterly disappointed by the succession of summits that prove to be not the main top, which, when it finally appears in view, is dwarfed by the second summit.

GLARAMARA
BORROWDALE
second summit
tarn
stony slope
grassy depression
third summit
stony plateau
2500
2400
2300
marshy depression (stepping-stones)
stony plateau
2200
tarn
depression
Lincomb Tarns
High House Tarn
the tarn illustrated above
depression
tarn
tarn
2200
grassy slope
2300
ALLEN CRAGS
2500
2400

N

ONE MILE

The second summit (left) and the main summit come into view as the third summit is passed

Great End
from Allen Crags

Allen Crags from Grains Gill

Black Fell

1056'

Ambleside ●
Skelwith ● Bridge

▲
BLACK FELL

Hawkshead ●

● Coniston

MILES
0 1 2 3 4

from Tarn Hows

MAP

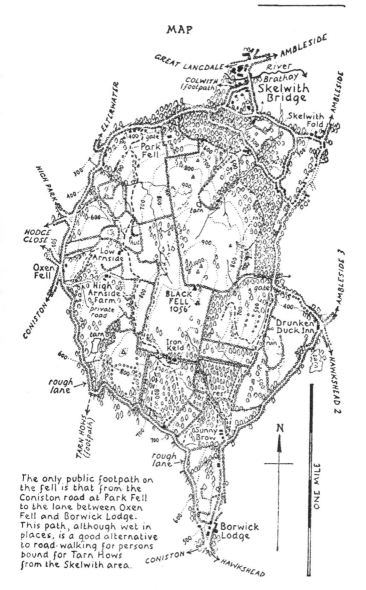

The only public footpath on the fell is that from the Coniston road at Park Fell to the lane between Oxen Fell and Borwick Lodge. This path, although wet in places, is a good alternative to road-walking for persons bound for Tarn Hows from the Skelwith area.

NATURAL FEATURES

Everybody knows Tarn Hows, but few the summit of the fell rising behind, above immature plantations and slopes richly clothed in bracken, to the north-east. This is Black Fell, springing rather steeply in dense woodlands from the Brathay at Skelwith and occupying a considerable area between the Ambleside-Coniston road on the west and the fields of Outgate to the east. It is thus isolated from other high ground, and because it is the first substantial elevation west of the head of Windermere the view in that direction is particularly good.

ASCENTS

None of the paths on the fell is continuous to the summit; a simple walk across grass from the main bridleway west of Iron Keld, however, soon brings it underfoot, and this is the easiest route to the top. Starts up the east flank may quickly lead to desperate manœuvres in thick plantations. *

THE SUMMIT

The highest point is a small outcrop with the ambitious name of Black Crag, and is given further distinction by the erection thereon of a triangulation column of the standard pattern to which has been affixed the extra adornment of the familiar metal symbol of the National Trust (this has been defaced by the scratched initials of visitors of the type who seem to see in this practice a chance of immortality.

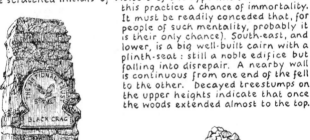

It must be readily conceded that, for people of such mentality, probably it is their only chance). South-east, and lower, is a big well-built cairn with a plinth-seat: still a noble edifice but falling into disrepair. A nearby wall is continuous from one end of the fell to the other. Decayed treestumps on the upper heights indicate that once the woods extended almost to the top.

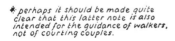

* perhaps it should be made quite clear that this latter note is also intended for the guidance of walkers, not of courting couples.

The south-east cairn

THE VIEW

The lovely countryside around the head of Windermere is delightfully pictured, this being the best viewpoint for the sylvan charms of the area between Ambleside, Wray Castle and Hawkshead. Southwards, Coniston Water is seen above the indented and wooded shores of Tarn Hows, which appears as beautiful as ever but a trifle foreign to the district. The mountain scene, although restricted, is good, the Langdale Pikes being especially well displayed. There is a peep of Scafell Pike, just overtopping the north ridge of the Crinkles. North, the various tops of the Helvellyn range are not seen distinctively, the mass appearing as a single mountain.

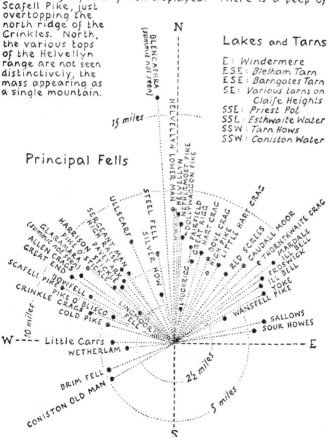

Lakes and Tarns

E : Windermere
ESE : Blelham Tarn
ESE : Barngates Tarn
SE : Various tarns on Claife Heights
SSE : Priest Pot
SSE : Esthwaite Water
SSW : Tarn Hows
SSW : Coniston Water

Principal Fells

Bowfell

'Bow·Fell' (two words)
on Ordnance Survey maps

2960'

from Lingmoor Fell

NATURAL FEATURES

A favourite of all fellwalkers, Bowfell is a mountain that commands attention whenever it appears in a view. And more than attention, respect and admiration, too; for it has the rare characteristic of displaying a graceful outline and a sturdy shapeliness on all sides. The fell occupies a splendid position at the hub of three well-known valleys, Great Langdale, Langstrath and Eskdale, rising as a massive pyramid at the head of each, and it is along these valleys that its waters drain, soon assuming the size of rivers. The higher the slopes rise the rougher they become, finally rearing up steeply as a broken rim of rock around the peaked summit and stony top. These crags are of diverse and unusual form, natural curiosities that add an exceptional interest and help to identify Bowfell in the memory. Under the terraced northern precipices, in a dark hollow, is Angle Tarn.

As much as any other mountain, the noble Bowfell may be regarded as affording an entirely typical Lakeland climb, with easy walking over grass giving place to rough scrambling on scree, and a summit deserving of detailed exploration and rewarding visitors with very beautiful views.

Rank Bowfell among the best half-dozen! ✳

✳The author is not prepared to say, at this stage, which he considers to be the other five. This opinion will be given in the last pages of Book Seven.

● Stonethwaite

▲ GLARAMARA

Wasdale ●
Head

▲ ESK PIKE

▲
SCAFELL PIKE

▲ BOWFELL

● Dungeon Ghyll

CRINKLE CRAGS ▲

Boot ●

MILES

0 1 2 3 4 5

MAP

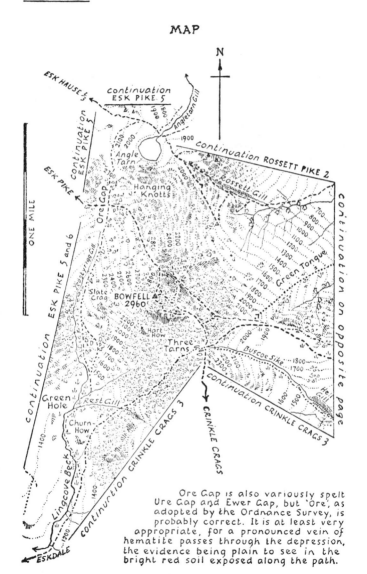

Ore Gap is also variously spelt Ure Gap and Ewer Gap, but 'Ore', as adopted by the Ordnance Survey, is probably correct. It is at least very appropriate, for a pronounced vein of hematite passes through the depression, the evidence being plain to see in the bright red soil exposed along the path.

MAP

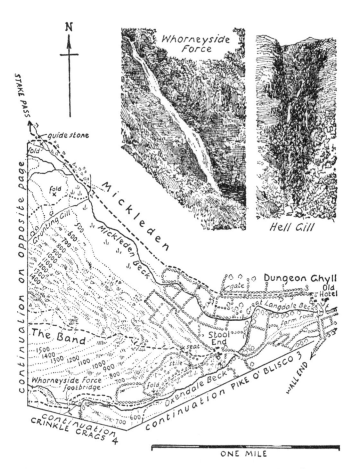

Whorneyside Force

Hell Gill

ONE MILE

The county boundary between Cumberland and Westmorland passes over the top of Bowfell, coming up from Wrynose Pass via Crinkle Crags and Three Tarns. From the summit it follows the height of land to Hanging Knotts, where the main ridge is left in favour of the lesser watershed of Rossett Pass, whence it continues the circuit of Mickleden. Thus, Great Langdale and all the waters thereof are wholly within Westmorland.

ASCENT FROM DUNGEON GHYLL
2700 feet of ascent : 3 miles (3¼ via Three Tarns)

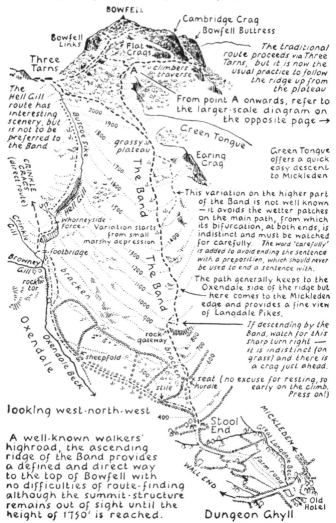

BOWFELL

Bowfell Links

Cambridge Crag
Bowfell Buttress

Flat Crags

Three Tarns

A

climbers traverse

The traditional route proceeds via Three Tarns, but it is now the usual practice to follow the ridge up from the plateau

From point A onwards, refer to the larger-scale diagram on the opposite page →

The Hell Gill route has interesting scenery, but is not to be preferred to the Band

CRINKLE CRAGS (direct route)

Buscoe Sike

2000
1900
1800
1700
1600
1500

grassy plateau

The Band

Green Tongue

Earing Crag

Green Tongue offers a quick easy descent to Mickleden

Crinkle Gill

Hell Gill

Whorneyside Force

Variation starts from small marshy depression

1400
1300
1200
1100
1000
900

footbridge

Browney Gill

rock tor

bracken

The Band

This variation on the higher part of the Band is not well known — it avoids the wetter patches on the main path, from which its bifurcation, at both ends, is indistinct and must be watched for carefully. The word 'carefully' is added to avoid ending the sentence with a preposition, which should never be used to end a sentence with.

The path generally keeps to the Oxendale side of the ridge but here comes to the Mickleden edge and provides a fine view of Langdale Pikes.

If descending by the Band, watch for this sharp turn right — it is indistinct (on grass) and there is a crag just ahead.

Oxendale

Oxendale Beck

rock gateway

800
700
600
500

sheepfold

bracken

stile

seat (no excuse for resting, so early on the climb. Press on!)

hurdle

looking west·north·west

400

Stool End

MICKLEDEN

Great Langdale Beck

A well-known walkers' highroad, the ascending ridge of the Band provides a defined and direct way to the top of Bowfell with no difficulties of route-finding although the summit·structure remains out of sight until the height of 1750' is reached.

WALL END

farm road

Old Hotel

Dungeon Ghyll

ASCENT FROM DUNGEON GHYLL

The upper section,
looking west

BB : Bowfell Buttress
CC : Cambridge Crag
FC : Flat Crag

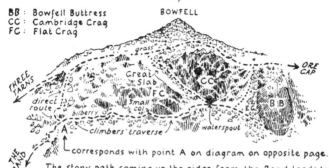

BOWFELL

grass

THREE TARNS

Great Slab

CC

ORE GAP

direct route

FC

Small col

bilberry

BB

EC

waterspout

A

climbers' traverse

THE BAND

└ corresponds with point A on diagram on opposite page.

The stony path coming up the ridge from the Band leads to, and is continued as, the climbers' traverse. Ten yards below the point where the horizontal traverse commences the direct route wiggles away up to the left and may be passed unnoticed.

The climbers' traverse is a very enjoyable high-level route leading to excellent rock-scenery. Two recent minor rockfalls have slightly disturbed the path but it is quite distinct and perfectly easy, with a very little very mild scrambling, hardly worth mentioning. The traverse is a series of little ups and downs, but generally keeps to a horizontal course. Except at the small col the ground falls away steeply on the valley side of the path.

The best way off the traverse to the summit lies up the fringe of a 'river' of boulders along the south side of Cambridge Crag, or, more tediously, the wide scree gully between Cambridge Crag and Bowfell Buttress may be ascended. (Cambridge Crag is identifiable, beyond all doubt, by the waterspout gushing from the base of the cliff — and nothing better ever came out of a barrel or a bottle).

The climbers' traverse

The striations of Flat Crags are of particular interest, even to non-geologists. Note how the angle of tilt is repeated in the slope of the Great Slab.

ASCENT FROM WASDALE

Although Bowfell is well hidden from Wasdale Head it is not too distant to be climbed from there in comfortable time, but the walk has the disadvantage (for those who object to re-tracing footsteps) that very little variation of route is possible on the return journey to Wasdale Head. Esk Pike stands in the way and must be climbed first (and traversed later).

FOR a diagram of the ascent of Esk Pike from Wasdale Head see Esk Pike 9

ASCENT FROM MICKLEDEN
2500 feet of ascent. 1¼ miles from the sheepfold

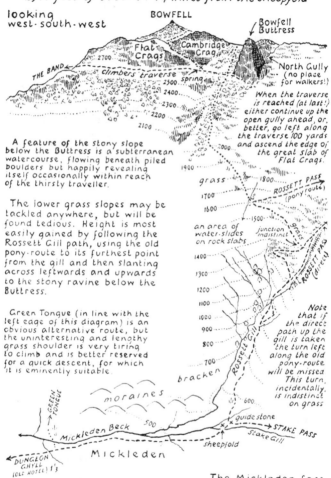

looking
west·south·west

BOWFELL

↓ Bowfell Buttress

THE BAND

Flat Crags

Cambridge Crag

climbers traverse

2700..

2500..

2400..

2300..

2200..

2100..

North Gully
(no place
for walkers!)

spring

When the traverse is reached (at last!) either continue up the open gully ahead, or, better, go left along the traverse 100 yards and ascend the edge of the great slab of Flat Crags.

A feature of the stony slope below the Buttress is a subterranean watercourse, flowing beneath piled boulders but happily revealing itself occasionally within reach of the thirsty traveller.

2000..

1900..

grass

1800..

ROSSETT PASS
(pony route)

1700..

1600..

1500..

The lower grass slopes may be tackled anywhere, but will be found tedious. Height is most easily gained by following the Rossett Gill path, using the old pony-route to its furthest point from the gill and then slanting across leftwards and upwards to the stony ravine below the Buttress.

an area of water-slides on rock slabs

junction indistinct

grass

1400..

1300..

1200..

1100..

1000..

900..

800..

ROSSETT PASS (direct)

Green Tongue (in line with the left edge of this diagram) is an obvious alternative route, but the uninteresting and lengthy grass shoulder is very tiring to climb and is better reserved for a quick descent, for which it is eminently suitable.

Note that if the direct path up the gill is taken the turn left along the old pony-route will be missed. This turn, incidentally, is indistinct on grass

700..

bracken

moraines

600..

500..

GREEN TONGUE

Mickleden Beck

Mickleden

guide stone

→ STAKE PASS

Stake Gill

sheepfold

← DUNGEON GHYLL
(OLD HOTEL) 1⅓

The Mickleden face, 2500 feet of continuous ascent, is a route for scramblers rather than walkers. The rock-scenery becomes imposing as height is gained, Bowfell Buttress in particular being an impressive object when seen at close quarters.

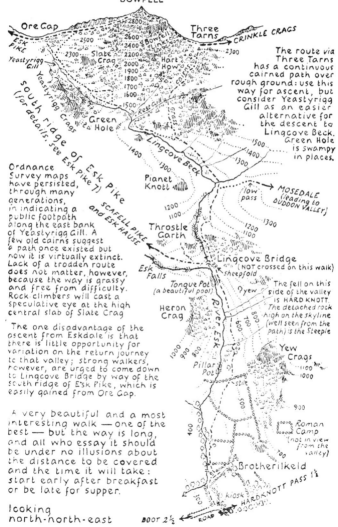

ASCENT FROM ESKDALE
2900 feet of ascent : 7½ miles from Boot

BOWFELL

Ore Gap

Three Tarns

CRINKLE CRAGS

ESK PIKE

2800
2700
2600
Bowfell 2500
Links 2400
Slate 2200
Crag 2100
Hart 2000
How 1900
1800
1700
1600
1500

2300

2300

Yeastyrigg Gill

Yeastyrigg Crags (for details, see Esk Pike 7)

south ridge of Esk Pike

Green Hole

Rest Gill

Lingcove Beck

1500
1400
1300

The route via Three Tarns has a continuous cairned path over rough ground: use this way for ascent, but consider Yeastyrigg Gill as an easier alternative for the descent to Lingcove Beck. Green Hole is swampy in places.

Ordnance Survey maps have persisted, through many generations, in indicating a public footpath along the east bank of Yeastyrigg Gill. A few old cairns suggest a path once existed but now it is virtually extinct. Lack of a trodden route does not matter, however, because the way is grassy and free from difficulty. Rock-climbers will cast a speculative eye at the high central slab of Slate Crag

SCAFELL PIKE AND ESK HAUSE

Planet Knott

1400
1300
1200
1100

low pass

MOSEDALE (leading to DUDDON VALLEY)

1300
1200
1100

Throstle Garth

Esk Falls

Tongue Pot (a beautiful pool)

Heron Crag

Lingcove Bridge (NOT crossed on this walk)
sheepfold

900 yew

River Esk

The fell on this side of the valley is HARD KNOTT. The detached rock high on the skyline (well seen from the path) is the Steeple

The one disadvantage of the ascent from Eskdale is that there is little opportunity for variation on the return journey to that valley; strong walkers, however, are urged to come down to Lingcove Bridge by way of the south ridge of Esk Pike, which is easily gained from Ore Gap.

Pillar Pot

1000
900

stile

800
700

600

Yew Crags

1100
1000

900

A very beautiful and a most interesting walk — one of the best — but the way is long, and all who essay it should be under no illusions about the distance to be covered and the time it will take: start early after breakfast or be late for supper.

500

400

Roman Camp (not in view from the valley)

700

Brotherilkeld

kiosk

HARDKNOTT PASS 1½

300

200

100

looking north-north-east

BOOT 2½

ROAD

ASCENT FROM STONETHWAITE
2650 feet of ascent : 6½ miles

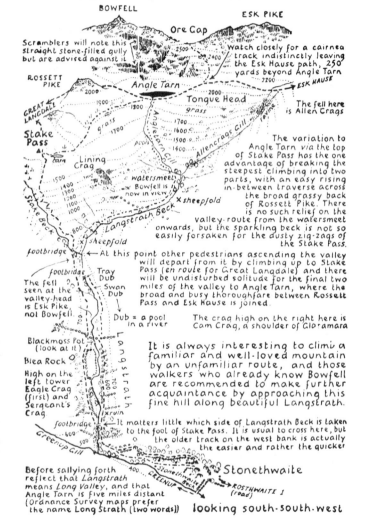

BOWFELL

ESK PIKE

Ore Gap

Scramblers will note this straight stone-filled gully but are advised against it

Watch closely for a cairned track indistinctly leaving the Esk Hause path, 250 yards beyond Angle Tarn

2500

2400

2200

ROSSETT PIKE

Angle Tarn

2000

ESK HAUSE

2000

1900

1800

Tongue Head   grass

The fell here is Allen Crags

GREAT LANGDALE

grass

1700

1600

1500

1400

Stake Pass

1700

Tarn

Lining Crag

watersmeet Bowfell is now in view

The variation to Angle Tarn via the top of Stake Pass has the one advantage of breaking the steepest climbing into two parts, with an easy rising in-between traverse across the broad grassy back of Rossett Pike. There is no such relief on the valley-route from the watersmeet onwards, but the sparkling beck is not so easily forsaken for the dusty zig-zags of the Stake Pass.

1500
1400
1300
1200
1100
1000

x sheepfold

Allencrags Gill

Angletarn Gill

Langstrath Beck

800

x sheepfold

footbridge

At this point other pedestrians ascending the valley will depart from it by climbing up to Stake Pass (en route for Great Langdale) and there will be undisturbed solitude for the final two miles of the valley to Angle Tarn, where the broad and busy thoroughfare between Rossett Pass and Esk Hause is joined

footbridge

Tray Dub

Swan Dub

The fell seen at the valley-head is Esk Pike, not Bowfell

Dub = a pool in a river

The crag high on the right here is Cam Crag, a shoulder of Glaramara

Blackmoss Pot (look at it)

Bica Rock

High on the left tower Eagle Crag (first) and Sergeant's Crag

Langstrath

600

It is always interesting to climb a familiar and well-loved mountain by an unfamiliar route, and those walkers who already know Bowfell are recommended to make further acquaintance by approaching this fine hill along beautiful Langstrath.

ruin

footbridge

600

Greenup Gill

500

It matters little which side of Langstrath Beck is taken to the foot of Stake Pass. It is usual to cross here, but the older track on the west bank is actually the easier and rather the quicker

Before sallying forth reflect that Langstrath means Long Valley, and that Angle Tarn is five miles distant (Ordnance Survey maps prefer the name Long Strath (two words))

400

GREENUP

Stonethwaite

Stonethwaite

ROSTHWAITE 1 (road)

looking south-south-west

Cambridge Crag and Bowfell Buttress
from the top of the Great Slab

THE SUMMIT

Bowfell's top is a shattered pyramid, a great heap of stones and boulders and naked rock, a giant cairn in itself.

The rugged summit provides poor picking for the Bowfell sheep, who draw the line at mosses and lichens and look elsewhere for their mountain greenery, and reserves its best rewards for the walkers who climb the natural rocky stairway to its upper limit for here, spread before them for their delectation, is a glorious panorama, which, moreover, may be surveyed and appreciated from positions of repose on the comfortable flat seats of stone (comfortable in the sense that everybody arriving here says how nice it is to sit down) with which the summit is liberally equipped. The leisurely contemplation of the scene will not be assailed by doubts as to whether the highest point has in fact been gained for rough slopes tumble away steeply on all sides.

The top pyramid stands on a sloping plinth which, to the east, extends beyond the base of the pyramid and forms a shelf or terrace where stones are less in evidence. It is from this shelf that Bowfell's main crags fall away, and from which, with care, they may be viewed; care is necessary because the boulders to be negotiated in carrying out this inspection are in a state of balance, in places, and liable to heel over and trap a leg.

It is possible, and does happen, that walkers ascend Bowfell and traverse its top quite unaware of the imposing line of crags overlooking Mickleden: from the summit and the shelf-track there is little to indicate the presence of steep cliffs. But to miss seeing the crags is to miss seeing half the glory of Bowfell.

THE SUMMIT

continued

KEY:

		for ROCK CLIMBERS	for WALKERS
NG :	North Gully	✓	-
BB :	Bowfell Buttress	✓	-
EG :	Easy Gully (scree)		✓
CC :	Cambridge Crag		✓
WS :	Waterspout	✓✓	✓✓
RB :	River of Boulders		✓
FC :	Flat Crags	✓	-
GS :	do Great Slab		✓
CT :	Climbers' Traverse		✓
WR :	Walkers' Route to avoid Traverse		✓
BL :	Bowfell Links	✓	-
▲	Summit		✓✓

PLAN OF THE SUMMIT

DESCENTS : The sloping grass shelf, east of the actual summit, carries the only path across the top : it links Ore Gap with Three Tarns. Two well-scratched tracks go down from the cairn and join this path : one, on the south, descends first in line with Three Tarns but is turned leftwards by the uncompromising rim of Bowfell Links ; the other, shorter, goes down north inclining north-east with many simple variations among the boulders. For Langdale the steep lower section of the Three Tarns path may be avoided by using a terrace on the left at a gap in the wall of rocks (WR on the plan above). Direct descents to Eskdale over the steepening boulder slopes are not feasible.

In mist, the only safe objectives are Ore Gap (for Wasdale, Borrowdale or Eskdale) and Three Tarns (for Langdale via the Band, or Eskdale) avoiding Bowfell Links on the way thereto.

The Great Slab of Flat Crags

RIDGE ROUTES

To CRINKLE CRAGS, 2816' : 1½ miles
SE, E, SE and then generally S
Main depression (Three Tarns) at 2320'
600 feet of ascent
A rough ridge walk of high quality

A bee-line for Three Tarns runs foul of Bowfell
Links, and the summit notes should be consulted
for getting down to the gap. From there onwards
the gradual climb to Crinkle Crags, with its many
turns and twists and ups and downs is entirely
delightful, *but not in mist.* (See Crinkle Crags 13)

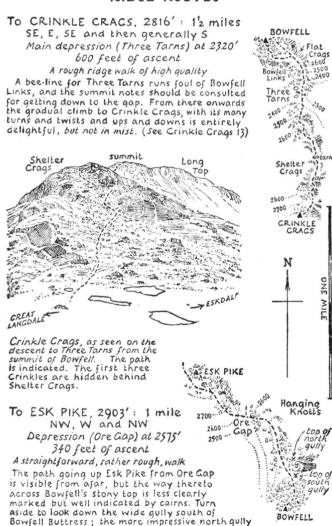

*Crinkle Crags, as seen on the
descent to Three Tarns from the
summit of Bowfell. The path
is indicated. The first three
Crinkles are hidden behind
Shelter Crags.*

To ESK PIKE, 2903' : 1 mile
NW, W and NW
Depression (Ore Gap) at 2575'
340 feet of ascent
A straightforward, rather rough, walk

The path going up Esk Pike from Ore Gap
is visible from afar, but the way thereto
across Bowfell's stony top is less clearly
marked but well indicated by cairns. Turn
aside to look down the wide gully south of
Bowfell Buttress ; the more impressive north gully
may also be reached by a short and easy detour.

Three views from the Band

Right:
Browney Gill and Cold Pike

Bottom Right:
Pike o' Blisco

Below:
Pike o' Stickle

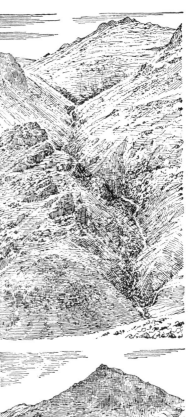

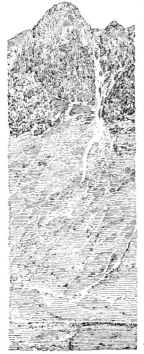

THE VIEW

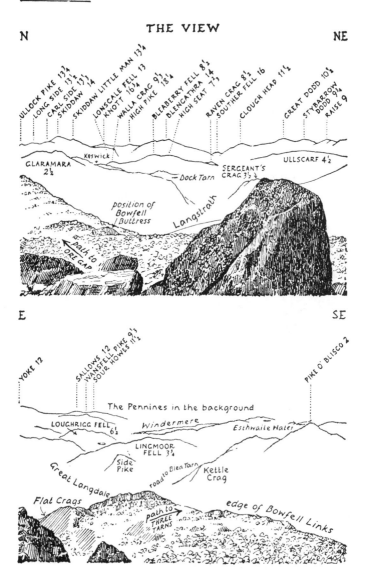

N   NE

ULLOCK PIKE 13¾
LONG SIDE 13½
CARL SIDE 13½
SKIDDAW 14
SKIDDAW LITTLE MAN 13¼
LONGSCALE FELL 13
KNOTT 16¼
WALLA CRAG 9½
HIGH PIKE 18¼
BLEABERRY FELL 8½
BLENCATHRA 14
HIGH SEAT 7¾
RAVEN CRAG 8½
SOUTHER FELL 16
CLOUGH HEAD 11½
GREAT DODD 10½
STYBARROW DODD 9¼
RAISE 9

GLARAMARA 2½

Keswick

— Dock Tarn

SERGEANT'S CRAG 3½

ULLSCARF 4½

position of Bowfell Buttress

Langstrath

path to ORE GAP

E   SE

YOKE 12
SALLOWS 12
WANSFELL PIKE 9¾
SOUR HOWES 11½
PIKE O' BLISCO 2

The Pennines in the background

LOUGHRIGG FELL 6½

Windermere

Esthwaite Water

LINGMOOR FELL 3¼

Side Pike

road to Blea Tarn

Kettle Crag

Great Langdale

Flat Crags

path to THREE TARNS

edge of Bowfell Links

THE VIEW

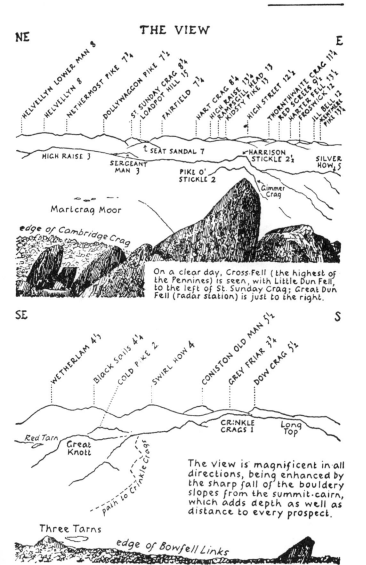

NE

E

HELVELLYN LOWER MAN 8
HELVELLYN 8
NETHERMOST PIKE 7¾
DOLLYWAGGON PIKE 7½
St SUNDAY CRAG 8¾
LOADPOT HILL 15
FAIRFIELD 7¼
HART CRAG 8¼
HIGH RAISE 13½
RAMPSGILL HEAD 13
KIDSTY PIKE 13
HIGH STREET 12½
THORNTHWAITE CRAG 11¼
RED SCREES 9½
HARTER FELL 13½
FROSTWICK 12
ILL BELL 12
KENTMERE PIKE 13¾

HIGH RAISE 3

SEAT SANDAL 7

HARRISON STICKLE 2½

SILVER HOW 5

SERGEANT MAN 3

PIKE O' STICKLE 2

Gimmer Crag

Martcrag Moor

edge of Cambridge Crag

On a clear day, Cross Fell (the highest of the Pennines) is seen, with Little Dun Fell, to the left of St. Sunday Crag; Great Dun Fell (radar station) is just to the right.

SE

S

WETHERLAM 4½
Black Sails 4¼
COLD PIKE 2
SWIRL HOW 4
CONISTON OLD MAN 5½
GREY FRIAR 3¾
DOW CRAG 5½

Red Tarn

Great Knott

path to Crinkle Crags

CRINKLE CRAGS 1

Long Top

The view is magnificent in all directions, being enhanced by the sharp fall of the bouldery slopes from the summit-cairn, which adds depth as well as distance to every prospect.

Three Tarns

edge of Bowfell Links

THE VIEW

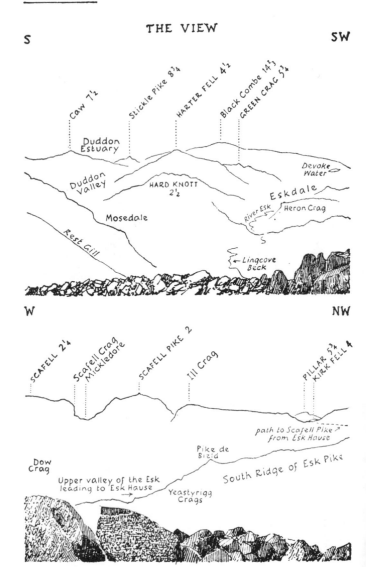

S   SW

Caw 7½   Stickle Pike 8¾   HARTER FELL 4½   Black Combe 14½   GREEN CRAG 5¾

Duddon Estuary

Duddon Valley   HARD KNOTT 2½   Devoke Water

Eskdale

Mosedale   River Esk   Heron Crag

Rest Gill   S

←Lingcove Beck

W   NW

SCAFELL 2¼   Scafell Crag Mickledore   SCAFELL PIKE 2   Ill Crag   PILLAR 5¾   KIRK FELL 4

path to Scafell Pike from Esk Hause →

Pike de Bield

Dow Crag   South Ridge of Esk Pike

Upper valley of the Esk leading to Esk Hause →   Yeastyrigg Crags

THE VIEW

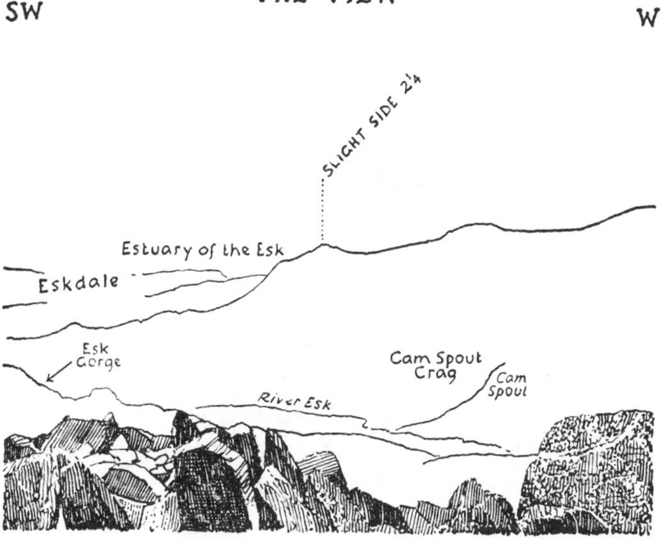

SW   W

SLIGHT SIDE 2¼

Estuary of the Esk

Eskdale

Esk Gorge

Cam Spout Crag

Cam Spout

River Esk

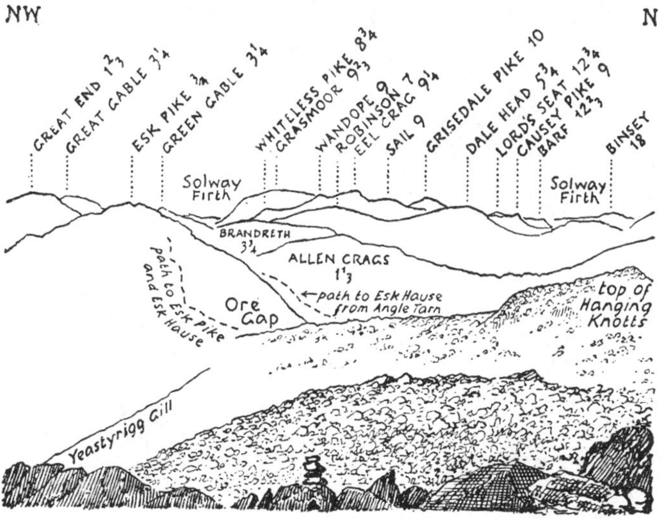

NW   N

GREAT END 1⅔
GREAT GABLE 3¼
ESK PIKE 3¾
GREEN GABLE 3¾
WHITELESS PIKE 8¾
GRASMOOR 9⅔
WANDOPE 9
ROBINSON 7
EEL CRAG 9¼
SAIL 9
GRISEDALE PIKE 10
DALE HEAD 5¾
LORD'S SEAT 12¾
CAUSEY PIKE 9
BARF 12⅔
BINSEY 18

Solway Firth

Solway Firth

BRANDRETH 3¼

ALLEN CRAGS 1⅓

path to Esk Pike and Esk House

path to Esk House from Angle Tarn

Ore Gap

top of Hanging Knotts

Yeastyrigg Gill

Brim Fell

from Little How Crags

WETHERLAM ▲

GREY ▲
FRIAR   ▲ SWIRL HOW

**BRIM
FELL** ▲

DOW ▲   ▲ CONISTON
CRAG   OLD MAN

● Coniston

MILES

0   1   2   3

1: *Great Carrs*
2: *Swirl How*
3: *Great How
Crags*

Swirl
House

The north-east cairn

NATURAL FEATURES

Brim Fell is the mile-long whalebacked ridge linking Coniston Old Man with Swirl How, the latter fell being joined at the narrow depression of Levers Hause, a high pass across the main watershed. Throughout its length the ridge is furnished with a most excellent turf, firm and dry and a pleasure to tread, but the featureless top, where a few stones intrude, is without interest. The western slope going steeply and roughly down amongst crags to Seathwaite Tarn is likewise dull, but the east face, craggy everywhere and narrowing quickly to the confluence of Low Water Beck and Levers Water Beck, is full of interesting detail, the best feature being the prominent buttress of Raven Tor thrusting out between the two attractive tarns of Low Water and Levers Water and the most fearsome a group of dangerous coppermine shafts in the vicinity of the sinister gash of Simon's Nick.

MAP

ONE MILE

The approaches from Coniston are illustrated in the diagram on the next page following →

ASCENT FROM CONISTON
2450 feet of ascent : 3 miles (3½ via Gill Cove)

CONISTON OLD MAN   BRIM FELL   looking west

Levers Hause

Gill Cove

Low Water

Raven Tor

Cove Beck

spoil

cave (shelter)

spoil

quarries

tunnel

Colt Crag

sheds

Boulder Valley

Pudding Stone

Levers Water

shafts (dangerous)

hut

quarry road

WALNA SCAR HUT ROAD

Turn right 20 yards after path joins quarry-road.

Low Water Beck

Water pipe

grass path

bracken

Coppermines Valley

juniper

bracken

stile

falls

Miners Bridge

YOUTH HOSTEL

Levers Water Beck

ROAD

CONISTON BECK

CHURCH BECK

gate

Sun Hotel   Coniston (Turn to the right behind the Sun Hotel)

Thus far the route is the same as that for Coniston Old Man.

Caves and shafts on this diagram are disused mine and quarry workings, and UNSAFE.

Brim Fell is the next summit northwards along the ridge from the Old Man, and is invariably attained (if at all) after first climbing the Old Man, the intervening ridge being a simple stroll on grass. However, the illustration gives two alternative ways of ascending Brim Fell direct, mercifully free from the din and clatter of the busy Old Man path through the quarries. Instead, turn off below the quarries to the quiet recess of Boulder Valley, and there follow one of the two routes shown — both of these entail some scrambling and neither is recommended for descent. In mist, the Old Man path is safer both ways.

Both routes give a much better idea of the structure of Brim Fell than is gained from a visit along the ridge.

THE SUMMIT

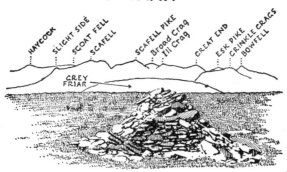

A big cairn, originally well built but becoming shattered, marks the highest part of the broad grassy plateau on top of the fell. 100 yards north-east is a second big cairn in an eruption of grey stones. There is nothing else to mention.

DESCENTS: The summit is usually left along the ridge, but it is useful to know that the north-east cairn stands at the head of a simple direct descent for Coniston (the only easy breach in the eastern escarpment): on this route aim for the col linking Raven Tor to the fell and here turn right down a grass slope to Low Water. But *in mist* go first to the Old Man and descend from there.

RIDGE ROUTES

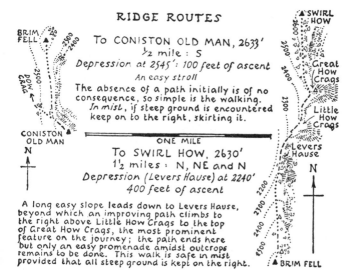

To CONISTON OLD MAN, 2633'
½ mile : S
Depression at 2545': 100 feet of ascent
An easy stroll

The absence of a path initially is of no consequence, so simple is the walking. *In mist, if steep ground is encountered keep on to the right, skirting it.*

ONE MILE

To SWIRL HOW, 2630'
1½ miles : N, NE and N
Depression (Levers Hause) at 2240'
400 feet of ascent

A long easy slope leads down to Levers Hause, beyond which an improving path climbs to the right above Little How Crags to the top of Great How Crags, the most prominent feature on the journey; the path ends here but only an easy promenade amidst outcrops remains to be done. This walk is safe in mist provided that all steep ground is kept on the right.

THE VIEW

The view, although extensive, suffers in comparison with that from the adjacent Old Man because of the broadness of the summit, there being no single vantage point that brings the surrounding tarns into the picture. The scene therefore depends for attractiveness on the far skyline of fells in the northern arc, with the other Coniston hills looming rather too largely to present a balanced view. A quite unexpected glimpse of Little Mell Fell is seen above Grisedale Hause; it is interesting also to see the atomic power plants on the coast neatly bisected by the peak of the Eskdale Harter Fell.

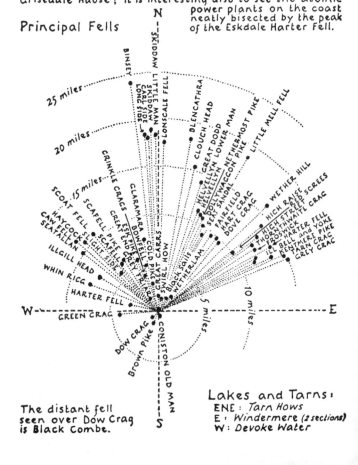

Principal Fells

The distant fell seen over Dow Crag is Black Combe.

Lakes and Tarns:
ENE: Tarn Hows
E: Windermere (2 sections)
W: Devoke Water

Simon's Nick (top left)
and the upper valley
of Levers Water Beck
from one of the old levels,
Paddy End Copper Works.

Raven Tor, the east
buttress of Brim Fell,
from the dam at
Levers Water

Cold Pike

2259'

from Pike o' Blisco

The true south ridge of Crinkle Crags follows the compass bearing to end in a long steep descent to Cockley Beck, but a spur running off south-east is more usually considered to continue the main spine of the mountain. This spur rises to the three rocky summits of Cold Pike before dropping down Wrynose Breast to the pass below; a concave eastern slope descends to the desolate upland hollow containing Red Tarn, so named from the rich colour of the shaly subsoil.

Although not of great significance, Cold Pike is prominent when seen from the north and east, and it has lovely views in those directions. All around, nearby, are higher fells, and they may be studied profitably from the triple peaks of this lowly one in their midst. Cold Pike is a Crinkle Crags in miniature.

CRINKLE
▲ CRAGS

● Dungeon Ghyll

▲ PIKE O' BLISCO

▲ COLD PIKE

Little Langdale ●

● Cockley Beck

MILES
0   1   2   3

MAP

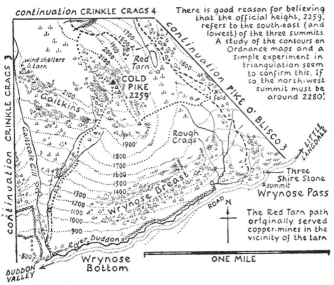

continuation CRINKLE CRAGS 4

continuation PIKE O'BLISCO 3

continuation CRINKLE CRAGS 3

Gaitscale Gill

wind shelters & tarn

Red Tarn

COLD PIKE 2259

Gaitkins

Rough Crags

1700
1600
1500
1400
1300
1200
1100
1000
900
800

Wrynose Breast

River Duddon

LITTLE LANGDALE

Three Shire Stone

▲ summit
Wrynose Pass

ROAD

N

DUDDON VALLEY

Wrynose Bottom

ONE MILE

There is good reason for believing that the official height, 2259, refers to the south-east (and lowest) of the three summits. A study of the contours on Ordnance maps and a simple experiment in triangulation seem to confirm this. If so, the north-west summit must be around 2280!

The Red Tarn path originally served copper-mines in the vicinity of the tarn

ASCENT FROM WRYNOSE

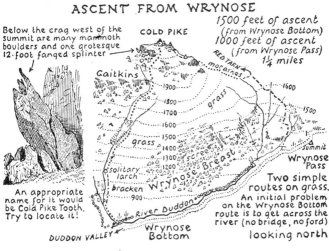

Below the crag west of the summit are many mammoth boulders and one grotesque 12-foot fanged splinter

COLD PIKE

Gaitkins

1900
1800
1700
1600
1500
1400
1300
1200
900

grass

grass

scree

Wrynose Breast

solitary larch

bracken

River Duddon

RED TARN moraines

1600
1500

grass

summit
Wrynose Pass

DUDDON VALLEY

Wrynose Bottom

An appropriate name for it would be Cold Pike Tooth. Try to locate it!

1500 feet of ascent (from Wrynose Bottom)
1000 feet of ascent (from Wrynose Pass)
1¼ miles

Two simple routes on grass.
An initial problem on the Wrynose Bottom route is to get across the river (no bridge, no ford)

looking north

THE SUMMIT

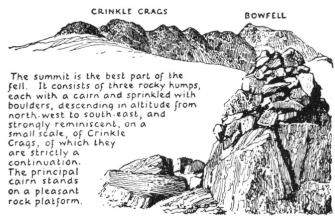

CRINKLE CRAGS

BOWFELL

The summit is the best part of the fell. It consists of three rocky humps, each with a cairn and sprinkled with boulders, descending in altitude from north-west to south-east, and strongly reminiscent, on a small scale, of Crinkle Crags, of which they are strictly a continuation. The principal cairn stands on a pleasant rock platform.

DESCENTS : The top of the fell is without paths, but in clear weather there is no difficulty in finding an easy way off through the outcrops. In mist, it is well to note that the summit ridge is buttressed by crags along its eastern fringe, and more distantly on the west, while Wrynose Breast is much too rough and steep to be considered as a route. The safest places to aim for are Red Tarn (for Oxendale) and Wrynose Pass, either of which may be reached by following the ridge south-east (in line with the three humps) as far as a cairn and a small tarn together, with rising ground beyond: here go down grass to the left and continue eastwards to join the path linking Red Tarn and Wrynose Pass.

RIDGE ROUTES

CRINKLE CRAGS

To CRINKLE CRAGS, 2816' : 1½ miles : NW
Depressions at 2100' and 2625'
850 feet of ascent
The first mile is dreary, then comes a sudden change
Nothing is gained by a beeline, the plateau being
marshy. Join the path at the streams. Consult
the Ridge Plan (see Crinkle Crags 11) at the
foot of the first Crinkle.

2500

To PIKE O' BLISCO, 2304' : 1¼ miles
NW, then N, E, SE and finally NE.
Depression at 1650'
700 feet of ascent
An easy, interesting walk

Join the path from Crinkle Crags to Red Tarn. The ascent starts directly opposite the junction with the Oxendale-Wrynose path

OXENDALE

PIKE O' BLISCO

1700

1800

2000

2100

Red Tarn

WRYNOSE

COLD PIKE

HALF A MILE

N

THE VIEW

The view between north and east is very extensive, but on the west side is severely restricted by the lofty south ridge coming down from Crinkle Crags. Perhaps the best features are the two splendid lowland prospects (1) over Little Langdale to Windermere and the distant Pennines, and (2) down the Duddan Valley to the estuary and the sea beyond.

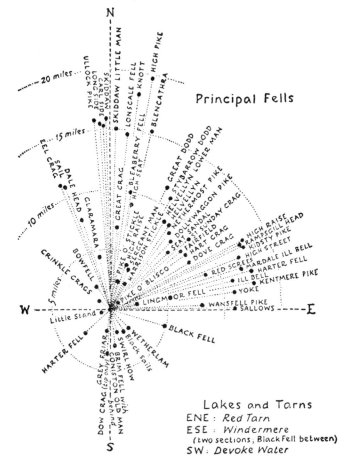

Principal Fells

Lakes and Tarns
ENE: Red Tarn
ESE: Windermere
(two sections, Black Fell between)
SW: Devoke Water

Coniston Old Man 2633'

properly
The Old Man of Coniston

from Red Dell Head

NATURAL FEATURES

The Coniston fells form a separate geographical unit. They are almost entirely severed from the adjacent mountainous parts of Lakeland by the Duddon and Brathay valleys, with the watershed between the two, Wrynose Pass, 1270', providing the only link with other fells. The whole of the Coniston group lies within Lancashire, the two valleys mentioned containing the boundaries of Cumberland (Duddon) and Westmorland (Brathay).

Whilst the characteristics of the Coniston fells are predominantly Lakeland, with lofty ridges, steep and craggy declivities, lovely waterfalls and lonely tarns and the general scenic charm so typical of the district, there has been a great deal of industrial exploitation here, principally in copper mining (now abandoned) and quarrying (still active), resulting in much disfigurement. So strongly sculptured are these fine hills, however, and so pronounced is their appeal that the scars detract but little from the attractiveness of the picture: many people, indeed, will find that the decayed skeletons of the mine-workings add an unusual, and if explored an absorbing, interest to their walks.

The western slopes are comparatively dull, and the appeal of these hills lies in their aspect to the east, where the village of Coniston, in an Alpine setting, is the natural base for explorations. The ridge-walking, on soft turf, is excellent, but all slopes are very rough down to valley-level. As viewpoints, the summits have the advantage of isolation between the main mass of Lakeland and the fine indented coastline of Morecambe Bay, the prospects in all directions being of a high quality.

Waterfalls
Church Beck

continued

NATURAL FEATURES

continued

The pattern of the Coniston Fells

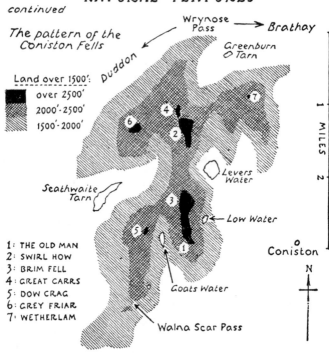

Wrynose Pass → Brathay

Greenburn Tarn

Duddon

Land over 1500':
- ■ over 2500'
- ▨ 2000'-2500'
- ▨ 1500'-2000'

Levers Water

Seathwaite Tarn

Low Water

Coniston

Goats Water

Walna Scar Pass

MILES 1 2 0

N

1: THE OLD MAN
2: SWIRL HOW
3: BRIM FELL
4: GREAT CARRS
5: DOW CRAG
6: GREY FRIAR
7: WETHERLAM

The northern Coniston Fells from Little Langdale

Wrynose Pass

NATURAL FEATURES

The highest (by a few feet) and best-known of the Coniston fells is the Old Man, a benevolent giant revered by generations of walkers and of particular esteem in the eyes of the inhabitants of the village he shelters, for he has contributed much to their prosperity.   The Old Man is no Matterhorn, nor is Coniston a Zermatt, but an affinity is there in the same close links between mountain and village, and the history of the one is the history of the other.   Coniston without its Old Man is unthinkable.

Yet the Old Man has little significance in the geographical arrangements hereabouts, the true hub of this group of hills being Swirl How, a summit of slightly lower elevation northwards. The Old Man is merely the termination of Swirl How's main ridge and ends high Lakeland in the south: the last outpost, looking far over the sea.

Although cruelly scarred and mutilated by quarries the Old Man has retained a dignified bearing, and still raises his proud and venerable head to the sky. His tears are shed quietly, into Low Water and Goats Water, two splendid tarns, whence, in due course, and after further service to the community in the matter of supplies of electricity and water, they ultimately find their way into Coniston's lake, and there bathe his ancient feet.

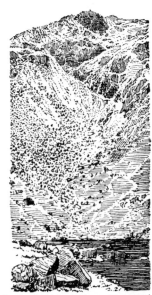

The Old Man from Low Water

Yet even during these peaceful ablutions the Old Man continues to be harassed.   On the day this page was prepared (November 10th. 1958) the world's water speed record was broken on Coniston Water. Thus, from tip to toe, the mountain serves man.

POSTSCRIPT: The speed record was later broken again here (May 1959)

MAP

MAP

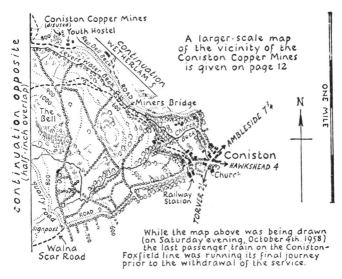

A larger-scale map of the vicinity of the Coniston Copper Mines is given on page 12

While the map above was being drawn (on Saturday evening, October 4th 1958) the last passenger train on the Coniston-Foxfield line was running its final journey prior to the withdrawal of the service.

Detail is not given of the territory south of the Walna Scar Road except in the vicinity of the approach from Torver. Here is little to tempt the fellwalker, for a broad and dreary moor declines to the cultivated shores of Coniston Water, but this rather desolate expanse nevertheless is fruitful ground for the antiquary, there being many evidences of a civilisation long past. Ancient cairns, walled enclosures and stone circles are all revealed to the eager and learned searcher amongst the bracken, and excavators have unearthed a Bronze Age cemetery. How odd that the scene of these mouldering relics should be also the place where an ultra-modern flying saucer was first photographed!

Somewhere in the area covered by the map on the opposite page, *but not indicated*, is a small upright memorial stone roughly inscribed 'CHARMER 1911' Charmer was a foxhound killed in a fall on Dow Crag, and it is rather nice to know that the memory of a faithful dog was revered in this way. But some visitors have seen nothing sacred in the stone and it has been uprooted and cast aside on occasion. For this reason it has been thought best not to disclose its exact location. Rest in peace, Charmer. They were happy days.........

Charmer's Grave

ASCENT FROM CONISTON (via BOO TARN)
2400 feet of ascent: 3 miles

CONISTON OLD MAN

looking north-west

2350'

south ridge

2100

quarries

water pipe

quarries

moss

2000

1900

At the points ● watch closely for the next cairns; they are not easily discerned in these places among the stones of the fellside.

stepping stones

1800

1700

cave

1600

tarn

1400

1300

old quarry (Bursting Stone Quarry)

1500

POSTSCRIPT:
Just as the book goes to press there is news that this quarry is soon to be re-opened.

1200

Timley Knott

1100

1000

bracken

WALNA SCAR 2

900

Braidy Beck

Boo Tarn
(a small reedy pool)

tarn

bracken

800

signpost

quarry road

The Cave, Bursting Stone Quarry

gate

CONISTON (road)

The signpost points along the quarry road to the Old Man, but take the Walna Scar path

For every hundred ascents of the Old Man by the signposted route through the labyrinth of big quarries on the east flank, perhaps one is made by the little-known alternative detailed above — and even this modest estimate may be too high. But here is a climb for which the discerning walker will cherish a strong preference over the usual quarries path, for the latter is not only unpleasantly stony but passes through a region of downright ugliness — hence its relegation to the next page.→ The way up from Boo Tarn is a succession of fascinating and unexpected zig-zags, making use of grassy terraces scented with thyme and tiny alpines on the south-east side of the fell. The path is mainly good as far as the old quarry (only a little one), beyond which dependence must be placed on a series of cairns, going first one way and then another and often seeming to be leading away from the objective, but, if trusted, in due course the walker will be unerringly led to the south ridge at a grassy saddle just below the summit. The man who worked out this delightful, well-graded and ingenious route clearly hated the sight of the big quarries.   He deserved a medal.

ASCENT FROM CONISTON (DIRECT)
2450 feet of ascent : 3 miles (2½ via Church Beck)

CONISTON OLD MAN

looking west

south ridge

BRIM FELL

2500
2400
2300
spoil

2200 cave ✕ (shelter)

Low Water
← a good place for giving up and going to sleep

2100
2000
1900

main quarry

water pipe

This is the way the crowds go: the day trippers, the courting couples, troops of earnest Boy Scouts, babies and grandmothers, the lot. On this stony parade fancy handbags and painted toenails are as likely to be seen as rucksacks and boots.   In its favour, it can be said that the route is absolutely safe in the worst weather — the densest mist cannot obscure the spiralling ribbon of stones.   But let's be fair — the scenery of Low Water is very good.

1700

tunnel ✕
1600
spoil heaps

Bursts in the waterpipe make attractive but noisy fountains

sheds
1500
Colt Crag

1400
1300

-1200

quarry road

1200

-1200
1100

BOULDER VALLEY — 5 minutes level walk to the giant Pudding Stone

900

grass path

800

WALNA SCAR

scanty ruins of ancient enclosure

1000
quarry road

hut

hut

juniper
700

800
bracken

signpost

gate

800

ROAD

700

600

Aspiring ascenders of the Old Man are directed by signposts to take the Walna Scar road and then the quarry road, but some relief from stones underfoot may be gained initially by using the much pleasanter route via Church Beck. (Turn right behind the Sun Hotel.)

Old path (wet)
new path (dry)

600

Levers Water

YOUTH HOSTEL

Miners Bridge waterfall

Meanwhile the discerning walker is enjoying a solitary and undisturbed climb on the sweet grass above Boo Tarn. The page to which he refers occasionally is Coniston Old Man 7 not 8.

500

400

Railway Station

300
signpost

Church Beck

CONISTON

200

Sun Hotel

BROUGHTON 9

Black Bull Hotel
Coniston

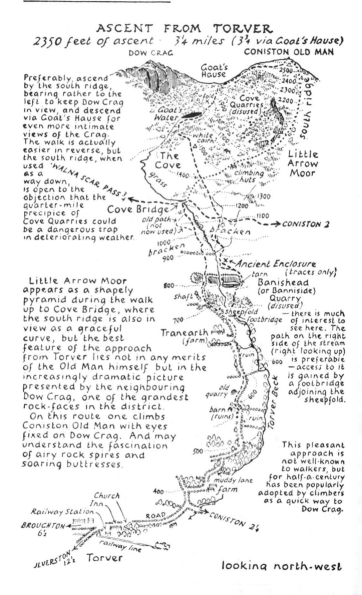

ASCENT FROM TORVER
2350 feet of ascent · 3¼ miles (3¾ via Goat's House)

DOW CRAG   CONISTON OLD MAN

Goat's House

Cove Quarries (disused)

2500·· 2400·· 2300·· 2200··

south ridge

fold

Goat's Water

white cairn

The Cove

grass 1400··

Little Arrow Moor

climbing huts

··1300

··1200

··1100

→ CONISTON 2

old path (not now used)

bracken

Cove Bridge

"WALNA SCAR PASS"?

1000 bracken 900

Ancient Enclosure (traces only)

tarn

800··

shaft

sheepfold footbridge

700··

Tranearth (farm)

old quarry

600

barn (ruins) ruin

500··

ruin

Torver Beck

600

Banishead (or Banniside) Quarry (disused)

Preferably, ascend by the south ridge, bearing rather to the left to keep Dow Crag in view, and descend via Goat's House for even more intimate views of the Crag. The walk is actually easier in reverse, but the south ridge, when used as a way down, is open to the objection that the quarter-mile precipice of Cove Quarries could be a dangerous trap in deteriorating weather.

Little Arrow Moor appears as a shapely pyramid during the walk up to Cove Bridge, where the south ridge is also in view as a graceful curve, but the best feature of the approach from Torver lies not in any merits of the Old Man himself but in the increasingly dramatic picture presented by the neighbouring Dow Crag, one of the grandest rock-faces in the district.
On this route one climbs Coniston Old Man with eyes fixed on Dow Crag. And may understand the fascination of airy rock spires and soaring buttresses.

— there is much of interest to see here. The path on the right side of the stream (right looking up) is preferable — access to it is gained by a footbridge adjoining the sheepfold.

This pleasant approach is not well-known to walkers, but for half-a-century has been popularly adopted by climbers as a quick way to Dow Crag.

Church Inn

Railway Station

BROUGHTON 6½

muddy lane farm

400··

ROAD

→ CONISTON 2½

railway line

ILVERSTON 12½   Torver

looking north-west

Boulder Valley

Low Water Beck falls in steep cascades from its tarn to a level shelf 600 feet below and there meanders uncertainly before resuming its hurried journey to join Levers Water Beck. This shelf is littered with boulders tumbled from the craggy slopes above, a scene common enough among the mountains, but in this particular instance several of the boulders are of quite uncommon size, big enough indeed to provide some entertainment and practice for rock-climbers, who name the area Boulder Valley.

The most massive and most prominent of the boulders is the Pudding Stone, 25 feet high and as big as a house, which has a dozen climbing routes, one of them being considered easy, but not by everybody, and the others, by walkers' standards, ranging between various grades of impossibility. The Pudding Stone may not have the overall dimensions of the Bowder Stone in Borrowdale, but certainly gives the impression of a greater bulk and weight.

The Pudding Stone
(the easy side)

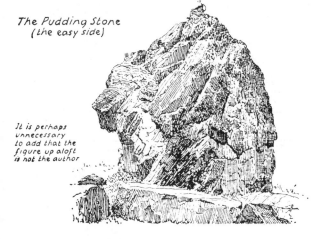

It is perhaps unnecessary to add that the figure up aloft is not the author

Coppermines Valley

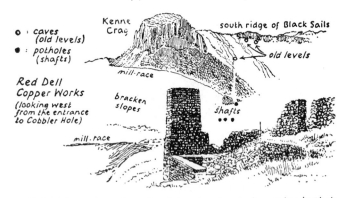

o : caves
(old levels)

● : potholes
(shafts)

Kenne
Crag

south ridge of Black Sails

old levels

mill-race

Red Dell
Copper Works
(looking west
from the entrance
to Cobbler Hole)

bracken
slopes

shafts
● ● ●

mill-race

    Fellwalkers based on Coniston need not sit moping in their lodgings if a wet day puts the high tops out of bounds for it is possible to occupy the mind and keep the body reasonably dry by dodging from one to another of the many caves, levels and tunnels of the Coppermines Valley, one mile distant.

    This hollow among the hills presents a surprising scene of squalid desolation, typical of the dreary outskirts of many coalmining towns but utterly foreign to the Lake District, and it says much for the quality of the encircling mountains that they can triumph over the serious disfigurement of ugly spoil heaps and gaping wounds, and still look majestic. Here, in this strange amphitheatre, where flowers once grew, one sees the hopeless debris of the ruins of industries long abandoned, where flowers will never grow again, and, as always in the presence of death, is saddened — but a raising of the eyes discloses a surround of noble heights, and then the heart is uplifted too.

    There is good fun and absorbing interest in locating all the tunnels and shafts of the old quarries and mines; *exploration must be carried no further than the entrances.* These workings, untouched for half a century or more, are in a state of decay and many are flooded. The shafts of the mines in particular, hideous potholes falling sheer into black depths, and without protecting fences, should be approached with great caution: we can't afford to lose any readers here, not with a further three volumes in this series still to be sold. Curious, too, are the mill-races, still coursing horizontally across steep slopes although their function has long since ended, and, in places where time has breached them, often squirting unnatural streams down fellsides not fashioned to accommodate them.

    The accompanying map indicates the various holes of one sort or another in the Coppermines Valley area. There are others elsewhere on the Coniston fells, notably on Wetherlam.

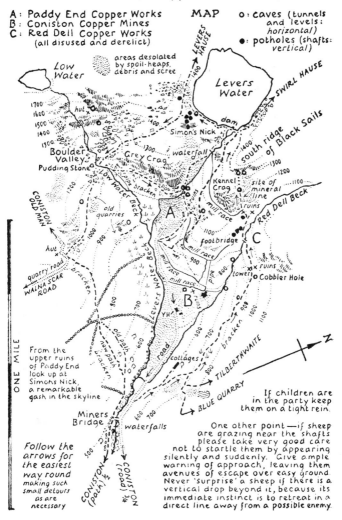

continuing *Coppermines Valley*

A: Paddy End Copper Works
B: Coniston Copper Mines
C: Red Dell Copper Works
  (all disused and derelict)

MAP

o: caves (tunnels and levels: horizontal)
•: potholes (shafts: vertical)

areas desolated by spoil-heaps, debris and scree

Low Water

LEVERS HAUSE

Levers Water

SWIRL HAUSE

1700
1600
1500
1400

hut

dam

Simon's Nick

Boulder Valley
Pudding Stone

Grey Crag

waterfall

south ridge of Black Sails

1300

1200

CONISTON OLD MAN

Low Water Beck

bracken

Kennel Crag

site of mineral line

1100

ruins

Red Dell Beck

old quarries

A

mill race

1500

hut

900

footbridge

C

quarry road
WALNA SCAR ROAD

bracken

mill race

900

pipe

800

mill race

tower

ruins · Cobbler Hole

1100

B

ruins

YH

800

700

900

Z

From the upper ruins of Paddy End look up at Simons Nick, a remarkable gash in the skyline

old path

bracken

road

cottages

TILBERTHWAITE

BLUE QUARRY

If children are in the party keep them on a tight rein.

ONE MILE

Miners Bridge

waterfalls

500 · 600 · 700

CONISTON (path)

CONISTON (road)

Follow the arrows for the easiest way round making such small detours as are necessary

One other point — if sheep are grazing near the shafts please take very good care not to startle them by appearing silently and suddenly. Give ample warning of approach, leaving them avenues of escape over easy ground. Never 'surprise' a sheep if there is a vertical drop beyond it, because its immediate instinct is to retreat in a direct line away from a possible enemy.

THE SUMMIT

Tourists looking for Blackpool Tower

Boy Scouts

Typical summit scene

Solitary fellwalker, bless him, looking north to the hills

There may be a cairn on the summit, or there may not.......
Sometimes there is, sometimes there isn't .... The frequent
visitor gains the impression that a feud rages here between
cairn-builders and cairn-destroyers, with the contestants
evenly matched, so that one week there will be a cairn, the
next week not, and so on. Indestructible, however, is a big
solidly-constructed slate platform on which the cairn, when
there is one, stands, and which has no counterpart on other
fells; into it a recess has been provided and this serves as a
shallow wind-shelter on occasions when it is not cluttered up
with the debris of shattered cairns, the latter circumstance
depending on which of the rival factions is, at the moment,
enjoying a temporary and fleeting triumph. One hesitates
to join in, if this is a private fight, but may perhaps suggest
that if the word 'man' means 'a summit cairn', as authorities
seem to be agreed, then, of all fells, the Old Man should be
allowed to have one and that it should be left alone to grow
hoary and ancient. But it never could. Not with those crowds.
 An Ordnance Survey column stands on the north side of the
platform. Recent editions of Survey maps are unanimous in
accrediting 2635 feet to the fell, but an older generation
of walkers was brought up to believe it was 2633.
 The summit is directly above
the very rough eastern slope,
which falls precipitously to
the black pool of Low Water;
in other directions gradients
are easy, predominantly with
a surface of grass but having
an occasional rash of stones.
 In places where the native
rock crops out, weathering
has reduced it to vertical
flakes occurring in series.

Typical rock formations on the summit

THE SUMMIT

DESCENTS:

TO CONISTON:

Although the start of the usual quarries path is indistinct for a few yards as it leaves the summit there should be no difficulty in finding and following it, even in the thickest mist: the path is one of the safest and surest (and stoniest) in the district.

The Boo Tarn route leaves the south ridge after 400 yards, at the first grassy depression: look for a cairn on the left marking the head of the path. Remember that this route has many acute turns and that the track disappears in places. This is a better way up than down, and is confusing in mist. Keep looking ahead for the next cairn.

TO TORVER:

Follow the south ridge (no path) to hit the Walna Scar Road anywhere, after which it is easy going; but the lower slopes of the ridge are rough and thick with bracken and are best avoided by inclining to the right *after Cove Quarries are passed* to join the good path from Goats Water near Cove Hut. *The quarries are an ugly trap in mist.*

Alternatively, a way may be found directly to the Cove by using an abominable track going straight down a scree slope from the top and indicated by a series of white (quartz) cairns, *which must be found before starting down.* Halfway down the steep slope, an old cairn on the left (NOT quartz) indicates a possible traverse (rough) to the uppermost of Cove Quarries, whence an interesting quarry path leads down to Cove Hut.

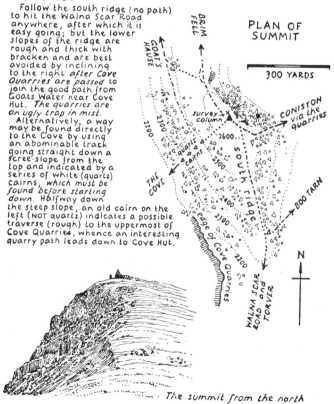

PLAN OF SUMMIT

300 YARDS

The summit from the north

The Coniston Fells : looking north along the ridge from the Old Man

A note on the names of fells:

Newcomers to Lakeland may wonder why many names of fells are prominently inscribed on Ordnance Survey maps yet rarely find mention in guidebooks and other literature descriptive of the district. This neglect of official names can be explained by reference to the Coniston area as an example. Thus the compact group of hills known to walkers as the Coniston Fells is, according to the Ordnance Survey, more properly described as a part of the Furness Fells, and this latter title appears in widely-spaced capital letters on their maps. So far all right, but then this general name of the whole has several sub-titles in smaller but quite prominent letters for particular (but ill-defined) sections — Cockley Beck Fell, Seathwaite Fells, Tilberthwaite Fells, Troutal Fell, Coniston Fells (an area east of the principal ridge), Above Beck Fells, and so on. These names mean little to the walker, who soon trains his eye, when looking at the map, to ignore them. His interest is in the names of the separate hills and summits.

Of course the Ordnance Survey is correct in using the local names of fells, which indicate not hills but indefinite areas of uncultivated high ground and other rough pastures: in general, sheep-grazing areas. Walkers are quite wrong in applying the name of a summit to the whole fell as they do. Wetherlam, for instance, is the name of the top of a fell only, the fell itself being named variously according to its different sections, e.g. Tilberthwaite High Fell, Low Fell, Above Beck Fells. These local distinctions are of no use to walkers, who want one name per hill, although, on occasion, in the absence of a name for a summit, one of them may be adopted, e.g. Brim Fell.

The ideal map for fellwalkers would omit detail of purely local interest (and parish and other boundaries), and name all summits distinctively. *Do one for us, O.S., please.*

RIDGE ROUTES

To BRIM FELL, 2611´ : ½ mile : N
Depression at 2545´ : 80 feet of ascent

A ten minutes' stroll on excellent turf
Brim Fell is the rounded top next on the
ridge northwards. As is often the case on
easy ground, where the feet are free to
wander without impediment, no path
has been formed on the grassy incline
beyond the slight depression.

To DOW CRAG, 2555´ : 1 mile :
NW, W, SW and S
*Depression (Goat's Hause) at 2130´
425 feet of ascent*

A walk of increasing interest
An expert rockclimber who is also a good swimmer might attempt
a straight course between the two summits, but ordinary mortals are
forced to make a considerable detour *via* Goat's Hause. There is no
path at first from the top of the Old Man, but a good one is picked
up at a patch of boulders. Note that, after crossing the Hause, a
simple but 98% stony horizontal traverse (the start of which, at a
cairn not seen from the ridge-path, must be looked for) may be made
to the base of the great crag for a close view of the rock buttresses.

*Dow Crag
from the Old Man*

THE VIEW

A vast seascape makes a glorious sweep across the southern horizon, ranging from the Pennines to Black Combe, and, further west, to the Isle of Man. A rare beauty is added to the scene by the silver waters of the Kent, Leven and Duddon estuaries.

Most people who climb the Old Man, not being fellwalkers, fix their eyes in this direction, and squeals of joy announce the sighting of Calder Hall Power Station, Blackpool Tower, Morecambe Battery, the monument on Ulverston's Hoad Hill, Millom and sundry other man-made monstrosities. This book does not deign to cater for such tastes.

The fellwalker will prefer to gaze across the gulf of Eskdale to the natural and unmarred grandeur of the Scafell group, but, this scene apart, the mountain panorama, although very extensive, is a little disappointing due to the intervening bulk of the other Coniston fells. The peep over the edge at the path zig-zagging upwards from Low Water, the tarn directly below, is, however, striking — the best bird's-eye view of an ascent-route in Lakeland.

Swirl How is a much better viewpoint for the man who would rather look at hills than at Millom, and moreover, the peace will not be disturbed by squealing women and children and by knowledgeable males who noisily identify wrongly every hill in sight. Before fleeing to this sanctuary, however, wander a little way down the western slope until out of earshot of the congregation on the summit and so come face to face with the magnificent front of Dow Crag — and agree that nature fashions the finest architecture whatever the folk on the top may say.

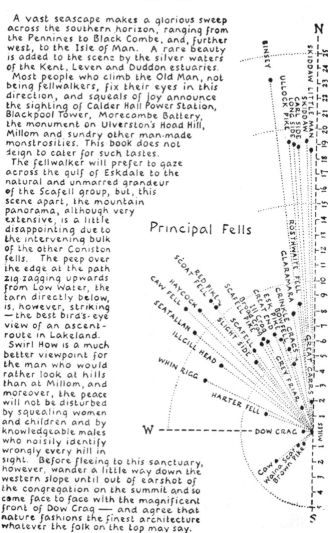

THE VIEW

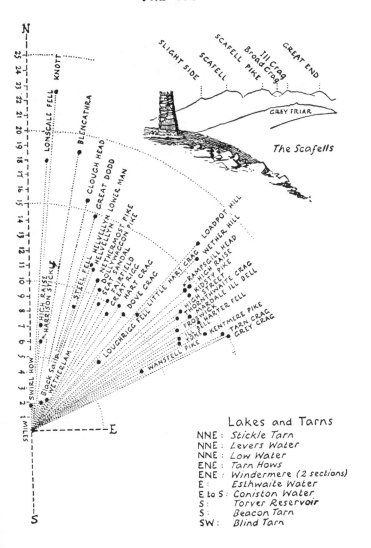

The Scafells

Labels on the skyline drawing: SLIGHT SIDE, SCAFELL, SCAFELL PIKE, BROAD CRAG, ILL CRAG, GREAT END, GREY FRIAR

N
55 24 23 22 21 20 19 18 17 16 15 14 13 12 11 10 9 8 7 6 5 4 3 2 1 MILES

KNOTT
LONSCALE FELL
BLENCATHRA
CLOUGH HEAD
GREAT DODD
HELVELLYN LOWER MAN
HELVELLYN
STEEL FELL
NETHERMOST PIKE
DOLLYWAGGON PIKE
SEAT SANDAL
FAIRFIELD
GREAT RIGG
HART CRAG
DOVE CRAG
HIGH RAISE
HARRISON STICKLE
LOUGHRIGG FELL
LITTLE HART CRAG
LOADPOT HILL
WETHER HILL
RAMPSGILL HEAD
HIGH RAISE
KIDSTY PIKE
HIGH STREET
THORNTHWAITE CRAG
MARDALE ILL BELL
FROSWICK
ILL BELL
HARTER FELL
YOKE
KENTMERE PIKE
WANSFELL PIKE
TARN CRAG
GREY CRAG
SWIRL HOW
BLACK SAILS
WETHERLAM

E

S

Lakes and Tarns

NNE:	*Stickle Tarn*
NNE:	*Levers Water*
NNE:	*Low Water*
ENE:	*Tarn Hows*
ENE:	*Windermere (2 sections)*
E:	*Esthwaite Water*
E to S:	*Coniston Water*
S:	*Torver Reservoir*
S:	*Beacon Tarn*
SW:	*Blind Tarn*

Crinkle Crags

2816'

from Pike o' Blisco

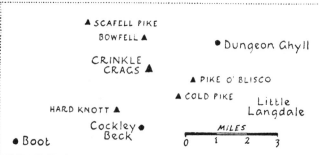

▲ SCAFELL PIKE

BOWFELL ▲

● Dungeon Ghyll

CRINKLE
CRAGS ▲

▲ PIKE O' BLISCO

▲ COLD PIKE

Little
Langdale

HARD KNOTT ▲

Cockley ●
Beck

● Boot

MILES

0   1   2   3

NATURAL FEATURES

Some mountains are obviously named by reference to their physical characteristics. Crinkle Crags is one of these, and it was probably first so called by the dalesfolk of the valleys to the east and around the head of Windermere, whence its lofty serrated ridge, a succession of knobs and depressions, is aptly described by the name. These undulations, seeming trivial from a distance, are revealed at close range as steep buttresses and gullies above wild declivities, a scene of desolation and rugged grandeur equalled by few others in the district. Nor is the Eskdale flank any gentler, for here too are gaunt shattered crags rising from incredibly rough slopes. The high pass of Three Tarns links the ridge with Bowfell to the north while southwards Wrynose Bottom is the boundary.

Crinkle Crags is much too good to be missed. For the mountaineer who prefers his mountains rough, who likes to see steep craggy slopes towering before him into the sky, who enjoys an up-and-down ridge walk full of interesting nooks and corners, who has an appreciative eye for magnificent views, this is a climb deserving of high priority. But it is not a place to visit in bad weather for the top is confusing, with ins and outs as well as ups and downs and a sketchy path that cannot be relied on. Crinkle Crags merits respect, and should be treated with respect; then it will yield the climber a mountain walk long to be remembered with pleasure.

Is it 'Crinkle Crags IS ...' or 'Crinkle Crags ARE ...' ?
Is it 'Three Tarns IS ....' or 'Three Tarns ARE ...' ?
                    IS sounds right but looks wrong!

The outline of Crinkle Crags from Great Langdale

C : The five Crinkles   GC : Great Cove
T : Rock tower near Three Tarns   SC : Shelter Crags

The highest Crinkle (2816') is second from the left on the diagram. When seen from the valley it does not appear to be the highest, as it is set back a little from the line of the others.

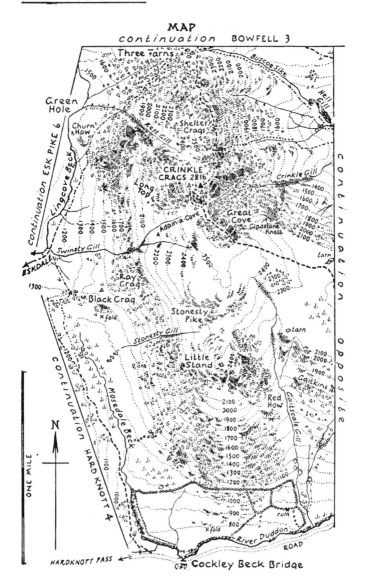

MAP

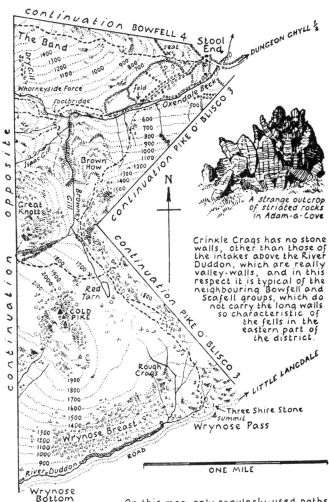

A strange outcrop of striated rocks in Adam-a-Cove

Crinkle Crags has no stone walls, other than those of the intakes above the River Duddon, which are really valley-walls, and in this respect it is typical of the neighbouring Bowfell and Scafell groups, which do not carry the long walls so characteristic of the fells in the eastern part of the district.

ONE MILE

On this map, only regularly-used paths are shown. Other routes are suggested, with qualifications, on the diagrams of ascents.

ASCENT FROM DUNGEON GHYLL (via RED TARN)
2600 feet of ascent : 4 miles

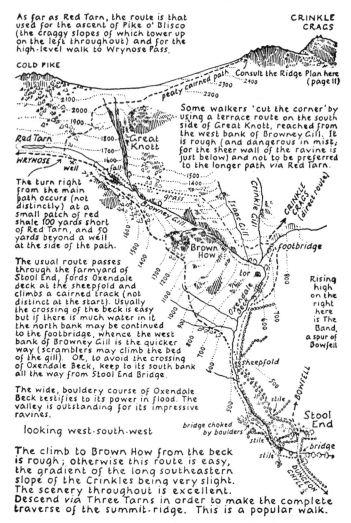

As far as Red Tarn, the route is that used for the ascent of Pike o' Blisco (the craggy slopes of which tower up on the left throughout) and for the high-level walk to Wrynose Pass.

COLD PIKE

CRINKLE CRAGS

Consult the Ridge Plan here (page 11)

Some walkers 'cut the corner' by using a terrace route on the south side of Great Knott, reached from the west bank of Browney Gill. It is rough (and dangerous in mist; for the sheer wall of the ravine is just below) and not to be preferred to the longer path via Red Tarn.

Red Tarn

Great Knott

WRYNOSE

well

fall

The turn right from the main path occurs (not distinctly) at a small patch of red shale 100 yards short of Red Tarn, and 50 yards beyond a well at the side of the path.

The usual route passes through the farmyard of Stool End, fords Oxendale beck at the sheepfold and climbs a cairned track (not distinct at the start). Usually the crossing of the beck is easy but if there is much water in it the north bank may be continued to the footbridge, whence the west bank of Browney Gill is the quicker way (scramblers may climb the bed of the gill). OR, to avoid the crossing of Oxendale Beck, keep to its south bank all the way from Stool End Bridge.

The wide, bouldery course of Oxendale Beck testifies to its power in flood. The valley is outstanding for its impressive ravines.

looking west-south-west

Browney Gill

grass

Crinkle Gill

Isaac Gill

CRINKLE CRAGS (direct route)

footbridge

Brown How

tor

Oxendale

Rising high on the right here is The Band, a spur of Bowfell

sheepfold

BOWFELL

stile

bridge choked by boulders

stile

stile

Stool End

bridge

DUNGEON GHYLL

The climb to Brown How from the beck is rough; otherwise this route is easy, the gradient of the long southeastern slope of the Crinkles being very slight. The scenery throughout is excellent.
Descend via Three Tarns in order to make the complete traverse of the summit-ridge. This is a popular walk.

ASCENT FROM DUNGEON GHYLL (via THREE TARNS)
2650 feet of ascent : 4 miles

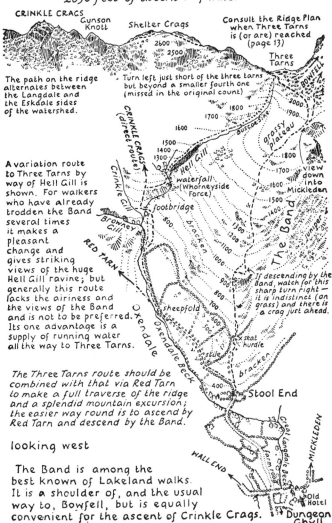

CRINKLE CRAGS
Gunson Knott
Shelter Crags

Consult the Ridge Plan when Three Tarns is (or are) reached (page 13)

2600
2500

Three Tarns

The path on the ridge alternates between the Langdale and the Eskdale sides of the watershed.

Turn left just short of the three tarns but beyond a smaller fourth one (missed in the original count)

BOWFELL

CRINKLE CRAGS (direct route)

Buscoe Sike

1800
1700
1600
1500
1400
1300

2000
1900

grassy plateau

1800

1700
view down into Mickleden

Hell Gill

waterfall (Whorneyside Force)

footbridge

Browney Gill

RED TARN

Crinkle Gill

bracken

1600
1500
1400
1300

The Band

juniper

1200
1100
1000
900

800

700

A variation route to Three Tarns by way of Hell Gill is shown. For walkers who have already trodden the Band several times it makes a pleasant change and gives striking views of the huge Hell Gill ravine; but generally this route lacks the airiness and the views of the Band and is not to be preferred. Its one advantage is a supply of running water all the way to Three Tarns.

If descending by the Band, watch for this sharp turn right — it is indistinct (on grass) and there is a crag just ahead.

Oxendale

Oxendale Beck

sheepfold

seat
hurdle

stile

bracken

500
600
400

The Three Tarns route should be combined with that via Red Tarn to make a full traverse of the ridge and a splendid mountain excursion; the easier way round is to ascend by Red Tarn and descend by the Band.

Stool End

looking west

The Band is among the best known of Lakeland walks. It is a shoulder of, and the usual way to, Bowfell, but is equally convenient for the ascent of Crinkle Crags.

WALL END

Great Langdale Beck

MICKLEDEN

Old Hotel

Dungeon Ghyll

ASCENT FROM DUNGEON GHYLL
(DIRECT CLIMB FROM OXENDALE)
2550 feet of ascent : 3½ miles

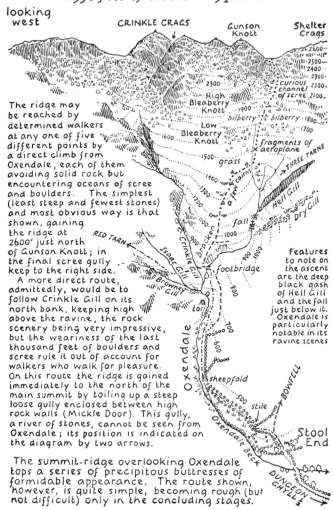

looking west

CRINKLE CRAGS

Gunson Knott

Shelter Crags

2600
2500
2400
2300
curious channel of scree 2200
2100

High Bleaberry Knott

1900
bilberry bilberry 1800

Low Bleaberry Knott

1700
fragments of aeroplane

1600

1500

grass

THREE TARNS

1400

a few cairns

1300

1200

Hell Gill

Dry Gill

fall

1100

1000

RED TARN

900

Isaac Gill

Crinkle Gill

Bracken

1000

footbridge

Browney Gill

800

tor

Oxendale

700

600

500

sheepfold

stile

BOWFELL

Oxendale Beck

Stool End

DUNGEON GHYLL

The ridge may be reached by determined walkers at any one of five different points by a direct climb from Oxendale, each of them avoiding solid rock but encountering oceans of scree and boulders. The simplest (least steep and fewest stones) and most obvious way is that shown, gaining the ridge at 2600' just north of Gunson Knott; in the final scree gully keep to the right side.

A more direct route, admittedly, would be to follow Crinkle Gill on its north bank, keeping high above the ravine, the rock scenery being very impressive, but the weariness of the last thousand feet of boulders and scree rule it out of account for walkers who walk for pleasure. On this route the ridge is gained immediately to the north of the main summit by toiling up a steep loose gully enclosed between high rock walls (Mickle Door). This gully, a river of stones, cannot be seen from Oxendale; its position is indicated on the diagram by two arrows.

Features to note on the ascent are the deep black gash of Hell Gill and the fall just below it. Oxendale is particularly notable in its ravine scenes.

The summit-ridge overlooking Oxendale tops a series of precipitous buttresses of formidable appearance. The route shown, however, is quite simple, becoming rough (but not difficult) only in the concluding stages.

ASCENT FROM ESKDALE
2650 feet of ascent : 7½ miles from Boot
(8 miles via Three Tarns)

CRINKLE CRAGS

Shelter Crags

Three Tarns

2500
2400
2300
1900
1800
1700

Long Top

spring

Adam-a-Cove

2500
2400
2300
2200
2100

bristly rocks

grass

2000

Ray Crag

Rest Gill

Green Hole

1400 1500 1600
1300

Swinsty Gill

1800

grass

1300

* In Adam-a-Cove an uncharacteristic outcrop of striated rocks is marked by two cairns.

Rest Gill is identifiable by its very bouldery bed.

Lingcove Beck

low pass

MOSEDALE (for the DUDDON VALLEY)

1300

SCAFELL PIKE and ESK HAUSE

Throstle Garth

1200 1300
1100

Esk Falls

Lingcove Bridge (which is NOT crossed on this walk)

Tongue Pot

sheepfold

yew

The fell on this side of the valley is HARD KNOTT. The detached rock high on the skyline is the Steeple.

Heron Crag

1000
900
800
700
600

River Esk

1100
1000
900

Yew Crags

Pillar Pot

500

stile

Roman Camp

700

• A study of the map suggests Long Top, the western shoulder of the highest Crinkle, as an obvious approach to the summit from Eskdale, but the wild appearance of its lower crags makes a less inviting proposition when seen 'in the flesh'. Nevertheless the cliff can be by-passed by a bouldery scramble up the bilberry slope alongside Rest Gill, and a series of stony rises then leads to the top; this is a rough but interesting route, suitable only in fine weather.

• The usual route proceeds to Three Tarns and then follows the ridge, so taking the fullest advantage of paths. The section between Rest Gill and Three Tarns is rough, but most ingeniously and delightfully cairned.

• The easiest route follows Swinsty Gill up into Adam-a-Cove. This is everywhere grassy — a surprising weakness in the armour of the Crinkles — and it is just possible to come within a few feet of the summit-cairn without handling rock or treading on stones.

Brotherilkeld

400

300

kiosk

HARDKNOTT PASS 1½

BOOT 2½

ROAD

looking north-east

ASCENT FROM COCKLEY BECK BRIDGE
2350 feet of ascent : 3 miles

CRINKLE CRAGS

Long Top
2700
2500

CRINKLE CRAGS

2700
2500

tarns
grass
RED TARN

If desired, the first Crinkle may be by-passed by skirting its base, but it is better to traverse it by joining the path coming from Red Tarn.

Stonesty Pike

2400
2300
2200
2100

south ridge

On a hot day, when copious supplies of water are considered essential to survival, there is much to be said, as an alternative to the south ridge, in favour of following Gaitscale Gill to its source. There are no difficulties on either bank and the rock scenery is very good

This grassy depression (¼ mile beyond the cairn on Little Stand) is the only place where the ridge can be left, if necessary, without encountering crags.

Little Stand
tarns

Strictly, the top of the south ridge (here shown as Little Stand) has no official name. The name 'Red How' is often applied to this part of the fell.

grass shelf
2000

1800
1700
1600
1500

Red How

1900
1800
1700
1600
1500
1400
1300

Gaitscale Gill

Mosedale

LINGCOVE BECK

1200
1100

landslip

1000

sheepfold

big boulder

1200

1100

1000

900

800

The approach to the south ridge above the intake wall is very rough and bouldery, but it is just possible to thread a way through the stones, keeping to the grass. This should be done; some of the boulders are unstable.

1000
900

HARDKNOTT PASS 1

Mosedale Beck

ROAD

700

R. Duddon

ROAD

Cockley Beck Bridge

WRYNOSE PASS 1½

looking north

DUDDON VALLEY

The scenery of the south ridge is good, with crags and outcrops in abundance, but the approach is fatiguing. This route should not be attempted in bad weather: there is no path to, or on, the ridge, which has escarpments on both flanks.

ASCENT FROM WRYNOSE PASS
1650 feet of ascent : 2¼ miles

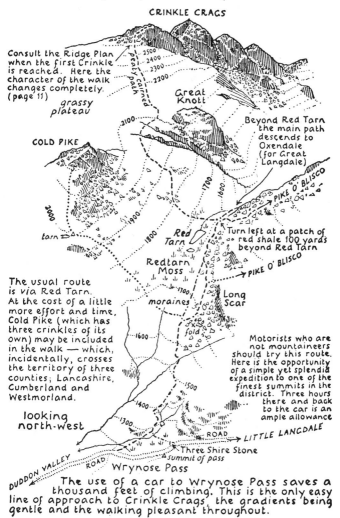

CRINKLE CRAGS

Consult the Ridge Plan when the first Crinkle is reached. Here the character of the walk changes completely. (page 11)

grassy plateau

Great Knott

Beyond Red Tarn the main path descends to Oxendale (for Great Langdale)

COLD PIKE

2100
2000
1900
1800
1700
1600

2500
2400
2300
2200

peaty cairned path

tarn

PIKE O' BLISCO

Red Tarn

Turn left at a patch of red shale 100 yards beyond Red Tarn

Redtarn Moss

PIKE O' BLISCO

The usual route is via Red Tarn. At the cost of a little more effort and time, Cold Pike (which has three crinkles of its own) may be included in the walk — which, incidentally, crosses the territory of three counties; Lancashire, Cumberland and Westmorland.

moraines

1700

Long Scar

fold

1600

Motorists who are not mountaineers should try this route. Here is the opportunity of a simple yet splendid expedition to one of the finest summits in the district. Three hours there and back to the car is an ample allowance

looking north-west

1500

1400

1300

ROAD → LITTLE LANGDALE

Three Shire Stone summit of pass

Wrynose Pass

DUDDON VALLEY   ROAD

The use of a car to Wrynose Pass saves a thousand feet of climbing. This is the only easy line of approach to Crinkle Crags, the gradients being gentle and the walking pleasant throughout.

RIDGE PLAN
for use when traversing the ridge from SOUTH to NORTH

• Read upwards from the bottom

All heights ending in 0 are approximate and unofficial

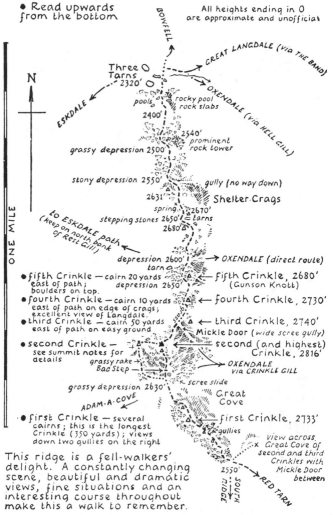

BOWFELL

GREAT LANGDALE (via THE BAND)

Three O Tarns 2320'

ESKDALE

N

OXENDALE (via HELL GILL)

pools

rocky pool rock slabs

2400'

2540' prominent rock tower

grassy depression 2500'

stony depression 2550'

gully (no way down)

2631'

Shelter Crags

spring 2670'

stepping stones 2650' tarns

to ESKDALE path (keep on north bank of Rest Gill)

ONE MILE

2680'

depression 2600' tarn

OXENDALE (direct route)

• fifth Crinkle — cairn 20 yards east of path; boulders on top.

depression 2650'

fifth Crinkle, 2680' (Gunson Knott)

• fourth Crinkle — cairn 10 yards east of path on edge of crags; excellent view of Langdale.

fourth Crinkle, 2730'

• third Crinkle — cairn 50 yards east of path on easy ground

third Crinkle, 2740' Mickle Door (wide scree gully)

• second Crinkle — see summit notes for details

second (and highest) Crinkle, 2816'

grassy rake Bad Step

OXENDALE via CRINKLE GILL

grassy depression 2630'

scree slide

Great Cove

ADAM-A-COVE

• first Crinkle — several cairns; this is the longest Crinkle (350 yards); views down two gullies on the right

first Crinkle, 2733'

gullies

View across Great Cove of second and third Crinkles with Mickle Door between

2550'

SOUTH RIDGE

RED TARN

This ridge is a fell-walkers' delight. A constantly changing scene, beautiful and dramatic views, fine situations and an interesting course throughout make this a walk to remember.

Looking NORTH along the ridge ....

*The second (and highest)
Crinkle, Mickle Door,
and the third Crinkle,
seen across Great Cove*

*The fourth and fifth
Crinkles (Shelter Crags
and Bowfell behind), seen
from the third Crinkle*

RIDGE PLAN
for use when traversing the ridge from NORTH to SOUTH

● Read Upwards from the bottom

This is, of course, the same plan as that already given for the south-to-north traverse but reversed for easier reference. Reading upwards, left and right on the plan will agree with left and right as they appear to the walker.

All heights ending in 0 are approximate and unofficial.

RED TARN

SOUTH RIDGE

2550'

viewpoint ·x· (fourth and third Crinkles, with Mickle Door between)

gullies

Great Cove

fifth Crinkle, 2733' — the longest Crinkle; several cairns along its top

grassy depression 2630'

ADAM-A-COVE

Bad Step

grassy rake

OXENDALE via CRINKLE GILL

fourth Crinkle — see summit notes for details

fourth (and highest) Crinkle

Mickle Door (wide scree gully)

2816'

third Crinkle, 2740'

● third Crinkle — cairn 50 yards east of path on easy ground

second Crinkle, 2730'

2650'

● second Crinkle — cairn on edge of crags 10 yards east of path; excellent view of Langdale

first Crinkle, 2680' (Gunson Knott)

tarn

● first Crinkle — cairn 20 yards east of path; boulders (shelter) on top

OXENDALE (direct route)

2600'

easy route to ESKDALE path (keep on north bank of Rest Gill)

first four Crinkles come into sight

2680'

tarns

2670'

stepping stones 2650'

spring

Shelter Crags

2631'

gully

2550' stony depression

Note that the arrow is upside-down, too

2500' grassy depression

prominent rock tower 2540'

2400'

Some writers have greatly exaggerated the dangers of the ridge. Nowhere is it anything but a pleasantly rough walk — except for the Bad Step, which can be avoided. (Bowfell and Scafell Pike are rougher)

rock slabs rocky pool

pools

OXENDALE (via HELL GILL)

ESKDALE

HALF A MILE

N

Three Tarns 2320'

GREAT LANGDALE (via THE BAND)

BOWFELL

Introducing Lakeland's best ridge-mile!

Looking SOUTH along the ridge.........

Four Crinkles come
suddenly into view from
the path as it rounds a
corner of Shelter Crags

The fifth Crinkle
as seen from the main
Crinkle on the descent
to the Bad Step

THE SUMMIT

← BOWFELL

There are five Crinkles (not counting Shelter Crags) and therefore five summits, each with its own summit-cairn. The highest is, however, so obviously the highest that the true top of the fell is not in doubt in clear visibility, and this is the Crinkle (the fourth from the north and second from the south) with which these notes are concerned. It is not the stoniest of the five, nor the greatest in girth, but, unlike the others, it extends a considerable distance as a lateral ridge (Long Top) descending westwards. On the actual summit are two principal cairns separated by 40 yards of easy ground; that to the north, standing on a rock platform, is slightly the more elevated. The eastern face descends in precipices from the easy grass terraces above it; there are crags running down steeply from the south cairn also, but in other directions the top terrain is not difficult although everywhere rough.

1 : grassy rake (easy way)
2 : direct route (steep scree)
3 : the Bad Step (see next page)
4 : detour to avoid the Bad Step.

The highest Crinkle, from the south

continued

THE SUMMIT

continued

DESCENTS

to GREAT LANGDALE: The orthodox routes are (1) *via* Red Tarn and Brown How, and (2) *via* Three Tarns and the Band, both excellent walks, and in normal circumstances no other ways should be considered. If time is very short, however, or if it is necessary to escape quickly from stormy conditions on the ridge, quick and sheltered routes are provided by (3) the scree gully of Mickle Door or (4) the Gunson Knott gully, which is easier: both are very rough initially but lead to open slopes above Oxendale.

to ESKDALE: Much the easiest way, and much the quickest, is to descend from Adam-a-Cove (no path), keeping *left* of Swinsty Gill where it enters a ravine. Long Top is a temptation to be resisted, for it leads only to trouble.

to COCKLEY BECK BRIDGE: The south ridge is interesting (no path and not safe in mist), but tired limbs had better take advantage of the easy way down from Adam-a-Cove, inclining left below Ray Crag into Mosedale

to WRYNOSE PASS: Reverse the route of ascent. Cold Pike may be traversed with little extra cost in energy.

In mist, take good care to keep to the ridge-path, which, in many places, is no more than nail-scratches on rocks and boulders but is generally simple to follow. Go nowhere unless there is evidence that many others have passed that way before. (The exception to this golden rule is Adam-a-Cove, which is perfectly safe *if it is remembered to keep to the left bank of the stream*).

The Bad Step

Caution is needed on the descent southwards from the summit. A walker crossing the top from the north will naturally gravitate to the south cairn and start his descent here. A steep path goes down rock ledges to a slope of loose scree, which spills over the lip of a chockstone (two, really) bridging and blocking a little gully. Anyone descending at speed here is asking for a nasty fall. The impasse is usually avoided and the gully regained below the chockstone by an awkward descent of the rock wall to the left, which deserves the name 'The Bad Step', for it is 10 feet high and as near vertical as makes no difference. This is the sort of place that everybody would get down in a flash if a £5 note was waiting to be picked up on the scree below, but, without such an inducement, there is much wavering on the brink. Chicken-hearted walkers, muttering something about discretion being the better part of valour, will sneak away and circumvent the difficulty by following the author's footsteps around the left flank of the buttress forming the retaining wall of the gully, where grassy ledges enable the foot of the gully to be reached without trouble; here they may sit and watch, with ill-concealed grins, the discomfiture of other tourists who may come along.

The Bad Step is the most difficult obstacle met on any of the regular walkers' paths in Lakeland.

The Bad Step from below

continued

THE SUMMIT

continued

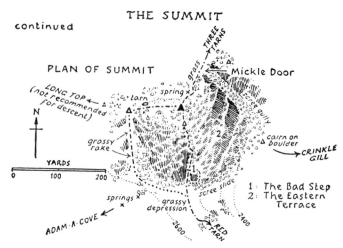

PLAN OF SUMMIT

LONG TOP → (not recommended for descent)

tarn

spring

Mickle Door

grassy rake

N

YARDS

0   100   200

springs ×

grassy depression

ADAM·A·COVE ←

cairn on boulder

CRINKLE GILL →

scree slide

2400

RED TARN

2600

1: The Bad Step
2: The Eastern Terrace

Note that the steep direct descent from the south cairn may be by-passed altogether (it was formerly customary to do so) by proceeding west from the main cairn for 140 yards to another on grass in a slight depression, whence a grassy rake on the left goes down, skirting completely the rocks of the Crinkle, to join the direct route at its base

The welcome spring on the summit (usually reliable after recent rain) is remarkable for its proximity to the top cairn (30 yards north-east, in the bend of the path); it is only 20 feet lower than the top cairn, and has a very limited gathering-ground. Find it by listening for it — it emerges as a tiny waterfall from beneath a boulder. This is not the highest spring in the district but it is the nearest to a high summit.

The Eastern Terrace

A conspicuous grass terrace slants at an angle of 30° across the eastern cliffs of the main Crinkle, rising from the screes of the Mickle Door gully to the direct ridge-route just above the Bad Step. It is not seen from the ridge but appears in views of the east face clearly, being the middle of three such terraces and most prominent. It is of little use to walkers, except those who (in defiance of advice already given) are approaching the summit from Crinkle Gill: for them it offers

1: the Bad Step
2: the Eastern Terrace
3: Mickle Door
4: scree slide

cairn on boulder

The Eastern Face

a way of escape from the final screes. The terrace (identified by a little wall at the side of the gully) is wide and without difficulties but is no place for loitering, being subject to bombardments of stones by bloody fools, if any, on the summit above. It is well to remember, too, that the terrace is bounded by a precipice. At the upper end the terrace becomes more broken near the Bad Step and is not quite easy to locate when approached from this direction.

RIDGE ROUTES

To BOWFELL, 2960': 1½ miles : Generally N, then WNW
Five depressions; final one (Three Tarns) at 2320': 850 feet of ascent
Positively one of the finest ridge-walks in Lakeland.

The rough stony ground makes progress slow, but this walk is, in any case, deserving of a leisurely appreciation; it is much too good to be done in a hurry. Every turn of the fairly distinct track is interesting, and in places even exciting, although no difficulty is met except for an occasional awkward stride on rock. *In mist,* the walker will probably have to descend to Three Tarns anyway, but should give Bowfell a miss, especially if the route is unfamiliar.

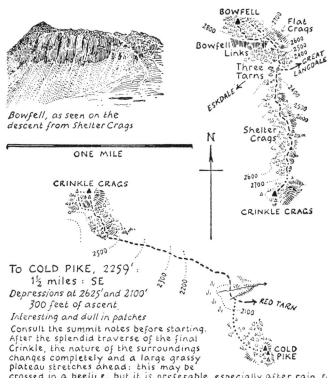

Bowfell, as seen on the descent from Shelter Crags

ONE MILE

To COLD PIKE, 2259':
1½ miles : SE
Depressions at 2625' and 2100'
300 feet of ascent
Interesting and dull in patches
Consult the summit notes before starting. After the splendid traverse of the final Crinkle, the nature of the surroundings changes completely and a large grassy plateau stretches ahead: this may be crossed in a beeline, but it is preferable, especially after rain, to keep to the Red Tarn path until a gentle slope, becoming craggy, leads easily to the attractive triple summit of Cold Pike.

THE VIEW

The view is not quite as comprehensive as might be expected, the western and north-western fells (with the exception of Eel Crag) being out of sight behind the bulky Scafell group and Bowfell, but is excellent nevertheless. Of special distinction is the supremely beautiful view of the valleys of the Duddon and the Esk winding down to the sea: from no other summit are they so well seen. There is a more dramatic but less attractive picture of Great Langdale, best seen from the edge of the eastern cliffs.

Intruding in the fine array of mountains and lakes and valleys and sea is a comparatively new feature — the cooling towers of the Calder Hall atomic power station, neatly framed in the dip of the skyline between Whin Rigg and Illgill Head, the two heights above Wastwater Screes. The summit of Crinkle Crags is ageless, the cooling towers are symbols of one particular age. Here, on this rugged mountain-top, is an everlasting permanence, something simple, and we can understand; but *there*, on the horizon, is something that is temporary, and complicated beyond our comprehension. Those modern structures, out of place in a landscape that is constant and unchanging, will vanish from the scene with the passing years. The mountains, nature's symbols of power and strength, will remain.

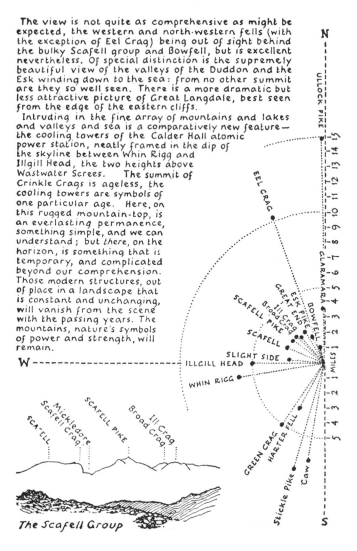

The Scafell Group

THE VIEW

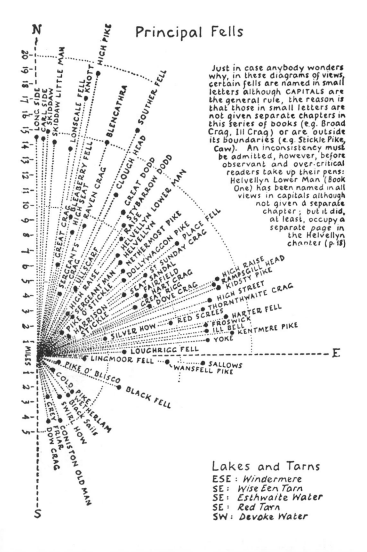

Principal Fells

Just in case anybody wonders why, in these diagrams of views, certain fells are named in small letters although CAPITALS are the general rule, the reason is that those in small letters are not given separate chapters in this series of books (e.g. Broad Crag, Ill Crag) or are outside its boundaries (e.g. Stickle Pike, Caw). An inconsistency must be admitted, however, before observant and over-critical readers take up their pens: Helvellyn Lower Man (Book One) has been named in all views in capitals although not given a separate chapter; but it did, at least, occupy a separate page in the Helvellyn chapter (p. 18)

Lakes and Tarns
ESE: *Windermere*
SE: *Wise Een Tarn*
SE: *Esthwaite Water*
SE: *Red Tarn*
SW: *Devoke Water*

Dow Crag

2555'

GREY
FRIAR ▲

SWIRL HOW
▲

Troutal
●

CONISTON
OLD MAN
▲

DOW ▲
CRAG

Coniston
●

● Seathwaite

MILES

0   1   2   3

from the Cove

NATURAL FEATURES

Second only to Scafell Crag in the magnificence of its rock architecture is the imposing precipice towering above the stony hollow of Goat's Water, a favourite climbing ground hallowed by memories of the earliest and greatest of Lakeland cragsmen and so obviously the supreme natural attraction hereabouts that its name is given to the whole of the fell of which it is a part. Controversy raged at one time on the spelling of the name, DOW or DOE, but the former is now generally accepted. The fell is extensive, and in marked contrast to the near-vertical eastern face is the smooth and gentle contour of the western slope descending to the little valley of Tarn Beck. The northern flank is easy too, except for a fringe of crag overlooking Seathwaite Tarn. South of the top, on a well-defined ridge, are the subsidiary summits of Buck Pike and Brown Pike, and beyond the latter is the lofty pass of Walna Scar, not now a traffic route since the closing of nearby quarries but remaining a most excellent walkers' highway.

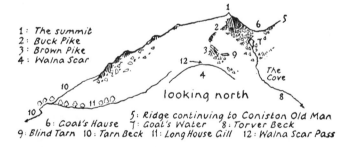

1: The summit
2: Buck Pike
3: Brown Pike
4: Walna Scar

looking north

5: Ridge continuing to Coniston Old Man
6: Goat's Hause   7: Goat's Water   8: Torver Beck
9: Blind Tarn   10: Tarn Beck   11: Long House Gill   12: Walna Scar Pass

Although really beyond the boundaries of fellwalking country, and therefore outside the area covered by this book, the ridge continuing south-west from the Walna Scar Pass deserves some attention. The 2000' contour occurs twice on Walna Scar itself and then across a wide depression rises the splendid little peak of Caw (1735') followed by a switchback ridge over the miniature Matterhorn of Stickle Pike (1231') and so ultimately, in a wealth of bracken, down to Duddon Bridge at the head of the estuary.

For seven miles this ridge forms the eastern watershed of the Duddon Valley and offers to strong walkers starting from Duddon Bridge a natural high-level approach to Dow Crag. Anyone doing this walk — a day's march in itself — will have fully merited his feeling of achievement when the top rocks are finally reached.

Dow Crag 3

NATURAL FEATURES

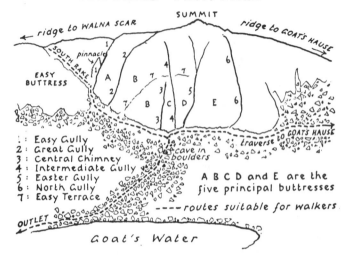

1: Easy Gully
2: Great Gully
3: Central Chimney
4: Intermediate Gully
5: Easter Gully
6: North Gully
7: Easy Terrace

A B C D and E are the
five principal buttresses

---- routes suitable for walkers

THE PATTERN OF DOW CRAG
as seen from the slopes of Coniston Old Man

The Crag is the preserve of rock-climbers, but walkers may visit the base of the great cliff by taking the climbers' path from the outlet of Goat's Water. A simple traverse to the right across a scree slope then leads to the ridge just above Goat's Hause. This route, although involving boulder-hopping, is much more interesting than the usual way to the Hause on the eastern shore of the tarn.

Easy Buttress, Easy Gully and *Easy Terrace* are easy by rock-climbing, not walking, standards. Rock-climbers don't seem to know the meaning of easy. True, most walkers would manage to get up these places if a mad bull was in pursuit, but, if there is no such compelling circumstance, better they should reflect soberly....and turn away.

There is, however, a coward's way to the top of the crag. From the lowest point of the cliff turn up left past the striking entrance to Great Gully and then more roughly up to the foot of Easy Gully, which is choked with stones. Here, unexpectedly, (it is not seen until reached) a straight ribbon of scree in a shallow gully goes up to the left (at a right-angled tangent to Easy Gully) — this route, although steep and loose, leads directly to the ridge above all difficulties. Climbers often use this as a quick way down, and it is comfortably within the capacity of most walkers. Lacking a name, but deserving one. SOUTH RAKE is suggested.

The entrance to Great Gully

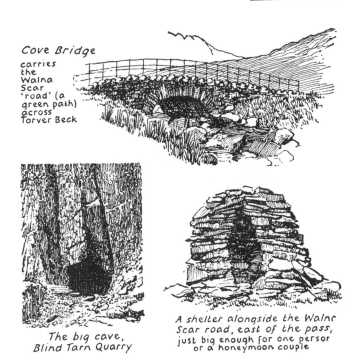

Cove Bridge carries the Walna Scar 'road' (a green path) across Torver Beck

The big cave, Blind Tarn Quarry

A shelter alongside the Walna Scar road, east of the pass, just big enough for one person or a honeymoon couple

Brown Pike and Blind Tarn from Buck Pike
Brown Pike has a fine cairn. Blind Tarn is one of the few tarns without an outlet — hence its name.

MAP

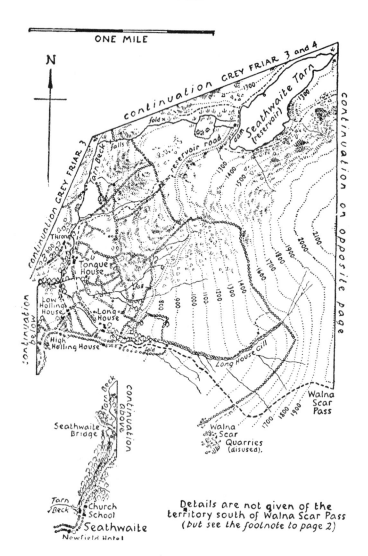

ONE MILE

N

continuation GREY FRIAR 3 and 4

continuation GREY FRIAR 3

Seathwaite Tarn

continuation on opposite page

fold

reservoir road

dam

Seathwaite Tarn (reservoir)

Tarn Beck

falls

1300

1300

1400

1500

1600

1700

1800

1900

2000

2100

continuation below

Throng

Tongue House

fall

Low Holling House

Long House

High Holling House

fold

1800

900

1000

1100

1200

1300

1400

1500

1600

1700

Long House Gill

Walna Scar Pass

1700 1800 1900

continuation above

Tarn Beck

Seathwaite Bridge

Walna Scar Quarries (disused).

Tarn Beck

Church School

Seathwaite

Newfield Hotel

Details are not given of the
territory south of Walna Scar Pass
(*but see the footnote to page 2*)

MAP

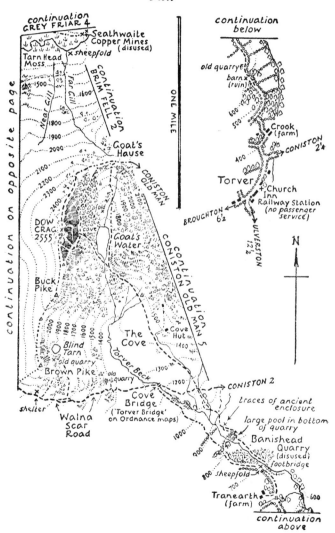

continuation
GREY FRIAR 4

Seathwaite
Copper Mines
(disused)

Tarn Head
Moss

× sheepfold

continuation
BRIM FELL 2

Near Gill

Tar Gill

1500
1600
1800
1900
2000

Goat's
Hause

continuation on opposite page

ONE MILE

2100
2200
2300
2400

DOW
CRAG
2555

fold

cove

CONISTON OLD MAN

2000
1900
1800

Goat's
Water

Buck
Pike

CONISTON OLD MAN 5

continuation

2000
1800
1600
1500
1400

Blind
Tarn
old quarry

Brown Pike

The
Cove

Cove Hut
1400

Torver Beck

1500

1300

1200

shelter

Walna
Scar
Road

Cove
Bridge
('Torver Bridge'
on Ordnance maps)

old
quarry

CONISTON 2

continuation
below

old quarry

barn ×
(ruin)

600
500

Crook
(farm)

400

CONISTON 2¼

Torver

Church
Inn

Railway Station
(no passenger
service)

BROUGHTON
6½

ULVERSTON
12½

N

1000

900

800
700

700

600

traces of ancient
enclosure

large pool in bottom
of quarry

Banishead
Quarry
(disused)

footbridge

sheepfold

Tranearth
(farm)

continuation
above

ASCENT FROM TORVER
2250 feet of ascent: 3¾ miles

DOW CRAG

Buck Pike

Brown Pike

Goat's Hause

CONISTON OLD MAN

Walna Scar Pass

2100
2000
Red Screes
cave
fold

Goat's Water

Blind Tarn
old quarries

shelter

1900

1800

1700

1600

The Cove

Goat Crag

white cairn (quartz)
hut
old quarries

Little Arrow Moor

hut
bracken
1300
1200

grass

old quarry

Cove Bridge

1400

Some altitudes:
Summit 2555'
Buck Pike 2430'
Brown Pike 2237'
Goat's Water 1646'
Goat's Hause 2130'
Walna Scar Pass 1995'

1300
old path (not now used)

1200
1100
1000
900

CONISTON 2

900

Ancient Enclosure

800
shaft

Banishead (or Baniside) Quarry (disused)
— there is much of interest to see here

sheepfold

700

Tranearth (farm)

ruin

600

old quarry

600

barn (ruins)
ruin

Torver Beck

500

Many walkers will not be familiar with this approach but it has long been popular with rock-climbers — a favourite way to a favourite crag!

From Cove Bridge, either go forward into the Cove, joining the white-cairn path, or go left to the top of Walna Scar Pass and thence follow the ridge over Brown Pike. The latter is the easier route, with pleasant walking, and is particularly good for descent.

If the Cove is entered, then from the outlet of Goat's Water either continue to Goat's Hause, there turning left to the summit (simple walking), or take the climbers' track to the base of the crags (some boulder-hopping) and traverse to the right below them, across scree, to join the other route on the skyline. There is an alternative way from the base of the crags *for scramblers* (South Rake — see page 3) not shown on this diagram.

This is the natural line of approach, following upstream the beck issuing from Goat's Water; it is also the most attractive, for when the pleasant woods of Torver are left behind the view forwards to the great buttresses of Dow Crag grows more dramatic with every step.

Church
Inn

muddy lane
farm

400

Railway Station
BROUGHTON
6½

ROAD

CONISTON 2½

ULVERSTON 12½

railway line

Torver

looking north-west

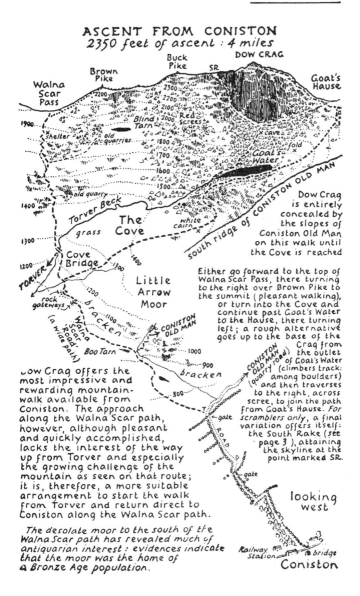

ASCENT FROM CONISTON
2350 feet of ascent : 4 miles

DOW CRAG

Walna Scar Pass

Brown Pike

Buck Pike

SR

Goat's Hause

1900

2200

2300

2200

2100

shelter

old quarries

Blind Tarn

Red Screes

2000

1800

cave

1700

Goat Water

1600

fold

1500

old quarry

1400

Torver Beck

The Cove

grass

white cairn

south ridge of CONISTON OLD MAN

Dow Crag is entirely concealed by the slopes of Coniston Old Man on this walk until the Cove is reached

1300

1200

TORVER

Cove Bridge

1400

1300

Little Arrow Moor

rock gateways

1200

bracken

1100

Walna Scar Road (a wide path)

CONISTON OLD MAN

Either go forward to the top of Walna Scar Pass, there turning to the right over Brown Pike to the summit (pleasant walking), or turn into the Cove and continue past Goat's Water to the Hause, there turning left; a rough alternative goes up to the base of the Crag from

Boo Tarn

1000

bracken

900

800

CONISTON OLD MAN (quarry road)

the outlet of Goat's Water (climbers track: among boulders) and then traverses to the right, across scree, to join the path from Goat's Hause. For scramblers only, a final variation offers itself: the South Rake (see page 3), attaining the skyline at the point marked SR.

Dow Crag offers the most impressive and rewarding mountain-walk available from Coniston. The approach along the Walna Scar path, however, although pleasant and quickly accomplished, lacks the interest of the way up from Torver and especially the growing challenge of the mountain as seen on that route; it is, therefore, a more suitable arrangement to start the walk from Torver and return direct to Coniston along the Walna Scar path.

gate

ROAD

gate

looking west

The desolate moor to the south of the Walna Scar path has revealed much of antiquarian interest: evidences indicate that the moor was the home of a Bronze Age population.

Railway Station

bridge

Coniston

ASCENT FROM THE DUDDON VALLEY
2300 feet of ascent : 3¾ miles from Seathwaite

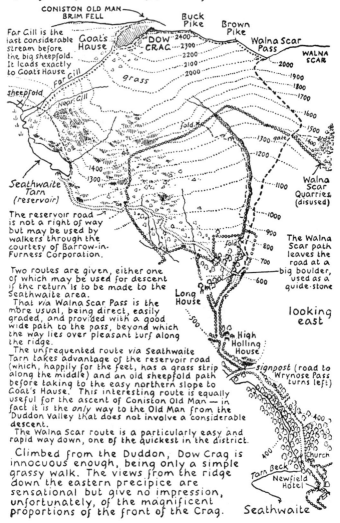

CONISTON OLD MAN
BRIM FELL

Buck Pike

Brown Pike

Walna Scar Pass

Far Gill is the last considerable stream before the big sheepfold. It leads exactly to Goat's Hause

Goat's Hause

DOW CRAG

WALNA SCAR

Far Gill

grass

sheepfold

Near Gill

Seathwaite Tarn (reservoir)

The reservoir road is not a right of way but may be used by walkers through the courtesy of Barrow-in-Furness Corporation.

Walna Scar Quarries (disused)

fold

fold

Long House

looking east

The Walna Scar path leaves the road at a big boulder, used as a guide-stone

Two routes are given, either one of which may be used for descent if the return is to be made to the Seathwaite area.

That via Walna Scar Pass is the more usual, being direct, easily graded, and provided with a good wide path to the pass, beyond which the way lies over pleasant turf along the ridge.

The unfrequented route via Seathwaite Tarn takes advantage of the reservoir road (which, happily for the feet, has a grass strip along the middle) and an old sheepfold path before taking to the easy northern slope to Goat's Hause. This interesting route is equally useful for the ascent of Coniston Old Man — in fact it is the only way to the Old Man from the Duddon Valley that does not involve a considerable descent.

The Walna Scar route is a particularly easy and rapid way down, one of the quickest in the district.

High Holling House

signpost (road to Wrynose Pass turns left)

Church

Tarn Beck

Newfield Hotel

Seathwaite

Climbed from the Duddon, Dow Crag is innocuous enough, being only a simple grassy walk. The views from the ridge down the eastern precipice are sensational but give no impression, unfortunately, of the magnificent proportions of the front of the Crag.

THE SUMMIT

Count this amongst the most delectable and exhilarating of Lakeland summits, for the sublime architecture of the great crag directly below is manifest in the topmost rocks also, forming an airy perch on a fang of naked stone elevated high above the tremendous precipice: a scene that cannot fail to exalt the minds of those who have lifted their bodies to it. An easy scramble gives access to the highest point: there is no room for a cairn. For peeps down the vertical rifts of Great Gully and Easy Gully follow a crumbled wall south along the ridge for 200 yards.

DESCENTS: Use the two ridges only: north curving east to Goat's Hause (fair path) for Coniston Old Man or Seathwaite Tarn, keeping steep ground on the right hand; or south over Buck Pike and Brown Pike to Walna Scar Pass (intermittent path ceases on Brown Pike) for Coniston or the Duddon, keeping steep ground on the left hand. Both routes are easy.

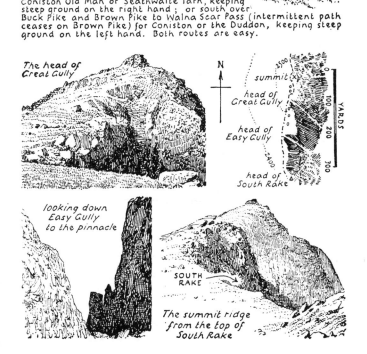

The head of Great Gully

N

2500

summit ✕

head of Great Gully

head of Easy Gully

2400

head of South Rake

YARDS

0
100
200
300

looking down Easy Gully to the pinnacle

SOUTH RAKE →

The summit ridge from the top of South Rake

THE VIEW

This is not the best of mountain views, but the outlook over the foothills of the Duddon and Esk is unexcelled, while across the southern horizon is a wide sweep of glittering sea beyond an interesting coastline. The Isle of Man, when visible, appears over Devoke Water.

Lakes and Tarns

E : Goat's Water
ESE : Windermere
E-S : Coniston Water
S : Beacon Tarn
W : Devoke Water

Principal Fells

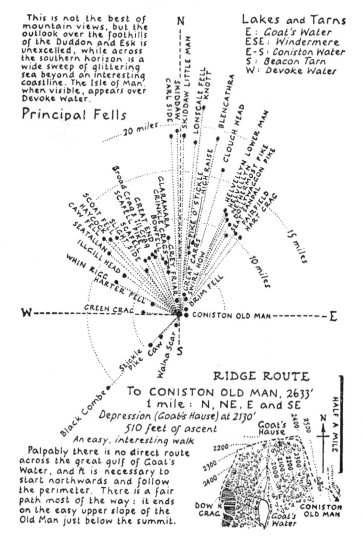

RIDGE ROUTE

To CONISTON OLD MAN, 2633'
1 mile : N, NE, E and SE
Depression (Goat's Hause) at 2130'
510 feet of ascent
An easy, interesting walk

Palpably there is no direct route across the great gulf of Goat's Water, and it is necessary to start northwards and follow the perimeter. There is a fair path most of the way: it ends on the easy upper slope of the Old Man just below the summit.

Dow Crag from Goat's Water

Esk Pike

not named on maps of
the Ordnance Survey

from Rest Gill.
Crinkle Crags

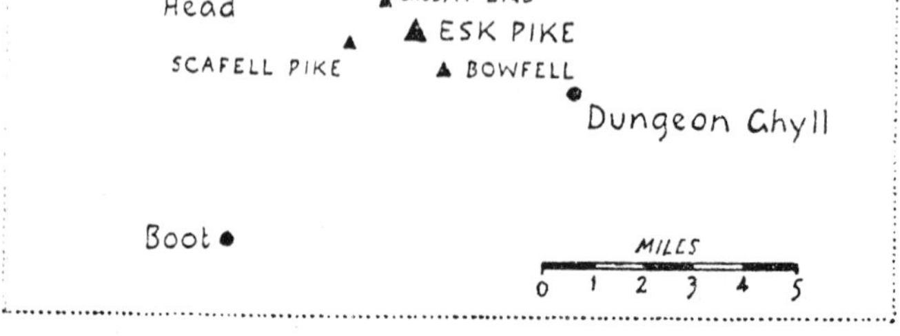

Seatoller ● ● Stonethwaite

Seathwaite ●

▲ CLARAMARA

Wasdale ●
Head
▲ GREAT END

▲ ESK PIKE

SCAFELL PIKE ▲ ▲ BOWFELL

● Dungeon Ghyll

Boot ●

MILES
0 1 2 3 4 5

NATURAL FEATURES

The central height in the semi-circle of fine peaks around the lonely head of upper Eskdale, nameless on Ordnance Survey maps, has long been known to walkers as Esk Pike. In the splendid panorama of the Eskdale skyline the fell is the least prominent, not because it competes for attention with popular favourites such as the Scafells and Bowfell and the Crinkles but rather because its top is the furthest removed from the valley and appears dwarfed in relation to the others. Yet this is, in fact, a most attractive summit, deserving a separate ascent but invariably combined with a greater objective, Bowfell. Did it but stand alone, away from such enticing neighbours, Esk Pike would rank highly among the really worth-while mountain climbs.

The outstanding feature is a lengthy south ridge, bounded by the River Esk westwards, and to the east by Yeastyrigg Gill and Lingcove Beck: a ridge with many abrupt crags. Northwards a short steep tongue of land goes down into Langstrath, enclosed between Allencrags Gill and Angletarn Gill.   Lofty ridges, crossed by the passes of Esk Hause and Ore Gap, connect with Great End and Bowfell.

1 : The summit
2 : Ridge continuing to Great End
3 : Ridge continuing to Bowfell
4 : Esk Hause
5 : Ore Gap
6 : Pike de Bield
7 : Yeastyrigg Crags
8 : Greenhole Crags
9 : High Gait Crags
10 : Low Gait Crags
11 : Long Crag
12 : Planet Knott
13 : Throstlehow Crag
14 : Throstle Garth
15 : Green Hole
16 : Yeastyrigg Gill
17 : Lingcove Beck
18 : Esk Falls
19 : River Esk
20 : Great Moss

looking north-west

Esk Hause

Sooner or later every fellwalker finds himself for the first time at Esk Hause, the highest, best-known and most important of Lakeland foot-passes, and he will probably have read, or been told, that this is a place where it is easy to go astray. There should be no danger of this, however, even in bad conditions.

Nevertheless the lie of the land is curious (but not confusing). Esk Hause is a tilted grass plateau, high among the mountains. The unusual thing about it is that *two* passes have their summits on the plateau, two passes carrying entirely different routes: in fact, in general direction they are at right angles. If these routes crossed at the highest point of the plateau there would be a simple 'crossroads', but they do not: one is a hundred feet higher than the other and 300 yards distant.

The name Esk Hause is commonly but incorrectly applied to the lower of the passes, a much-trodden route, but properly belongs to the higher and less-favoured pass. What is almost always referred to as Esk Hause is not Esk Hause at all; the true Esk Hause is rarely so named except by the cartographers. The true Esk Hause (2490') is the head of Eskdale, a shallow depression between Esk Pike and Great End, and is an infrequently-used pass between Eskdale and Borrowdale; the general direction is south-west to north-east. The false Esk Hause (2386', with a wall shelter in the form of a cross) is a shallow depression in the high skyline between the true Esk Hause and Allen Crags, and is a much used pass between Great Langdale and Wasdale, general direction being south-east to north-west.

Esk Pike, from the wall-shelter

There may, or may not, be a signpost near the shelter. Signposts erected at this point never survive long, winter gales and campfires being the chief agents of destruction.

Esk Hause ↗

path to Scafell Pike ↗

continued

Esk Hause

continued

The likeliest mistake in bad weather is that a walker approaching from Langdale and bound for Wasdale may continue along the plain path beyond the shelter and so unwittingly be ascending Scafell Pike when he should be going down to Wasdale. (The path to Scafell Pike from the shelter, incidentally, first goes up to the *true* Esk Hause and there swings away to the right; fortunately there is no track leading down into Eskdale from the Hause, otherwise it might be thought that the valley below is Wasdale — which would be a still worse mistake). The correct continuation to Wasdale is indistinct on the grass for 30 yards beyond the shelter before becoming clear. Here is an example of a bifurcation (to Scafell Pike) having become better marked on the ground than the original path (to Wasdale). It is well to remember that the shelter is the *highest* point attained on the Langdale - Wasdale route.

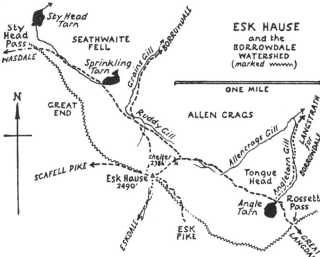

The greater importance of the higher pass as a watershed is well seen from a study of the map. All streams crossed on the Langdale-Wasdale route within the area between Rossett Pass and Sty Head Pass find their way into Borrowdale, although the latter valley is largely screened by Allen Crags. No water from this wide area flows into Langdale or Wasdale, and the lower pass therefore has little geographical significance: it is merely an intrusion in the vast system of the Eskdale-Borrowdale gathering grounds. The one function of the spurious Esk Hause is to deflect the plateau's waters into Borrowdale either by way of Langstrath or Grains Gill.

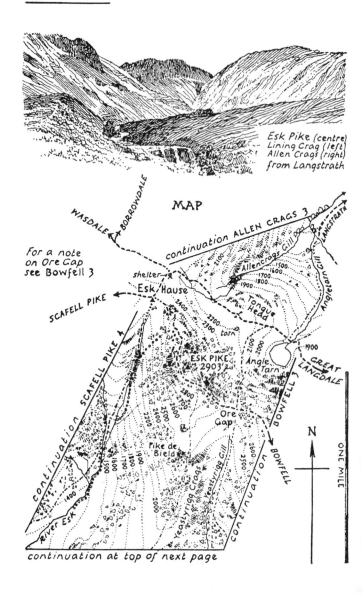

Esk Pike (centre)
Lining Crag (left)
Allen Crags (right)
from Langstrath

MAP

WASDALE
BORROWDALE

continuation ALLEN CRAGS 3

LANGSTRATH

Angletarn Gill

For a note
on Ore Gap
see Bowfell 3

shelter

Esk Hause

SCAFELL PIKE

Allencrags Gill

1500
1600
1700
1800
1900

2100

2400

2300 tarn

Tongue
Head

ESK PIKE
2903

Angle
Tarn

2100
2000

1900

GREAT LANGDALE

continuation SCAFELL PIKE 4

2800

2700

2600

2400

2500

1600

Ore
Gap

BOWFELL 3

Pike de
Bield

Yeastyrigg Crag

Yeastyrigg Gill

1500
1600
1700
1800
1900
2000

1400

2000

2600

2500

continuation BOWFELL

N

ONE MILE

River Esk

continuation at top of next page

MAP

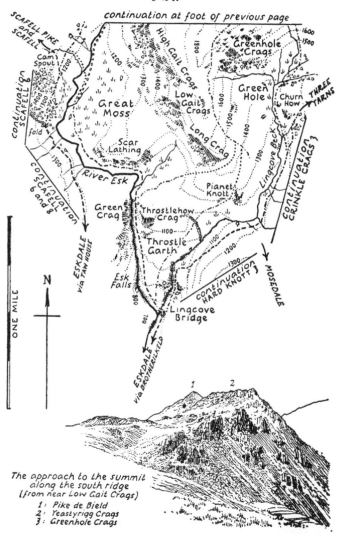

continuation at foot of previous page

SCAFELL PIKE and SCAFELL

Cam Spout

Great Moss

fold

continuation SCAFELL 6

continuation SCAFELL 6 and 8

River Esk

High Gait Crags

Low Gait Crags

Long Crag

Scar Lathing

Green Crag

ESKDALE VIA TAW HOUSE

Esk Falls

Throstlehow Crag

Throstle Garth

Pianet Knott

Greenhole Crags

Green Hole

Churn How

THREE TARNS

continuation CRINKLE CRAGS 3

Lingcove Beck

continuation HARD KNOTT 3

MOSEDALE

Lingcove Bridge

ESKDALE via BROTHERILKELD

ONE MILE

N

The approach to the summit along the south ridge (from near Low Gait Crags)

1 : Pike de Bield
2 : Yeastyrigg Crags
3 : Greenhole Crags

ASCENT FROM ESKDALE
2800 feet of ascent : 8½ miles from Boot
looking north-north-east

ESK PIKE

GREAT END · Esk Hause · Ore Gap → BOWFELL

SCAFELL PIKE · 2500 · 2700 · 2600 · 2400 · 2300 · 2200

Coldkeld Knotts · path in ravine · Pike de Bield · tarn · 2100 · 2000 · 1900 · 1800 · 1700 · 1600 · Yeastyrigg Crags

Cockly Pike · Little Narrowcove · 2000 grass · Yeastyrigg Gill · THREE TARNS

Scafell, Scafell Pike and Ill Crag tower above in succession on the left during the walk from the sheepfold to Esk Hause

Dow Crag · SCAFELL · SCAFELL PIKE · 1600 · SOUTH RIDGE · 1500 · Green Hole · grass track · 1400

Cam Spout · Cam Spout Crag · 1300 · 1400 · Great Moss · Long Crag · Pianet Knott · Lingcove Beck

sheepfold · Esk · Esk Gorge · 1000 · 900 · 1200

Esk Pike is the middle height of the five great summits forming a semi-circle around the head of upper Eskdale, and is the most distant. Although the south ridge going up above Lingcove Bridge is an obvious and natural route, it is better reserved as a quick way down and the ascent made via the Cowcove zig-zags, Cam Spout and Esk Hause, thus avoiding treading the same ground twice.
   This is a walk of exceptional beauty and interest, but make no mistake — it is a very long one.

Silverybield Crag · 1300 · 1200 · 1100 · Esk Falls · Tongue Pot · Lingcove Bridge · sheepfold · Heron Crag · Brock Crag · Pillar Pot · Yew Crags · stile

Cowcove Beck · sheepfold · gate · 900 · 800 · 700

Here is a specimen timetable for the walk, travelling comfortably (slowly on the last lap).
Boot .... 10 a m
Wha House 10.30
Cam Spout 12 30
Esk Hause 2 30
Esk Pike 3
Lingcove Bridge 4 30
Brotherilkeld 5 10
Wha House 5 30
Boot (direct) 6 15
Boot (via the bar of the Woolpack Inn) ?

Taw House farm, which always seems densely populated with yelping dogs, may be avoided by using a gate on the left and keeping above the wall.

gate · Taw House · Brotherilkeld · ESK · HARDKNOTT PASS 1½ · ROAD · 700 · 800 · 600

farm road · BOOT 1½ · Whahouse Bridge · Wha House · 300

ASCENT FROM WASDALE HEAD
2700 feet of ascent : 4¼ miles

This is also the route of ascent to Bowfell from Wasdale Head — it is reached by going on along the ridge from the top of Esk Pike south east, crossing the depression of Ore Gap.

ESK PIKE   BOWFELL

ALLEN CRAGS

2600   2700

Esk Hause

SCAFELL PIKE

shelter

2300

GREAT END

Esk Pike remains concealed by Great End almost until Esk Hause is reached

Ruddy Gill

2200

2100

2300
2200

BORROWDALE

Sprinkling Tarn   2000

2000

1900

1800

1700

1600

The Band

Skew Gill

SCAFELL PIKE

1500
grass

Sty Head Tarn

1500

Sty Head

1400

Kern Knotts

Spouthead Gill

Grainy Gill

1300

1200

1100

While nothing should be said that might be thought to detract from this excellent climb there will be no doubt in the mind of anybody who does it that the finest scenes are met in the vicinity of Sprinkling Tarn and the towering cliffs of Great End and that, in comparison with these awesome surroundings, the way beyond deteriorates in quality — which is rather a pity, for those climbs are best that grow in interest throughout, the climax coming only as the final steps are taken

Looking back and upwards to the Napes from this point, the Needle can just be discerned. The prominent rock like a sitting cat on the skyline is the Sphinx.

scree slope

Piers Gill

The fell on the right is LINGMELL

beautiful small pools

1000

Towering high into the sky on the left here is GREAT GABLE. The crags are the Napes Ridges

fold

bracken

900

800

700

600

500

Lingmell Beck

Strongly recommended as an alternative to the busy path to Sty Head rising across the screes of Great Gable is the old now-neglected valley track, a route of delightful grassy zig-zags. (For a description and eulogy of this forgotten path see Great End 7)

400

Burnthwaite

HOTEL

looking east

Wasdale Head

ASCENT FROM BORROWDALE
2550 feet of ascent : 4¾ miles from Seatoller

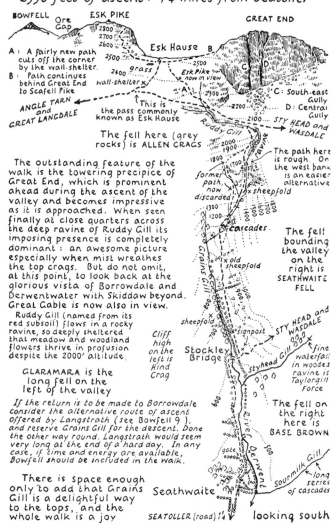

BOWFELL Ore ESK PIKE GREAT END
Gap

A : A fairly new path cuts off the corner by the wall-shelter.
B : Path continues behind Great End to Scafell Pike

ANGLE TARN and GREAT LANGDALE

Esk Hause

grass

Esk Pike now in view

wall-shelter

This is the pass commonly known as Esk Hause

C : South-east Gully
D : Central Gully

STY HEAD and WASDALE

The fell here (grey rocks) is ALLEN CRAGS

Ruddy Gill

The path here is rough. On the west bank is an easier alternative

former path, now discarded

sheepfold

Cascades

The outstanding feature of the walk is the towering precipice of Great End, which is prominent ahead during the ascent of the valley and becomes impressive as it is approached. When seen finally at close quarters across the deep ravine of Ruddy Gill its imposing presence is completely dominant : an awesome picture especially when mist wreathes the top crags. But do not omit, at this point, to look back at the glorious vista of Borrowdale and Derwentwater with Skiddaw beyond. Great Gable is now also in view.

Ruddy Gill (named from its red subsoil) flows in a rocky ravine, so deeply sheltered that meadow and woodland flowers thrive in profusion despite the 2000' altitude.

old sheepfold

The fell bounding the valley on the right is SEATHWAITE FELL

Grains Gill

GLARAMARA is the long fell on the left of the valley

sheepfold

signpost

STY HEAD and WASDALE

Styhead Gill

Cliff high on the left is Hind Crag

Stockley Bridge

fine waterfall in wooded ravine is Taylorgill Force

The fell on the right here is BASE BROWN

If the return is to be made to Borrowdale consider the alternative route of ascent offered by Langstrath (see Bowfell 9), and reserve Grains Gill for the descent. Done the other way round, Langstrath would seem very long at the end of a hard day. In any case, if time and energy are available, Bowfell should be included in the walk.

River Derwent

gate

sourmilk Gill

long series of cascades

There is space enough only to add that Grains Gill is a delightful way to the tops, and the whole walk is a joy

Seathwaite

SEATOLLER (road) 1¼

looking south

ASCENT FROM GREAT LANGDALE
2800 feet of ascent : 4¼ miles (from Dungeon Ghyll Old Hotel)

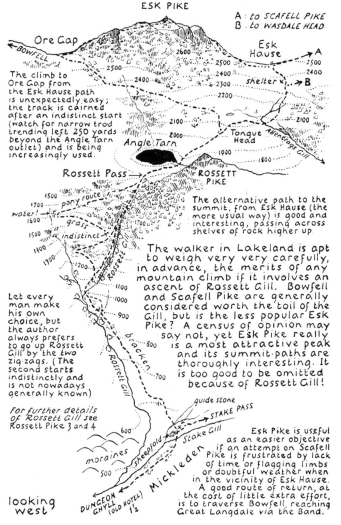

ESK PIKE

A : to SCAFELL PIKE
B : to WASDALE HEAD

Ore Gap

BOWFELL

Esk Hause

2600   2500
2500   2400   2400
2400   2300   shelter   B
2200
2100   2100
2000

Angle Tarn   Tongue Head

Allencrags Gill

1900   1800

The climb to Ore Gap from the Esk Hause path is unexpectedly easy; the track is cairned after an indistinct start (watch for narrow trod trending left 250 yards beyond the Angle Tarn outlet) and is being increasingly used.

Rossett Pass →   ROSSETT PIKE

1800
1700   pony route
water! →   1600
1500   grass
indistinct
1400
1300   1200

Rossett G.

1100
1000
900

bracken

800

Rossett Gill

700

guide stone
STAKE PASS

Stake Gill

moraines

600
500

sheepfold

Mickleden

DUNGEON GHYLL (OLD HOTEL) 1½

Let every man make his own choice, but the author always prefers to go up Rossett Gill by the two zig-zags. (The second starts indistinctly and is not nowadays generally known)

For further details of Rossett Gill see Rossett Pike 3 and 4

The alternative path to the summit, from Esk Hause (the more usual way) is good and interesting, passing across shelves of rock higher up.

The walker in Lakeland is apt to weigh very very carefully, in advance, the merits of any mountain climb if it involves an ascent of Rossett Gill. Bowfell and Scafell Pike are generally considered worth the toil of the Gill, but is the less popular Esk Pike? A census of opinion may say not, yet Esk Pike really is a most attractive peak and its summit paths are thoroughly interesting. It is too good to be omitted because of Rossett Gill!

Esk Pike is useful as an easier objective if an attempt on Scafell Pike is frustrated by lack of time or flagging limbs or doubtful weather when in the vicinity of Esk Hause. A good route of return, at the cost of little extra effort, is to traverse Bowfell, reaching Great Langdale via the Band.

looking west

THE SUMMIT

The summit is characterised by its colourful rocks, which, unlike those of the other tops in this area of 'Borrowdale volcanics,' are sharp and splintery, in predominantly brown or coppery hues with generous splashes of white and heavily stained with vivid patches of green lichen. These stones are profusely scattered and it is from a debris of flakes and fragments that the highest point, a craggy outcrop, emerges. In the lee of this small crag, which is cut away vertically to the north, is the most effective of all summit shelters, formed by two short but substantial walls: a good refuge in storm.
The path across the top of the fell does not visit the outcrop, its obvious purpose being to link Esk Hause and Bowfell and not to lead its passengers to the summit of Esk Pike. Most walkers adhere to the path and by-pass the highest rocks; they miss also the short and easy detour on grass to the pleasant tops of the buttresses forming the abrupt northern edge of the summit.

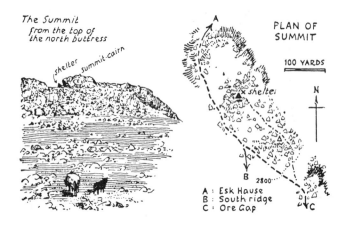

The Summit
from the top of
the north buttress

shelter   summit cairn

PLAN OF
SUMMIT

100 YARDS

N

A : Esk Hause
B : South ridge
C : Ore Gap

2800

A
B
C

× shelter

RIDGE ROUTES

To BOWFELL, 2960': 1 mile
SE, E and SE
Depression (Ore Gap) at 2575'
400 feet of ascent
Rough in places but path generally good.

A faint track skirts the north side of the next prominent outcrop along the top and then goes down to join the ridge-path, when the walk across Ore Gap (note red soil here, due to presence of hematite) and onwards is straightforward. If the day is clear and time permits, a good alternative from Ore Gap is to bear left and over the top of Hanging Knotts to get views of Angle Tarn and Rossett Pass, which will otherwise not be seen during the walk.

To GREAT END, 2984':
1¼ miles : N, NNW. W and N
Depression (Esk Hause) at 2490'
525 feet of ascent
A pleasant high-level walk

An interesting path goes down to Esk Hause (the *true* Esk Hause) where the well-trodden route to Scafell Pike is joined: this may be followed into and out of Calf Cove, when turn right up an easy ridge to the stony top of Great End. A more direct finish, avoiding Calf Cove, will encounter rougher ground.

looking north-west to Great End

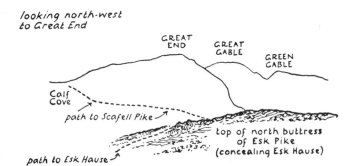

GREAT END   GREAT GABLE   GREEN GABLE

Calf Cove
path to Scafell Pike
top of north buttress of Esk Pike (concealing Esk Hause)
path to Esk Hause

THE VIEW

The excellent view is little inferior to that from the neighbouring Bowfell, and in some respects is even better, notably in the fine sight of the Scafells rising out of the depths of upper Eskdale, while the scene northwards is enhanced by the inclusion of Derwentwater, which is not seen from the loftier Bowfell. Southwards the Duddon estuary makes a pleasing picture over the slender peak of Stickle Pike.

There is an interesting viewpoint 60 yards north of the cairn and above a craggy buttress, where upper Langstrath is well displayed beyond and below Tongue Head, the shelf carrying the path between Rossett Pass and Esk Hause, which can also be seen fully. Two other buttresses to the left are easily visited: the further one has a view of Sprinkling Tarn.

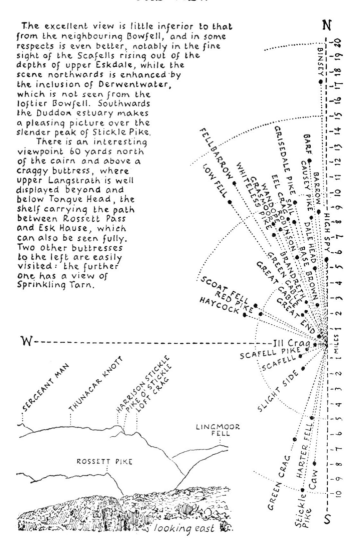

looking east

THE VIEW

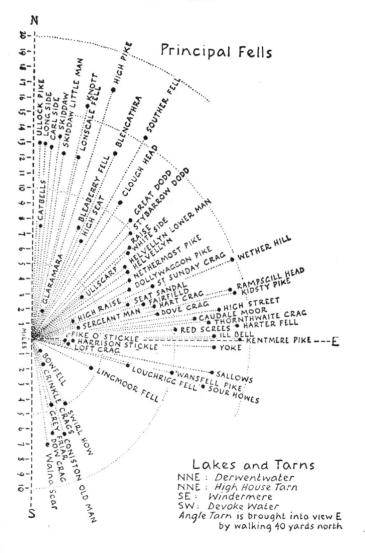

Principal Fells

Lakes and Tarns
NNE : Derwentwater
NNE : High House Tarn
SE : Windermere
SW : Devoke Water
Angle Tarn is brought into view E
by walking 40 yards north

Claramara 2560'

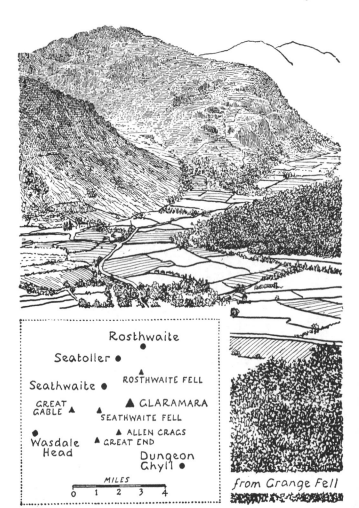

Rosthwaite •
Seatoller •
ROSTHWAITE FELL ▲
Seathwaite •
GREAT ▲
GABLE ▲ CLARAMARA ▲
▲ SEATHWAITE FELL
▲ ALLEN CRAGS
Wasdale • ▲ GREAT END
Head
Dungeon •
Ghyll

MILES
0 1 2 3 4

from Grange Fell

NATURAL FEATURES

Prominent in the mid-Borrowdale scene is the bulky fell of Glaramara, which, with an ally in Rosthwaite Fell, seems, on the approach from the north, to throw a great barrier across the valley; although in fact the level strath turns away to the right to persist as far as Seathwaite, two miles further, while a shorter branch goes left to Stonethwaite. Seen from the north the most notable feature is a gigantic hollow scooped out of the craggy mountain wall — this is Comb Gill, a splendid example of a hanging valley caused by glacial erosion and containing in its recesses the biggest cave of natural origin in the district. Considering the short distance from the road, the charmingly-wooded climb to its portals, and the impressive surround of crags, the Gill is surprisingly little visited.

Comb Gill apart, Glaramara exhibits sterile slopes of scree and rock on both east and west sides, where deep valleys, Langstrath and Grains Gill, effectively sever it from other high ground, but southwards a broad grass ridge continues with many undulations but with little general change in altitude over Allen Crags to join, at Esk Hause, a high link with the Scafell mass, of which, geographically, Glaramara and Rosthwaite Fell form the northern extremity.

The ancient and beautiful name really applies only to the grey turret of rock at the summit but happily has been commonly adopted for the fell as a whole, and it is pleasing to record that no attempt has been made to rob it of this heritage of the past, as in the case of Blencathra.

Much of Lakeland's appeal derives from the very lovely names of its mountains and valleys and lakes and rivers, which fit the scenery so well. These names were given by the earliest settlers, rough men, invaders and robbers: they were here long before Wordsworth — but they, too, surely had poetry in their hearts?

Comb Head and Raven Crag

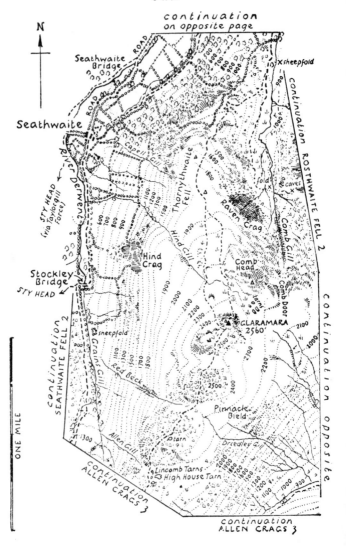

MAP

continuation
on opposite page

MAP

A new generation seems to have sprung up that knows not the pleasant path from Mountain View to Seathwaite, at first along the lane almost to Thornythwaite and then on through the fields; indeed it is unusual nowadays to see anyone using it, even though the hard road to Seathwaite yearly becomes busier and busier with pedestrian and motor traffic and, in the season, is a trial to walk upon. The field-path is an excellent start to a day's walk on the hills; returning, when one no longer has strength left even to climb stiles and ambition has narrowed to the sole objective of reaching the bus terminus before collapse is complete, the road will be rather the easier.

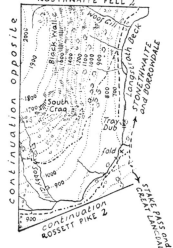

Tray Dub

ASCENT FROM BORROWDALE
2300 feet of ascent : 3¾ miles (from Rosthwaite)

looking
south-south-east

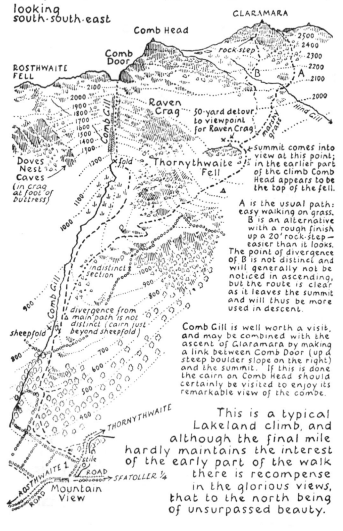

CLARAMARA

Comb Head

Comb Door

ROSTHWAITE FELL

2500
2400
2300
2200
2100
2000

rock-step

B   A

Hind Gill

mossy grass

2100
2000
1900
1800
1700
1600
1500
1400
1300

Comb Gill

Raven Crag

50-yard detour to viewpoint for Raven Crag

Doves Nest Caves
(in crag at foot of buttress)

1200

fold

Thornythwaite Fell

1100

summit comes into view at this point; in the earlier part of the climb Comb Head appears to be the top of the fell.

A is the usual path: easy walking on grass. B is an alternative with a rough finish up a 20' rock-step — easier than it looks. The point of divergence of B is not distinct and will generally not be noticed in ascending, but the route is clear as it leaves the summit and will thus be more used in descent.

1000

indistinct section

1000
900
800

900

divergence from main path is not distinct (cairn just beyond sheepfold)

sheepfold

800

700
600
500
400

Comb Gill is well worth a visit, and may be combined with the ascent of Glaramara by making a link between Comb Door (up a steep boulder slope on the right) and the summit. If this is done the cairn on Comb Head should certainly be visited to enjoy its remarkable view of the combe.

THORNYTHWAITE

stile

ROSTHWAITE 1

ROAD
SEATOLLER ¼

Mountain View

ROAD

This is a typical Lakeland climb, and although the final mile hardly maintains the interest of the early part of the walk there is recompense in the glorious views, that to the north being of unsurpassed beauty.

ASCENT FROM LANGSTRATH
2300 feet of ascent : 4½ miles (from Stonethwaite)

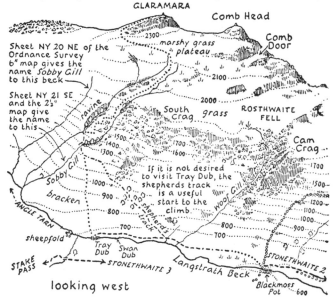

GLARAMARA
Comb Head
Comb Door

Sheet NY 20 NE of the Ordnance Survey 6" map gives the name Sobby Gill to this beck

Sheet NY 21 SE and the 2½" map give the name to this

marshy grass plateau

2300
2100
2000

South Crag   grass   ROSTHWAITE FELL

Cam Crag

Sobby Gill

bracken

If it is not desired to visit Tray Dub, the shepherds track is a useful start to the climb.

Woof Gill

shepherds track

ANGLE TARN

sheepfold
Tray Dub   Swan Dub
STAKE PASS   ←STONETHWAITE 3   Langstrath Beck   STONETHWAITE 2→

Blackmoss Pot   600

looking west

This route is submitted without recommendation that it should be tried: it lacks interest above Tray Dub and does not favourably compare with the usual approach over Thornythwaite Fell.   One purpose it serves, and serves well, is to introduce Langstrath but otherwise the climb from the valley-floor is dull, although the route will satisfy purists who like to traverse their mountains. Sobby Gill marks the first real break in the long escarpment above Langstrath and the climbing here, pathless on grass, is straightforward, simple and trouble-free: in fact the only easy route on this flank. (Woof Gill looks inviting, but is all stones)

1: Bowfell
2: Esk Pike
3: Rossett Pike
4: Tongue Head
5: Allen Crags
6: Angletarn Gill
7: Allencrags Gill
8: Langstrath Beck
9: Ore Gap

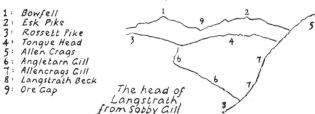

The head of Langstrath from Sobby Gill

THE SUMMIT

Twin summits of rock rise from a surrounding ocean of grass, each within its own circle of crags. They are much alike, and of similar elevation, but indisputably the finer is that to the north-east, the top of which is a rocky platform bearing two cairns: this is Glaramara proper, a pleasant halting-place on the right sort of day. The other summit, strictly, is nameless.

DESCENTS: All descents must lead to Borrowdale because all the flanking valleys flow thereto.   The usual route starts indistinctly (cairn) down a little ravine from the slight hollow between the two summits.   The alternative route, initially rough, goes sharply down north-east from the main cairn and breaches the escarpment at a 20' rock-step, which is easier than it looks. (Ladies wearing skirts, in mixed parties, can best preserve their decorum at this point by insisting on going down first and rejecting offers of male assistance.   Conversely, when *ascending* here, they must send the men up first) The alternative crosses much marshy ground, aided by stepping stones provided by various public benefactors, and joins the usual route 150 yards short of the cairn on Thornythwaite Fell.   Comb Gill is too rough and bumpy to give a good way down, and takes an hour longer.

In mist, neither path will be easy to follow, but it is most important that one or the other should be adhered to closely.

the 20' rock-step

PLAN OF SUMMIT
A: *BORROWDALE (usual route)*
B: *BORROWDALE (alternative route)*

A   B

20' rock-step

N

second summit

grass

tarn

ALLEN CRAGS

COMB DOOR

100 YARDS

RIDGE ROUTES

To ALLEN CRAGS, 2572': 1¾ miles : generally SSW
Five depressions : 500 feet of ascent

A delightful walk along a fascinating new path

The time when this ridge-walk was a rough and disagreeable scramble will be within the memory of many walkers, but in recent years a well-cairned and continuous path has come into being, skilfully planned so that the easy passages are linked together, resulting in a simple walk throughout; time formerly spent in hunting the route can now be employed in admiring the excellent views. The track, with many turns and twists and undulations, is fairly distinct (more so, for instance, than that up Claramara from the valley) and can be followed in any weather. Look out for a perfect mountain tarn in a rocky setting.

Which comes first, the line of cairns or the path? Usually, as here, the cairns, the path materialising gradually as walkers aim from one to the next. Paths often become, in due course, so distinct that the cairns lose their function except in deep snow.

To ROSTHWAITE FELL
(BESSYBOOT), 1807':
1¾ miles
ESE, then NE and N

Not as good as it looks on the map
200 feet of ascent

Confusing, marshy, pathless terrain makes this a disappointing walk. (Wanted : a line of cairns!). If the idea is to find an alternative way down to Borrowdale, it should be discarded. The easiest way lies on the Langstrath side. Definitely not a walk to attempt in mist.

Map labels:

CLARAMARA
depression — tarn
second summit — stony slope
grassy depression
third summit
stony plateau — 2500 — 2400 — 2300
marshy depression (stepping-stones)
stony plateau — 2200 — tarn
depression — Lincomb Tarns
High House Tarn — *a gem of a tarn!*
depression — tarn
tarn
grassy slope — 2200 — 2100
ALLEN CRAGS — 2500 — 2400

ROSTHWAITE FELL (BESSYBOOT)
1600
Tarn at Leaves
1700 — 1500
Rosthwaite Cam
1900 — 1700
Cam Crag
tarn — 2000
Comb Door
Comb Head
tarns — 2300 — 2200 — 2100 — 2000 — 1900
CLARAMARA

ONE MILE

N

THE VIEW

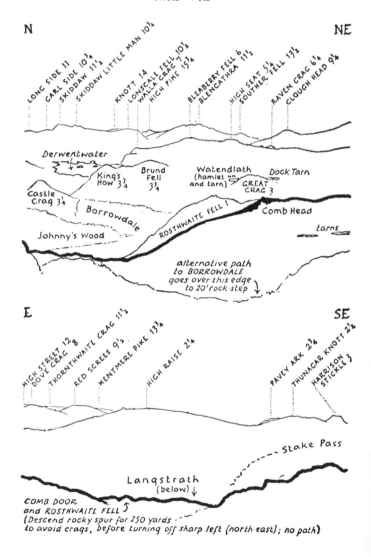

THE VIEW

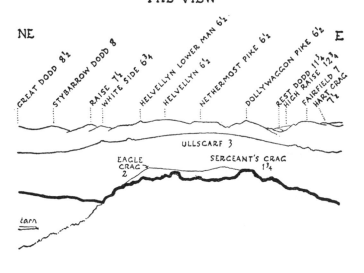

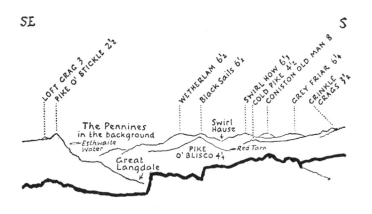

The thick line marks the visible boundaries
of the fell from the main cairn

THE VIEW

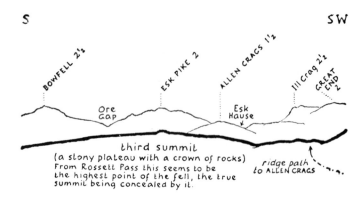

S — SW

BOWFELL 2½   ESK PIKE 2   ALLEN CRAGS 1½   Ill Crag 2½   GREAT END 2

Ore Gap

Esk Hause ↓

third summit
(a stony plateau with a crown of rocks)
From Rossett Pass this seems to be
the highest point of the fell, the true
summit being concealed by it.

ridge path
to ALLEN CRAGS

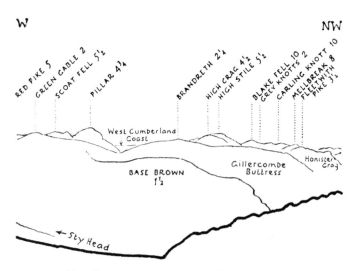

W — NW

RED PIKE 5   GREEN GABLE 2   SCOAT FELL 5½   PILLAR 4¾   BRANDRETH 2½   HIGH CRAG 4½   HIGH STILE 5½   BLAKE FELL 10   GREY KNOTTS 2   CARLING KNOTT 10   MELLBREAK 8   FLEETWITH PIKE 3½

West Cumberland Coast

BASE BROWN 1½

Gillercombe Buttress

Honister Crag

← Sty Head

*The figures accompanying the names of fells
indicate distances in miles*

THE VIEW

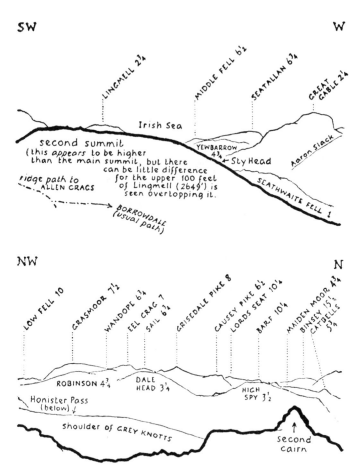

SW

W

LINGMELL 2¾

MIDDLE FELL 6½

SEATALLAN 6¾

GREAT GABLE 2¼

Irish Sea

second summit
(this appears to be higher
than the main summit, but there
can be little difference
for the upper 100 feet
of Lingmell (2649') is
seen overtopping it.

YEWBARROW 4¾
Sty Head

Aaron Slack

ridge path to
ALLEN CRAGS

BORROWDALE
(usual path)

SEATHWAITE FELL 1

NW

N

LOW FELL 10

GRASMOOR 7½

WANDOPE 6¾

EEL CRAG 7
SAIL 6¾

GRISEDALE PIKE 8

CAUSEY PIKE 6½
LORDS SEAT 10¼

BARF 10¼

MAIDEN MOOR 4¾
BINSEY 15½
CATBELLS 5¾

ROBINSON 4¾

DALE
HEAD 3¼

HIGH
SPY 3½

Honister Pass
(below)

shoulder of GREY KNOTTS

second
cairn

Glaramara's unique situation, in the heart of the district
yet isolated by deep valleys, is emphasised by the splendid
view. Overtopped by many fells but overshadowed by none,
the summit provides a spacious and interesting panorama.
But the best scene of all is that of the curve of Borrowdale
with Derwentwater and Skiddaw beyond: a superb picture.

Dungeon Ghyll

▲ PIKE O'BLISCO

Little Langdale

GREAT CARRS ▲

Cockley Beck ▲ WETHERLAM

▲ SWIRL HOW

GREY FRIAR ▲

CONISTON ▲ OLD MAN

Coniston

MILES
0 1 2 3 4

from Greenburn Beck

NATURAL FEATURES

Curved like a scythe, the shapely ridge springing from the fields of Little Langdale to the crest of Rough Crags and climbing gradually thence along the grassy rim of Wet Side Edge to a lofty altitude between deep valleys, has little to arouse interest until the mild excitement of a bouldery stairway skirting the edge of crags promises better things ahead. The airy summit of Great Carrs follows at once, a splendid perch on the edge of the profound abyss of Greenburn. A short distance beyond, the ridge terminates in the peak of Swirl How.

Apart from its eastern precipice Great Carrs has few features out of the ordinary and the western slopes going down to the valley of the Duddon are generally dull: on this flank the cliffs of Hell Gill Pike, below the subsidiary summit of Little Carrs, are more worthy of note.

The ridge, which bounds Wrynose Pass on the south, separates the waters of the Brathay from those of Greenburn, but they mingle finally in Little Langdale Tarn. Westwards, Hell Gill, in a steep ravine, is the most prominent of the early feeders of the Duddon.

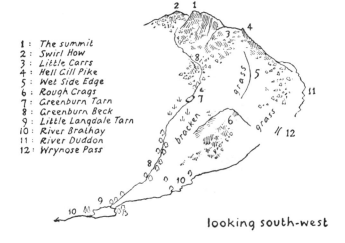

1 : The summit
2 : Swirl How
3 : Little Carrs
4 : Hell Gill Pike
5 : Wet Side Edge
6 : Rough Crags
7 : Greenburn Tarn
8 : Greenburn Beck
9 : Little Langdale Tarn
10 : River Brathay
11 : River Duddon
12 : Wrynose Pass

looking south-west

MAP

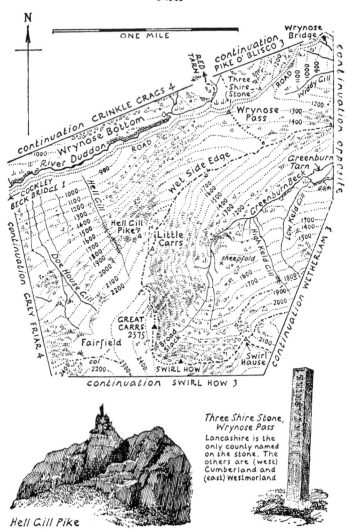

N

ONE MILE

continuation PIKE O' BLISCO 3

Wrynose Bridge

continuation opposite

RED TARN ¾

Three Shire (Stone)

ROAD

Widdy Gill

900

1100

1200

Wrynose Pass

1300

1400

continuation CRINKLE CRAGS 4

Wrynose Bottom

River Duddon

ROAD

Wet Side Edge

Greenburn Tarn

dam

1600

1700

1500

1400

1300

Greenburn Beck

1000

COCKLEY BECK BRIDGE 1

900

1000

1100

1200

1300

1400

1500

1600

1700

1800

1900

2000

2100

2200

Hell Gill

Doe House Gill

Hell Gill Pike

Little Carrs

sheepfold

High Keld Gill

Low Keld Gill

1300

1400

1500

1600

1700

1800

1900

2000

continuation WETHERLAM 3

continuation GREY FRIAR 4

GREAT CARRS: 2575

Fairfield

Broad Slack

col 2200

2300

2400

SWIRL HOW

Swirl Hause

2100

continuation SWIRL HOW 3

Hell Gill Pike

*Three Shire Stone,
Wrynose Pass*

Lancashire is the
only county named
on the stone. The
others are (west)
Cumberland and
(east) Westmorland

LANCASHIRE

MAP

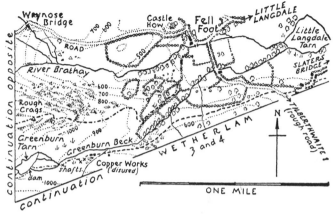

ONE MILE

Great Carrs from Little Carrs
(Swirl How in the background)

RIDGE ROUTES

To SWIRL HOW, 2630': ⅓ mile
S. then SE and E
Depression at 2500'
130 feet of ascent

To GREY FRIAR, 2536'
⅞ mile: W trending SW
Depression at 2275'
265 feet of ascent

Both easy walks, but Grey Friar is not a place to visit in mist.

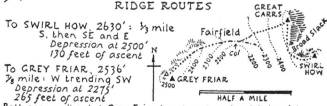

HALF A MILE

ASCENT FROM LITTLE LANGDALE
2350 feet of ascent
4 miles (from the village)

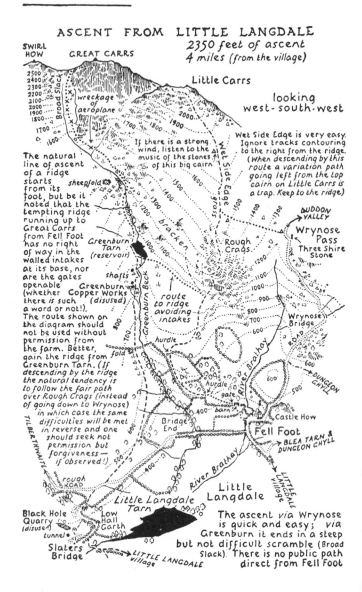

looking
west-south-west

SWIRL HOW

GREAT CARRS

Little Carrs

Broad Slack

2500 2400 2300 2200 2100 2000 1900 1800 1700 1600

wreckage of aeroplane

1700 1800 1900 2000

If there is a strong wind, listen to the music of the stones of this big cairn

Wet Side Edge

Wet Side Edge is very easy. Ignore tracks contouring to the right from the ridge. (When descending by this route a variation path going left from the top cairn on Little Carrs is a trap. Keep to the ridge)

Bracken

1600 1500 1400 1300 1200 1100

The natural line of ascent of a ridge starts from its foot, but be it noted that the tempting ridge running up to Great Carrs from Fell Foot has no right of way in the walled intakes at its base, nor are the gates openable (whether there *is* such a word or not!). The route shown on the diagram should not be used without permission from the farm. Better, gain the ridge from Greenburn Tarn. (If descending by the ridge the natural tendency is to follow the fair path over Rough Crags (instead of going down to Wrynose) in which case the same difficulties will be met in reverse and one should seek not permission but forgiveness — if observed!)

sheepfold

Greenburn Tarn (reservoir)

shafts

Greenburn Copper Works (disused)

Greenburn Beck

route to ridge avoiding intakes

hurdle

fold

Rough Crags

DUDDON VALLEY

Wrynose Pass
Three Shire Stone

1000 900 800 700 600 500

Wrynose Bridge

ROAD

600

DUNGEON GHYLL

River Brathay

hurdle

gate

barn

400

Castle How

Fell Foot

BLEA TARN & DUNGEON GHYLL

Bridge End

LITTLE LANGDALE village

500

400

River Brathay

Little Langdale

TILBERTHWAITE

rough ROAD

300

Little Langdale Tarn

Black Hole Quarry (disused)

tunnel

Low Hall Garth

Slaters Bridge

LITTLE LANGDALE village

The ascent *via* Wrynose is quick and easy; *via* Greenburn it ends in a steep but not difficult scramble (Broad Slack). There is no public path direct from Fell Foot

THE SUMMIT

1 : slope of Swirl How
2 : Coniston Old Man
3 : Brim Fell
4 : Dow Crag

south summit

The easily-graded upper western slope of Great Carrs breaks very abruptly into a long eastern precipice, the highest point of the fell therefore being on the rim, and here, on a small outcrop, is the cairn, airily perched in a splendid position high above the great hollow formed by the deep-set Greenburn valley in its circle of peaks. A short tour along the ridge, which is grassy on either side of the cairn, reveals striking gullies falling very steeply in the direction of Greenburn Tarn.

An unnatural and unwelcome adornment to the top is provided by the wreckage of an aeroplane, 150 yards south of the cairn. It is easy to reconstruct the accident. The aeroplane, travelling from west to east, failed to clear the ridge by a few feet only; at the place of impact the undercarriage was ripped off (and still lies there in a rough grave of stones) but the crippled machine went on over the edge to crash far down the precipice: the remains can be discerned from the top of Broad Slack.

DESCENTS : Go along the declining ridge, over Little Carrs, to Wet Side Edge, where incline *left* for Wrynose Pass, *right* for Greenburn Tarn — an easy descent, safe in mist.

The summit ridge, looking north

THE VIEW

looking north-west

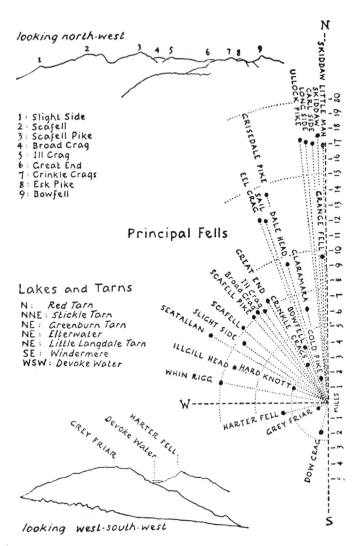

1 : Slight Side
2 : Scafell
3 : Scafell Pike
4 : Broad Crag
5 : Ill Crag
6 : Great End
7 : Crinkle Crags
8 : Esk Pike
9 : Bowfell

Principal Fells

Lakes and Tarns

N : *Red Tarn*
NNE : *Stickle Tarn*
NE : *Greenburn Tarn*
NE : *Elterwater*
NE : *Little Langdale Tarn*
SE : *Windermere*
WSW : *Devoke Water*

looking west-south-west

THE VIEW

This is an excellent view, well worth the easy walk up from Wrynose Pass, although to some extent unbalanced by the impending mass of Swirl How, which conceals the pleasant Coniston countryside (this defect being quickly remedied by going on to Swirl How itself).

The prospect across to the Scafell and Bowfell groups is magnificent. Greenburn is especially well displayed, directly below, but appears as a drab and unattractive hollow until its beck curves to join the Brathay in the brighter pastures of Little Langdale.

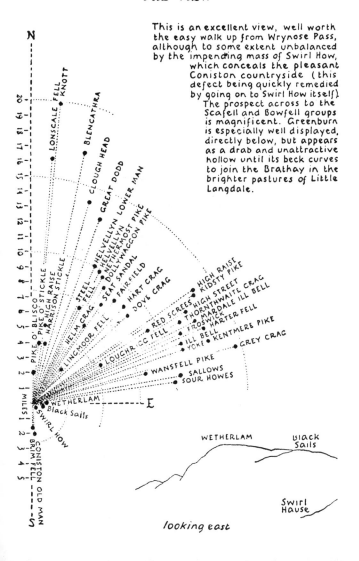

looking east

Great End

2984'

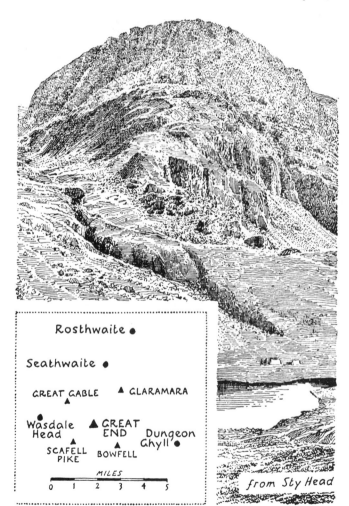

Rosthwaite ●

Seathwaite ●

GREAT GABLE ▲   ▲ GLARAMARA

Wasdale ●   ▲ GREAT
Head   END   Dungeon
        ▲   Ghyll ●
SCAFELL   BOWFELL
PIKE

MILES
0   1   2   3   4   5

from Sty Head

NATURAL FEATURES

Nobody who is familiar with the topography of the Scafell area will have any doubts why Great End was so named: there could not have been a more descriptive choice for the tremendous northern buttress of the mass. Great it is, and the end of the highest plateau in the country.

Without losing much altitude, the lofty spine of Scafell Pike extends north-eastwards a mile to the domed summit of Great End, which, when approached in this direction, has little to show other than a bouldery waste, a stony wilderness. But the vast northern fall of the mountain is one of the finest scenes in the district, awe-inspiring in its massive strength and all the more imposing for being eternally in shadow. The summit breaks immediately in a long cliff seamed by dark gullies, below which a broad shelf holds Sprinkling Tarn and continues as Seathwaite Fell, but a shoulder (the Band) also fiercely scarped and severed from the main fell by the deep ravine of Skew Gill, runs down to Sty Head.

When mist wreathes the summit and clings like smoke in the gullies, when ravens soar above the lonely crags, when snow lies deep and curtains of ice bejewel the gaunt cliffs, then Great End is indeed an impressive sight. Sunshine never mellows this grim scene but only adds harshness.

This is the true Lakeland of the fellwalker, the sort of terrain that calls him back time after time, the sort of memory that haunts his long winter exile.

It is not the pretty places— the flowery lanes of Grasmere or Derwentwater's wooded bays — that keep him restless in his bed; it is the magnificent ones. Places like Great End.....

South-east Gully · Central Gully · Cust's Gully · Long Pike

The Band

Skew Gill

footpath
ESK HAUSE
STY HEAD

stream from Sprinkling Tarn (usually regarded as the source of the Derwent)

Sty Head Tarn

Key to drawing opposite

Borrowdale
from the top of
Central Gully

MAP

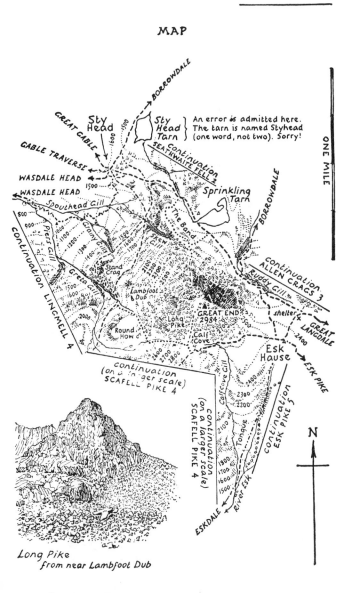

BORROWDALE

GREAT GABLE

Sty Head

Sty Head Tarn

An error is admitted here. The tarn is named Styhead (one word, not two). Sorry!

continuation SEATHWAITE FELL 2

GABLE TRAVERSE

WASDALE HEAD

WASDALE HEAD

1500

Spouthead Gill

800
900
Piers Gill
1100
1200
Grainy Gill
1300
1400
1500
Greta Gill
1500
1600
1700
2000

Stand Crag

Lambfoot Dub

Sprinkling Tarn

The Band

Skew Gill

2100
2200

BORROWDALE

continuation ALLEN CRAGS 3

Ruddy Gill

shelter ✕

GREAT LANGDALE

GREAT END 2984

2100
2200
2000

2400

Long Pike

Round How

Calf Cove

Esk Hause

ESK PIKE

continuation (on a larger scale) SCAFELL PIKE 4)

continuation (on a larger scale) SCAFELL PIKE 4)

Calfcove Gill

2300
2200

2400

continuation ESK PIKE 5

1800
1700
1600
1500

The Tongue

ESKDALE

River Esk

ONE MILE

N

Long Pike
from near Lambfoot Dub

Sty Head

Once upon a time Sty Head was a simple pass between Wasdale and Borrowdale, providing also a link with Great Langdale: the two routes served the dalesmen sufficiently and no others were needed in the vicinity to carry them about their business.

Then, a century ago, came the first walkers, in occasional twos and threes, hesitant to venture into this wild place; and later, in greater numbers, with growing confidence and much more often — for Sty Head became known as a convenient springboard for excursions into the surrounding mountains.

At the present time, it is doubtful whether Sty Head is without a visitor on any day of any year; and on most days scores, and, in high summer, hundreds of walkers pass this way — some, as the early dalesmen, seeking only an easy crossing from one valley to another, but the majority starting from this point to ascend the hills and win for themselves one more memorable experience. The needs of these happy wanderers could only be met by additional paths, and their boots have brought into existence a network of well-trodden tracks.

It is important to know these various tracks and the purpose and objective of each.

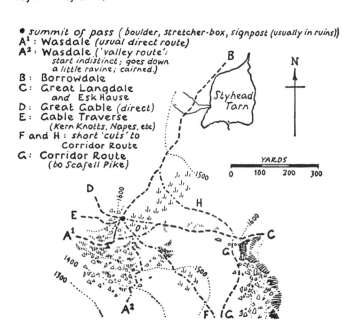

• summit of pass (boulder, stretcher-box, signpost (usually in ruins))
A¹ : Wasdale (usual direct route)
A² : Wasdale ('valley route':
  start indistinct; goes down
  a little ravine; cairned.)
B : Borrowdale
C : Great Langdale
  and Esk Hause
D : Great Gable (direct)
E : Gable Traverse
  (Kern Knotts, Napes, etc)
F and H : short 'cuts' to
  Corridor Route
G : Corridor Route
  (to Scafell Pike)

YARDS
0 100 200 300

ASCENT FROM STY HEAD
1450 feet of ascent : 1 mile

(from Wasdale Head : 2800 ft : 3¼ miles
from Seathwaite : 2650 ft : 3¼ miles)

GREAT END

A: Cust's Gully
B: branch gully

The fringe of boulders below the west summit calls for slow and careful placing of the feet.

head of Skew Gill (here only a shallow trough)

The Band (not to be confused with Bowfell's better-known Band)

2800
2700
2600
2500
2400
2300
2000
1900
1800
1700

A
B

Skew Gill

grass

ESK HAUSE

The Band is straightforward walking but the rugged final dome beyond the head of Skew Gill is mountaineering. Cust's Gully and it's branch may be inspected from below by a detour (and later from the top) but the recommended route goes up a narrow scree-filled cleft away to the right around an intervening buttress; above, a steep slope leads past the upper exit of the branch gully, and then, 50 yards higher and in the midst of boulders, a short traverse left crosses the head of Cust's Gully and reaches the welcome grass of the summit.

The simplest way onto the ridge of the Band is to first use the Esk Hause path and leave it for a grassy slope on the right at the point where the path crosses the stream.

This ascent should not be attempted in mist.

SCAFELL PIKE

Sty Head

note stretcher (just in case it is needed later in the day!)

1600

1500

Sty Head Tarn

BORROWDALE

1500

1600

looking south-south-east

Subject to the qualification that the last section is a very rough climb, this is an excellent ascent, giving a satisfying sense of achievement. The route depicted is within the capacity of energetic walkers; experienced scramblers may vary it by ascending Skew Gill (instead of the Band) and by finishing up the branch gully, both of which entail some handling of easy rocks.

The Valley Route
(Wasdale Head to Sty Head)

'Stee' (or 'Sty') means 'ladder' and the old original zigzag path here described may well be the stee that gave the Pass its name.

This page alone is worth the price of the book to those readers who frequent Wasdale Head and yet do not know the Valley Route, for it will introduce them to a new way of reaching Sty Head, on a wonderfully-graded grass path infinitely to be preferred to the usual direct route rising across the stony slopes of Great Gable, and bring pleasure in future to what is now commonly regarded as a detestable journey.

This is the old path, like many others abandoned in favour of a more direct course — but for walkers who walk for pleasure and move leisurely, who don't mind the extra 20 minutes, who find a fascination in a cleverly planned zigzag progression and who prefer to get away quietly from the crowds, it is a gem. Rarely used nowadays, and in fact not generally known, this path is not quite clear in the upper stages, but it will cause no difficulty if it is borne in mind that, everywhere, it takes the easiest line over the ground ahead. But one defect should be recorded: after rain it becomes spongy.

The point of divergence from the direct route (¼ mile beyond the footbridge)

There is as much difference between the Valley Route and the direct route as there is between sweet and sour.

It would be nice to keep the Valley Route a secret for the discerning few, and let the big parties continue to use the direct path (scar would be a better name for it), but as long as the present crazy urge for speedy methods persists (time is intended to be spent, not saved) there is little danger of the Valley Route becoming over-populated.

looking east

ASCENT FROM WASDALE HEAD
2750 feet of ascent: 4 miles

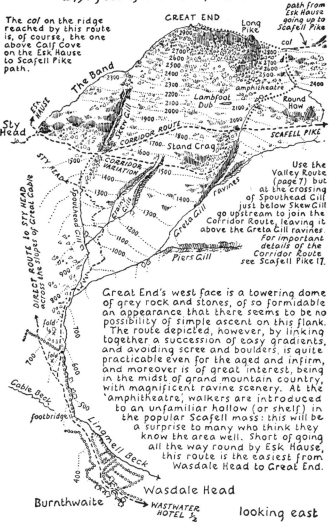

The *col* on the ridge reached by this route is, of course, the one above Calf Cove on the Esk Hause to Scafell Pike path.

path from Esk Hause going up to Scafell Pike

GREAT END

Long Pike

col

The Band

2900
2700
2500
2400
2300
2200
2100
2000
1900

ESK HAUSE

Lambfoot Dub

amphitheatre

Round How

2800
2700
2600
2400

Sty Head

STY HEAD

2100

2000

SCAFELL PIKE

CORRIDOR ROUTE

1800

1700

Stand Crag

1600

CORRIDOR VARIATION

1500

1500

Spouthead Gill

DIRECT ROUTE to STY HEAD across the slopes of Great Gable

Greta Gill ravines

Greta Gill

Grainy Gills

1300

1400

1300

1200

1100

1000

900

800

700

600

500

Piers Gill

Use the Valley Route (page 7) but at the crossing of Spouthead Gill just below Skew Gill go upstream to join the Corridor Route, leaving it above the Greta Gill ravines. For important details of the Corridor Route see Scafell Pike 17.

Great End's west face is a towering dome of grey rock and stones, of so formidable an appearance that there seems to be no possibility of simple ascent on this flank. The route depicted, however, by linking together a succession of easy gradients and avoiding scree and boulders, is quite practicable even for the aged and infirm, and moreover is of great interest, being in the midst of grand mountain country, with magnificent ravine scenery. At the 'amphitheatre', walkers are introduced to an unfamiliar hollow (or shelf) in the popular Scafell mass: this will be a surprise to many who think they know the area well. Short of going all the way round by Esk Hause, this route is the easiest from Wasdale Head to Great End.

Cable Beck

footbridge

fold

fold

Lingmell Beck

400

Wasdale Head

Burnthwaite

WASTWATER HOTEL ½

looking east

ASCENT FROM BORROWDALE
2650 feet of ascent : 5 miles from Seatoller

The path continues to Scafell Pike. Turn off (right) at the col above Calf Cove

SCAFELL PIKE →
GREAT END

Calf Cove 2600

Esk Hause

ESK PIKE

2500

fairly new path cuts off the corner by the shelter

shelter x

2400

A : South-east Gully
B : Central Gully

2400

GREAT LANGDALE →

2300

2200

2100

This is the pass commonly known as Esk Hause

Ruddy Gill

STY HEAD and WASDALE HEAD →

2000
1900
1800

Sprinkling Tarn

The fell here is ALLEN CRAGS

former path now discarded

1700

easier alternative on west bank

x sheepfold

1400

The fell bounding the valley on the right is SEATHWAITE FELL

Grains Gill is a beautiful approach to the high fells of the Scafell group.

Great End dominates the walk up the valley, almost oppressively so by the time Ruddy Gill is forded to join the Langdale - Wasdale path, and from this point it is difficult to believe that the top of the great wall of rock towering directly in front can be reached by the simplest of walking; but this is so, and in fact the steepest climbing is already at an end at 2000'.

1300

1200

cascades

old sheepfold

1100

1000

900

800

STY HEAD

signpost

The long fell on the left of the valley is GLARAMARA

Stockley Bridge

x

Styhead Gill

The fell on the right here is BASE BROWN

This route is an adaptation of a popular way to Scafell Pike (coinciding with the Langdale route thereto from Esk Hause onwards) and for anyone who sets forth for the Pike but finds his strength ebbing in the vicinity of Calf Cove it is a grand face-saver and will send him home with his tail wagging instead of between his legs, for nobody will regret a day that includes Great End in its itinerary: it is a magnificent mountain, scarcely inferior to the Pike, and, in some respects, to be preferred.

600

Grains Gill

River Derwent

500

Seathwaite

SEATOLLER (road) 1¼ ↓

looking south-south-west

ASCENT FROM GREAT LANGDALE
2900 feet of ascent : 5 miles (from Dungeon Ghyll Old Hotel)

GREAT END

SCAFELL PIKE ¾

col

2900

Keep to the path until the col above Calf Cove is reached, then turn off to the right up a grassy rake between boulders.

2500
2700

Calf
Cove

Resist this beeline (execrable stones)

ESKDALE

ESK PIKE

2600

2500

grass

2700

Esk
Hause

WASDALE
HEAD

ALLEN
CRACS

A disadvantage of the approach from Langdale is that there is little scope for variation on the return journey but strong walkers may well consider Esk Pike and Bowfell.

2400

shelter

2300
2200
2100

Tongue
Head

Angle Tarn

1900

LANGSTRATH

Rossett
Pass

ROSSETT
PIKE

pony route

1900

1500

1500
1400
1300

1200

For further details of Rossett Gill see Rossett Pike 3

1100
1000

900

800

700

Several thousand boots tread this well-known path every year, and all but a few pairs go along to its terminus at Scafell Pike's top. The very small minority of walkers turn off to Great End, an action regarded with incredulity by the following hordes of pedestrians, and they are doubtless thought to have gone astray. Nothing of the sort: they are instead exercising good judgment for Great End's quietness is much to be preferred to Scafell Pike's clatter on a day when hikers are out in quantity.
Although this is not the finest approach to Great End it is an excellent walk nevertheless; but it should be undertaken out of season if the idea is to get away from others of the species and commune with nature.

guide
stone

STAKE PASS

sheepfold

Stake Gill

moraines

Mickleden

DUNGEON
GHYLL (OLD HOTEL)
1½

looking west

Cust's Gully

Sooner or later, every Lakeland walker hears mention of Cust's Gully, but written references to it are confined to rock-climbing literature, which dismiss the place as of little consequence although grudgingly conceding that there is one small and insignificant pitch.

Looking up from the path near Sprinkling Tarn, Cust's Gully is situated high to the western end of the Great End cliffs, a clue to its position being given by the long conspicuous tongue of light-coloured stones debouching from it. On this approach the gully is concealed until its foot is reached, when it is revealed suddenly and impressively as a straight rising channel of scree between vertical walls that wedge a great boulder high above the bed of the gully and thereby provide a sure means of identification. There is no mistaking Cust's Gully.

Progress up the stony bed of the gully is easy but very rough for 50 yards to the pitch, where a chockstone blocks the way. Sloping shelves of rock, one on each side, lead up beyond the obstruction, that on the left requiring an awkward final movement, that on the right steepening for a few critical feet. The walls of the gully are here quite vertical, and directly above is poised the wedged boulder.

the pitch

This pitch is the one difficulty: above there is nothing but simple scrambling to the top of the gully. The pitch may therefore be visited from either exit and the splendid rock-scenes certainly justify an inspection.

from below

The author, after twice timorously attempting to climb the pitch with no real hope of succeeding, retired from Cust's Gully with a jeering conscience and went home to write, in capital letters, on page 11 of his Great End chapter:
NO WAY FOR WALKERS

from above

Note that the wedged boulder itself supports a number of smaller stones which can only be at temporary rest. Heaven help anybody in Cust's Gully when they fall off. It won't be the author, anyway: he's not going again.

The branch gully

On the direct climb from the path below Cust's Gully slants away to the left, but an ill-defined branch gully continues the line of ascent, its course after 20 yards being interrupted by a chockstone pitch, mossy and of formidable appearance. This can be avoided, but not easily and only by handling rocks, over broken ground (steep) immediately to the right; beyond is scree to the open fellside.

The branch gully cannot be described as a walkers route, either.

The pitch, branch gully

The pedestrian route

Frustrated and humbled by defeats in Cust's and the branch gully, the dispirited pedestrian, his ego in shreds, can still find a way to the top of the fell without losing more than 100 feet in height, by sneaking round the toe of the buttress to the right (west) of both gullies and ascending the first obvious breach in the crags, a short screefilled ravine, which will be found easy after what has just been endured and which gives access to a steep, simple slope above, where an incipient track will be found. Halfway up this slope the top exit of the branch gully is passed and higher a fringe of boulders is reached; by stumbling upwards over these wretched stones for 50 further yards and then traversing left the open top of Cust's Gully will be skirted and the grassy summit of the fell reached, with sighs of relief, immediately beyond.

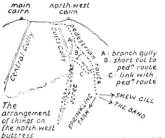

main cairn
north-west cairn
Central Gully
Cust's Gully
Pedestrian route
scree

A: branch gully
B: short cut to pedⁿ route
C: link with pedⁿ route

→ SKEW GILL
→ THE BAND
SPRINKLING TARN

The arrangement of things on the north-west buttress

Skew Gill

Skew Gill is a tremendous gash in the Wasdale side of Great End with proportions little inferior to those of Piers Gill. The floor of the ravine is littered with stones of all shapes and sizes which can be negotiated by agile walkers, but in the upper reaches the bed of the gill is composed of naked rock at an easy angle, calling for care; the final climb out, round a corner, is rather steeper. The sides of the ravine are loose; it is important to keep throughout in the company of the stream. In good conditions this may be regarded as a way for experienced scramblers. The author managed to ascend the gill (on the end of the publisher's rope) so there seems to be no good reason why everybody shouldn't, but his sufferings were such that he can NOT recommend it as a route for decent walkers.

in Skew Gill

the lower entrance, Skew Gill

THE SUMMIT

There are two cairns, each centred in a rash of stones, linked by a grassy saddle of slightly lower altitude. The main cairn (trigonometrical station) is that to the south-east, although the difference in elevation between the two can be a matter of inches only. There is little interest on the actual top of the fell but it would be almost a sin to go away without searching for the various upper exits of the gullies. Only the gaping main exit of Central Gully is likely to be noticed on a walk across the summit; the others have to be hunted and each in turn provides an excitement with its startling downward plunge and fine rock scenery.

north-west cairn   GREAT GABLE

The cliff is broken into small crags with areas of vegetation. Except at the rim, the angle of the slope is, in general, not excessive. This explains the wide extent of the cliff on the plan. Thus, although the two main gullies have a vertical height of 600 feet, it is that distance also horizontally between top and bottom — an average of 45°

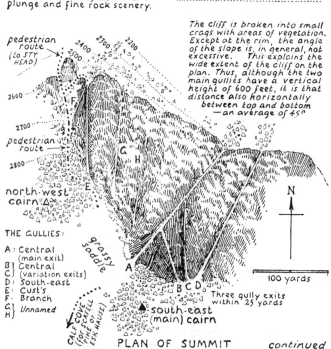

pedestrian route (to STY HEAD)

2400 2300 2200
2500
2600
2700
2800
F

pedestrian route

G
H
E

north-west cairn △

grassy saddle

N

A
B C D

THE GULLIES:
A: Central (main exit)
B) Central
C) (variation exits)
D: South-east
E: Cust's
F: Branch
G)
H) Unnamed

Three gully exits within 25 yards

100 yards

CALF COVE (for SCAFELL PIKE, ESK HAUSE)

south-east (main) cairn △

PLAN OF SUMMIT

continued

THE SUMMIT

continued

DESCENTS: There is only one simple way off Great End, and that is to proceed south-south-west, keeping to a grass strip between acres of stones, to the Calf Cove depression, where the path from Scafell Pike may be followed to Esk Hause for whatever destination is required. Although this way is roundabout and long, it is possible to work up a spanking pace on the easy gradient to Esk Hause.

The pedestrian route below the north-west cairn is not quite easy to determine from above, the stony ground is very rough, and progress is painfully slow. This route goes down parallel to and 30 yards west of Cust's Gully.

In mist, do be careful and sensible. Go round by Calf Cove to Esk Hause. The inviting openings in the edge of the cliff are all traps and will quickly lead to serious trouble. The pedestrian route is out of the question unless its location is already well known and its course has been followed recently.

RIDGE ROUTES

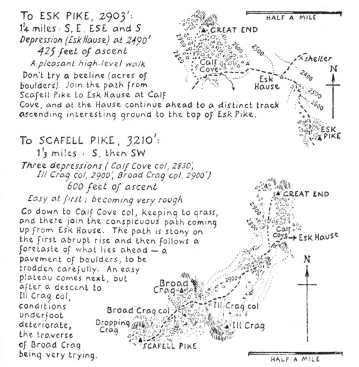

To ESK PIKE, 2903':
1¼ miles: S, SE, ESE and S
Depression (Esk Hause) at 2490'
425 *feet of ascent*
A pleasant high-level walk

Don't try a beeline (acres of boulders). Join the path from Scafell Pike to Esk Hause at Calf Cove, and at the Hause continue ahead to a distinct track ascending interesting ground to the top of Esk Pike.

To SCAFELL PIKE, 3210':
1⅓ miles : S, then SW
Three depressions (Calf Cove col, 2830';
Ill Crag col, 2900'; Broad Crag col, 2900')
600 *feet of ascent*
Easy at first ; becoming very rough

Go down to Calf Cove col, keeping to grass, and there join the conspicuous path coming up from Esk Hause. The path is stony on the first abrupt rise and then follows a foretaste of what lies ahead — a pavement of boulders, to be trodden carefully. An easy plateau comes next, but after a descent to Ill Crag col, conditions underfoot deteriorate, the traverse of Broad Crag being very trying.

THE VIEW

While the multitudes are milling around the top of nearby Scafell Pike, trying to find elbow-room to manipulate their field-glasses and telescopes, the cairn on Great End often remains lonely and here one may enjoy, uninterrupted, a view scarcely less extensive or interesting and certainly not less beautiful than that from the Pike. In one direction, to the north, the view is near perfection: this scene of Borrowdale and Derwentwater, backed by Skiddaw, is best surveyed from the crest of the cliff and is among the fairest of Lakeland pictures. The only blot on the wide landscape is Calder Hall Atomic Power Station, a reminder that, down on the plains, men's thoughts are not, as they are up here, of mountains and peace and the bountiful goodness of the Creator of this lovely district. Here, not there, is the supreme artistry.

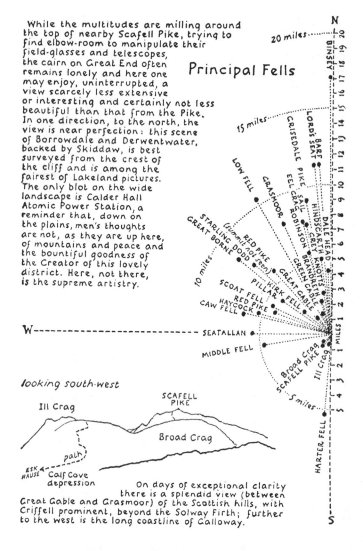

Principal Fells

looking south-west

On days of exceptional clarity there is a splendid view (between Great Gable and Grasmoor) of the Scottish hills, with Criffell prominent, beyond the Solway Firth; further to the west is the long coastline of Galloway.

THE VIEW

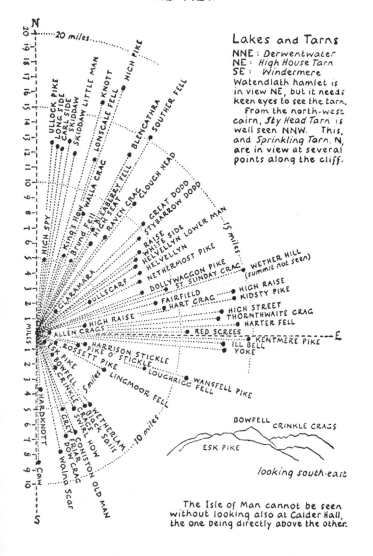

Lakes and Tarns

NNE: *Derwentwater*
NE: *High House Tarn*
SE: *Windermere*

Watendlath hamlet is in view NE, but it needs keen eyes to see the tarn.

From the north-west cairn, *Sty Head Tarn* is well seen NNW. This, and *Sprinkling Tarn*, N, are in view at several points along the cliff.

looking south-east

The Isle of Man cannot be seen without looking also at Calder Hall, the one being directly above the other.

Green Crag

from Birker Fell

from Boot

On the crest of the moorland between the Duddon Valley and Eskdale there rises from the heather a series of serrated peaks, not of any great height but together forming a dark and jagged outline against the sky that, seen from certain directions, arrest the eye as do the Black Coolin of Skye. The highest of these peaks is Green Crag, a single summit, and its principal associate is Crook Crag, with many separate tops. Together they provide an excellent objective for exploration, or as viewpoints, and, if the climb is made from Eskdale, as it should be for full enjoyment, the whole walk is a delight, best saved for a sunny afternoon in August.

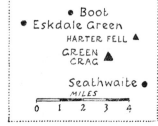

- ● Boot
- ● Eskdale Green
- HARTER FELL ▲
- GREEN CRAG ▲
- Seathwaite ●

MILES

0 1 2 3 4

on the approach from Eskdale

MAP

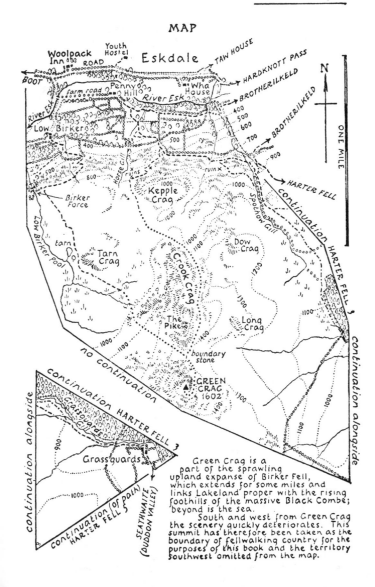

Green Crag is a part of the sprawling upland expanse of Birker Fell, which extends for some miles and links Lakeland proper with the rising foothills of the massive Black Combe; beyond is the sea.

South and west from Green Crag the scenery quickly deteriorates. This summit has therefore been taken as the boundary of fellwalking country for the purposes of this book and the territory southwest omitted from the map.

ASCENT FROM ESKDALE
1450 feet of ascent : 2½ miles from the Woolpack Inn

GREEN CRAG

The rocky top is most easily gained from the rear →

A standing stone → in the depression marks the parish boundary.

Crook Crag is a cockscomb ridge, interesting to follow, but it may be avoided on the east if desired

bracken

Crook Crag

bog myrtle

Low Birker Pool

Low Birker Tarn

the Low Birker peat-hut

many perched boulders in this area

Tarn Crag

plateau

fold

heathery swamps

Kepple Crag

In descent, the top of the Penny Hill peat road is not easy to locate. Keep left of the last bulky rise on the plateau (Kepple Crag)

heather

old fold

peat road

stone hut (ruin)

peat road

stone hut (ruin)

HARTER FELL ruins

Birker Force

Detour to foot of Birker Force (not a public path)

hurdle

juniper

gate

path to DALEGARTH

Crag Coppice

enclosure of rough bouldery ground (glacier debris?)

Low Birker

farm road

footpath to CHURCH

footpath to BROTHERILKELD

sheepfold

Penny Hill

farm road

Doctor Bridge

River Esk

looking south-south-east

UPPER ESKDALE

Woolpack Inn

BOOT 1

A wet morning in Eskdale need not necessarily mean a day's fellwalking lost, for if the sky clears by the early afternoon here is a short expedition well worth trying. The two old peat roads are excellent ways to the lip of the plateau; beyond is a heathery wilderness from which rise several rocky tors, the furthermost (and loftiest) being Green Crag. Preferably, ascend by Low Birker and return by Penny Hill: the walk is easier and less confusing done so.

An interesting feature of this walk is the acquaintance made with the old peat roads so characteristic of Eskdale. From most of the valley farms a wide, well graded 'road' (usually a grassy path) zig-zags up the fellside to the peaty heights above, and there ends; the stone huts used for storing a supply of peat are still to be seen, now in ruins or decay, on or just below the skyline. Time has marched fast in Eskdale: at the foot of the valley is the world's first atomic power station, and peat is out of fashion. Alas!

OTHER ASCENTS

FROM THE DUDDON VALLEY: Reach Grassguards by one of the three
routes mentioned on page Harter Fell 5, continuing onwards by the
Eskdale path until the open fell is gained beyond the last wall, and
there turning due west up a grassy, often wet, and very easy slope.

FROM THE BIRKER FELL ROAD: An obvious starting-point is the top of
the unenclosed road between Ulpha and Eskdale Green, whence simple
and straightforward walking leads to the summit. To avoid swamps
keep to the heights over Great Worm Crag.

THE SUMMIT

A ring of crags gives the appearance of
impregnability to the summit, but an easy
scramble reveals the highest point, a fine
place of vantage, as a small grassy sward,
with an old and hoary cairn occupying the
place of honour, and looking as though it
has stood there since the beginning of time.

THE VIEW

DESCENTS in mist:
Get down, with care, to
the grassy depression
between Green Crag
and Crook Crag (a
standing stone may
be noted here) and
walk east, down a
gentle gradient,
to join the path
connecting the
Duddon Valley
(right) and
Eskdale (left)

The view is better
than will generally
be expected, and in
some respects even
surpasses that from
Harter Fell, the high
Mosedale Fells being
seen to advantage over
the wide depression of
Burnmoor Tarn, while
the Scafell - Bowfell
groups lose nothing
in majesty at this
greater distance.
Seawards there
is a fine prospect
interrupted only by
the bulky Black Combe.

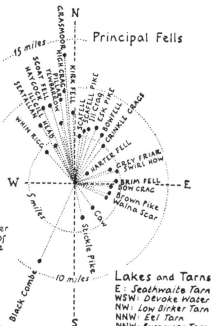

Principal Fells

N

15 miles

GRASMOOR
HIGH CRAG
PILLAR
YEWBARROW
SCOAT FELL
HAYCOCK
ILLGILL HEAD
SEATALLAN

KIRK FELL

SCAFELL
SCAFELL PIKE
ESK PIKE

ILL CRAG

BONFELL

CRINKLE CRAGS

WHIN RIGG

HARTER FELL

CREY FRIAR
SWIRL HOW

W — — — — — E

BRIM FELL
DOW CRAG
Brown Pike
Walna Scar

5 miles

Caw

Stickle Pike

10 miles

Black Combe

S

Lakes and Tarns
E: Seathwaite Tarn
WSW: Devoke Water
NW: Low Birker Tarn
NNW: Eel Tarn
NNW: Burnmoor Tarn

Grey Friar

2536'

from Hell Gill Pike

Cockley
Beck
GREY
FRIAR
Troutal
DOW
CRAG
Seathwaite

Little
Langdale
SWIRL HOW

CONISTON
OLD MAN

Coniston

MILES
0 1 2 3 4

NATURAL FEATURES

Grey Friar, like Dow Crag, stands aloof from the main spine of the Coniston Fells, but, unlike Dow Crag, has no great single natural feature to attract attention and is consequently the least-frequented of the group. Yet it is a fine mountain of considerable bulk, and forms the eastern wall of the Duddon Valley for several miles, rising high above the foothill series of knobbly tors and hanging crags that so greatly contribute to the unique beauty of that valley. In topographical fact, Grey Friar belongs exclusively to the Duddon, to which all its waters drain, and not to Coniston. Great Blake Rigg and Little Blake Rigg are extensive rock-faces in the neighbourhood of Seathwaite Tarn, and there are others, but generally the higher reaches are grassy and the summit assumes the shape of a rounded dome, which is of no particular interest except as a viewpoint, the scene westwards to the Scafells being magnificent.

Grey Buttress,
Great Blake Rigg

1 : The summit
2 : Wet Side Edge
3 : Great Blake Rigg
4 : Little Blake Rigg
5 : Troutal Tongue
6 : High Tongue
7 : Holling House Tongue
8 : Hinning House Plantation
(Hardknott National Park)
9 : Seathwaite Tarn
10 : Tarn Beck
11 : The valley of Tarn Beck
12 : Cockley Beck
13 : River Duddon
14 : Wallowbarrow Gorge

grass

bracken

looking
east·south·east

Grey Friar 3

MAP

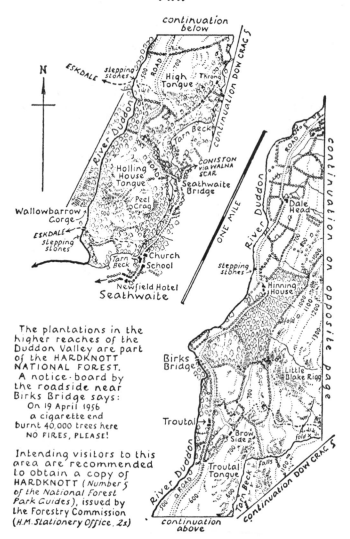

The plantations in the higher reaches of the Duddon Valley are part of the HARDKNOTT NATIONAL FOREST. A notice-board by the roadside near Birks Bridge says:

On 19 April 1956 a cigarette end burnt 40,000 trees here NO FIRES, PLEASE!

Intending visitors to this area are recommended to obtain a copy of HARDKNOTT (Number 5 of the National Forest Park Guides), issued by the Forestry Commission (H.M. Stationery Office. 2s)

MAP

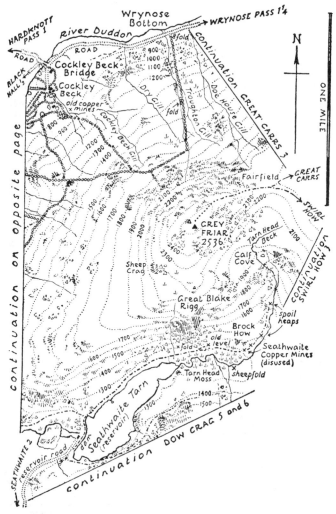

The Valley of Tarn Beck

The geography of the Duddon Valley above Seathwaite is confusing, and calls for a close study of the map. The tributary Tarn Beck is the cause of the perplexity: this considerable stream issues from Seathwaite Tarn and at first heads directly for the River Duddon in accordance with the natural instinct of all water to go downhill by the shortest route and has almost finished the journey when it runs up against the low rocky barrier of Troutal Tongue, which turns it south, parallel to the Duddon. A continuation of the Tongue then persists in keeping Tarn Beck away from its objective until gentler pastures are reached below Seathwaite, where the waters are finally united. Tarn Beck, after thousands of years of constant frustration, has carved out its own beautiful valley, so that for two miles the dale has twin parallel troughs running closely side by side.

Confusion is worse confounded because the road along the valley switches from one to the other, unobtrusively. Thus the river bordering the road north of the village of Seathwaite is Tarn Beck, not the Duddon as is commonly supposed, while higher, after the road has crossed again to the Duddon, the valley of Tarn Beck widens into a neat cultivated strath with a small farming community, but the main river hereabouts remains hidden in its wooded gorge.

Ancient footbridge over Long House Gill in the valley of Tarn Beck

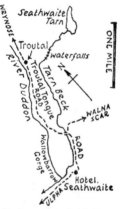

Man rarely beautifies nature, but the exception most certainly occurs in the cultivated valleys of Lakeland. Every walker on the hills must often have been stopped in his tracks by some entrancing glimpse of beautiful green pastures and stately trees in a valley below, a perfect picture of charm and tranquillity in utter contrast to his own rugged surroundings. So delightfully fresh and sparkling, those lovely fields and meadows, that they seem to be in sunshine even in rain; so trim and well-kept that they might be the lawns of some great parkland. But they were not always so. Before man settled here these same valleys were dreary marshes.

The little valley of Tarn Beck illustrates the 'before and after' effect very well. Beyond and around the walled boundaries of the cultivated area — a patchwork of level pastures — there is at once a morass of bracken and coarse growth littered with stones, with much standing water that cannot escape the choke of vegetation. Once all the dale was like this. So was Borrowdale, and Langdale, and other valleys that today enchant the eye. Hard work and long perseverance have brought fertility from sterility. Rough hands have won a very rare beauty from the wilderness.... Man here has improved on nature.

ASCENT FROM THE DUDDON VALLEY
2200 feet of ascent : 4 miles from Seathwaite
(2000 feet : 2¼ miles from Troutal)

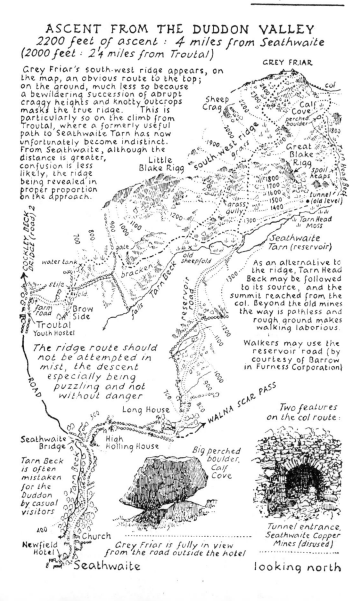

Grey Friar's south-west ridge appears, on the map, an obvious route to the top; on the ground, much less so because a bewildering succession of abrupt craggy heights and knotty outcrops masks the true ridge.   This is particularly so on the climb from Troutal, where a formerly useful path to Seathwaite Tarn has now unfortunately become indistinct. From Seathwaite, although the distance is greater, confusion is less likely, the ridge being revealed in proper proportion on the approach.

The ridge route should not be attempted in mist, the descent especially being puzzling and not without danger

As an alternative to the ridge, Tarn Head Beck may be followed to its source, and the summit reached from the col. Beyond the old mines the way is pathless and rough ground makes walking laborious.

Walkers may use the reservoir road (by courtesy of Barrow in Furness Corporation)

Two features on the col route:

Big perched boulder. Calf Cove

Tunnel entrance, Seathwaite Copper Mines (disused)

Tarn Beck is often mistaken for the Duddon by casual visitors

Grey Friar is fully in view from the road outside the hotel

Seathwaite

looking north

ASCENT FROM WRYNOSE PASS
1350 feet of ascent : 2¼ miles

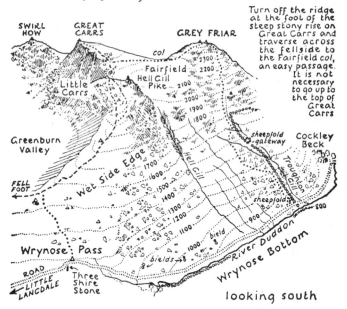

Turn off the ridge at the foot of the steep stony rise on Great Carrs and traverse across the fellside to the Fairfield col, an easy passage. It is not necessary to go up to the top of Great Carrs

looking south

Once the ridge is gained from the Pass (a matter of 15 minutes simple climbing over rough grass and mosses) the remainder of this walk, with views improving the whole way, is merely a stroll. Wet Side Edge is one of the easiest ridges in the district, and, in spite of its name, quite dry underfoot. In mist, keep to the edge and be content with Great Carrs instead.

The alternative route depicted (a direct climb from the road in Wrynose Bottom) is less interesting and rather spoiled by much wet ground alongside the wall (which, usefully, points straight to the unseen summit). When the wall turns away to the right, keep on ahead, first up a grassy rake between crags and then selecting a route between the several outcrops below the top.

Fairfield, well named, is a wide gently-contoured grassy expanse, and a favourite sheep-walk, sloping to a shallow col between Grey Friar and the main ridge.

Travellers along Wrynose Bottom may have their curiosity aroused by the short stone walls, only a few yards in length, built at intervals at right angles to the road and not far distant from it. These walls are BIELDS, shelters for sheep from strong winds and drifting snow.

THE SUMMIT

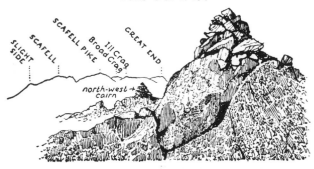

On the usual approach to the summit, from the Fairfield col, a long level promenade of excellent turf precedes a stonier area where two rock outcrops 40 yards apart, each bearing a cairn, are slightly elevated above the plateau: the one to the south-east is the true summit, having an advantage of a few feet in altitude, but the one north-west (which may be reached by a simple 20' rock-climb, if desired) commands the better view. Other outcrops carry smaller cairns, a source of confusion in mist.

DESCENTS: In clear weather there should be no difficulty in getting down by any of the routes given for ascent, but the south-west ridge may involve some trial and error in finding an easy passage at its extremity. In mist, it is advisable to go down first to the Fairfield col, whatever the ultimate aim, and take bearings there. The track to the col is so sketchy as to be virtually non-existent, and a few more cairns would be useful here: incline slightly right rather than left where the descent from the summit-plateau commences.

RIDGE ROUTES

To SWIRL HOW, 2630': 1 mile: NE, then E and ESE
Depression (Fairfield col) at 2275'
355 feet of ascent

To GREAT CARRS, 2575'
⅞ mile: NE, then E
Depression (Fairfield col) at 2275'
300 feet of ascent

Both routes may be described together, for they are twins. In either case go down to Fairfield col, where there is a faint and insignificant meeting of tracks. Very easy grass slopes lead upwards beyond the col without incident except for the remains of a crashed aeroplane just below the top of Great Carrs.

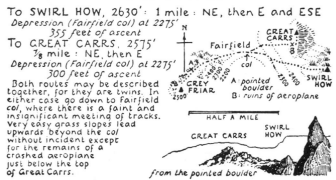

A: pointed boulder
B: ruins of aeroplane

HALF A MILE

from the pointed boulder

THE VIEW

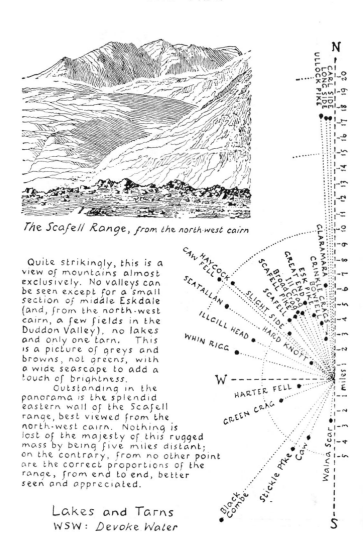

The Scafell Range, from the north-west cairn

Quite strikingly, this is a view of mountains almost exclusively. No valleys can be seen except for a small section of middle Eskdale (and, from the north-west cairn, a few fields in the Duddon Valley), no lakes and only one tarn. This is a picture of greys and browns, not greens, with a wide seascape to add a touch of brightness.

Outstanding in the panorama is the splendid eastern wall of the Scafell range, best viewed from the north-west cairn. Nothing is lost of the majesty of this rugged mass by being five miles distant; on the contrary, from no other point are the correct proportions of the range, from end to end, better seen and appreciated.

Lakes and Tarns
WSW: Devoke Water

THE VIEW

Principal Fells

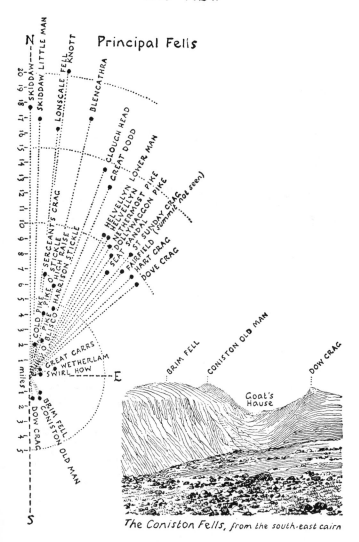

The Coniston Fells, from the south-east cairn

Hard Knott

from Whahouse Bridge

Hard Knott is well known for three features: the pass of the same name, a Roman camp, and the view of the Scafells from its summit. The fell itself is not especially remarkable, and is best described as a wedge of high ground dividing Eskdale and Mosedale, the latter running down into the Duddon Valley.

Hardknott Pass

Geographically, Hard Knott is a continuation of the north-eastern ridge of Harter Fell, with the pass occupying a depression thereon.

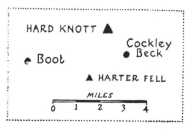

HARD KNOTT ▲

Cockley
● Beck

● Boot

▲ HARTER FELL

MILES
0   1   2   3   4

The Roman Fort

On the south-western slope of Hard Knott the rocky cliffs of Border End fall steeply to an inclined grassy shelf, which extends for half a mile and then breaks abruptly in a line of crags overlooking the Esk. This shelf, a splendid place of vantage commanding a view of the valley from the hills down to the sea, was selected by the Romans towards the end of the first century A.D. as a site for the establishment of a garrison to reinforce their military occupation of the district. Here they built a fort, MEDIOBOGDVM, which today is more usually, and certainly more easily, referred to as HARDKNOTT CASTLE. The main structure and outbuildings have survived the passing years sufficiently to provide a valuable source of information and study for the expert and an object of considerable interest for the layman. At present the walls of the fort are being rebuilt by the Ministry of Works, a slate course indicating the original wall below and the restored portion above. There is divided opinion as to whether this physical reconstruction is desirable: would not the mouldering ruins, left to their natural decay, have had a greater appeal to the imagination?

A : Commandant's House
B : Headquarters
C : Granaries
D : Bath-houses

mound (inspection platform)

open PARADE GROUND

road

900

N

walled FORT

HARDKNOTT PASS

800

D

ESKDALE   present motor road

YARDS

0   100   200

One wonders what were the thoughts of the sentries as they kept watch over this lonely outpost amongst the mountains, nearly two thousand years ago? Did they admire the massive architecture of the Scafell group as they looked north, the curve of the valley from source to sea as their eyes turned west? Or did they feel themselves to be unwanted strangers in a harsh and hostile land? Did their hearts ache for the sunshine of their native country, for their families, for their homes?

There is an informative article on the Roman fort in the publication of the Forestry Commission "HARDKNOTT: Number Five of the National Forest Park Guides" (H.M. Stationery Office, 2s.). This is an excellent book, dealing with the history, geology, wild life, botany, and so on, of Eskdale and the Duddon Valley. It isn't as good as "The Southern Fells," though, in its detail of the walking routes in the area, not by a long chalk.

MAP

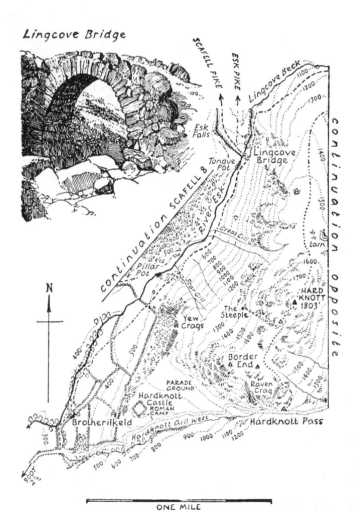

Lingcove Bridge

MAP

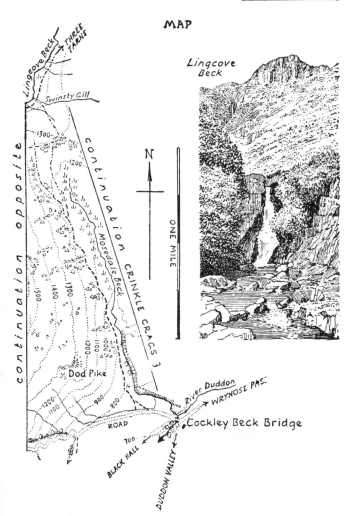

The present motor road across Hardknott Pass does not lie on the line of the Roman road. The latter generally lay to the north of the present road on the Eskdale side of the Pass (and, of course, went up to the fort), and on the Duddon side made a wide detour to the south, coming down to the valley where Black Hall now stands.

ASCENT FROM HARDKNOTT PASS
550 feet of ascent : ¾ mile

This short climb hardly calls for a diagram.   Leave the road exactly at the cairn on the highest point of the Pass — not from the rocky defile to the west, where crags bar the way. From the cairn a grass track slants up to the right, then left to a run of scree, above which easier ground is reached, amongst outcrops, and followed to the summit along an indefinite ridge. (There is a view of the Steeple, down on the left, at one place on the ridge). Memorise the position of the scree-run, if returning to the road : it is elusive when sought from above. While on the top it is worth while making the short detour to Border End for a glorious prospect of Eskdale.

The Steeple,
also known as
Eskdale Needle
(about 50' high
on its longest side,
facing the valley)

THE SUMMIT

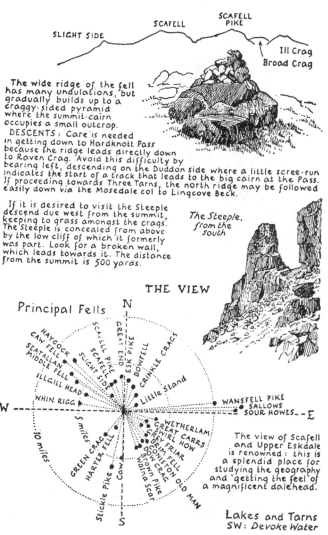

SLIGHT SIDE — SCAFELL — SCAFELL PIKE — Ill Crag — Broad Crag

The wide ridge of the fell has many undulations, but gradually builds up to a craggy-sided pyramid where the summit-cairn occupies a small outcrop.

DESCENTS: Care is needed in getting down to Hardknott Pass because the ridge leads directly down to Raven Crag. Avoid this difficulty by bearing left, descending on the Duddon side where a little scree-run indicates the start of a track that leads to the big cairn at the Pass. If proceeding towards Three Tarns, the north ridge may be followed easily down via the Mosedale col to Lingcove Beck.

If it is desired to visit the Steeple descend due west from the summit, keeping to grass amongst the crags. The Steeple is concealed from above by the low cliff of which it formerly was part. Look for a broken wall, which leads towards it. The distance from the summit is 500 yards.

The Steeple, from the south

THE VIEW

Principal Fells

N

HAYCOCK
CAW FELL
SEATALLAN
MIDDLE FELL
ILLGILL HEAD
WHIN RIGG
SCAFELL PIKE
SCAFELL
SLIGHT SIDE
GREAT END
ESK PIKE
BOWFELL
CRINKLE CRAGS
Little Stand
WANSFELL PIKE
SALLOWS
SOUR HOWES

W — — — — — — — E

5 miles
10 miles

GREEN CRAG
HARTER FELL
Stickle Pike
Caw
WETHERLAM
GREAT CARRS
SWIRL HOW
GREY FRIAR
DOW CRAG
CONISTON OLD MAN
BRIM FELL
DOON CRAG
WALNA SCAR

S

The view of Scafell and Upper Eskdale is renowned: this is a splendid place for studying the geography and 'getting the feel' of a magnificent dalehead.

Lakes and Tarns
SW: Devoke Water

Harter Fell

2140'

from Penny Hill

Birks Bridge

HARD KNOTT ▲

Cockley ● Beck

● Boot

▲ HARTER FELL

▲ GREEN CRAG

● Seathwaite

MILES

0 1 2 3 4

NATURAL FEATURES

Not many fells can be described as *beautiful*, but the word fits Harter Fell, especially so when viewed from Eskdale. The lower slopes on this flank climb steeply from the tree-lined curves of the River Esk in a luxurious covering of bracken, higher is a wide belt of heather, and finally spring grey turrets and ramparts of rock to a neat and shapely pyramid. The Duddon slopes are now extensively planted, and here too, thanks to the good taste of the Forestry Commission in this area, deciduous trees and evergreens amongst the crags will, in due course, make a colourful picture.

The fell is not only good to look at, but good to climb, interest being well sustained throughout and reaching a climax in the last few feet, an upthrust of naked rock where the walker must turn cragsman if he is to enjoy the magnificent panorama from the uttermost point.

Harter Fell rises between the mid-valleys of the Esk and the Duddon, not at the head, and is therefore not the source of either river although it feeds both.

The head of Eskdale, from the summit of Harter Fell

MAP

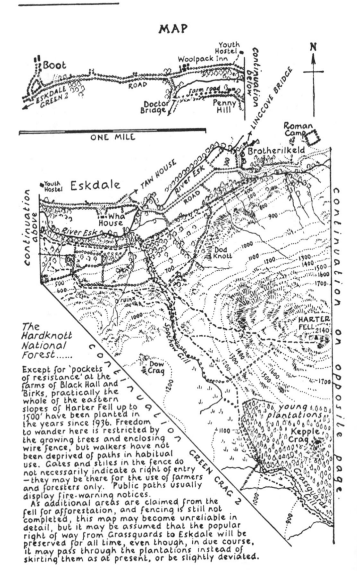

ONE MILE

The Hardknott National Forest......

Except for 'pockets of resistance' at the farms of Black Hall and Birks, practically the whole of the eastern slopes of Harter Fell up to 1500' have been planted in the years since 1936. Freedom to wander here is restricted by the growing trees and enclosing wire fence, but walkers have not been deprived of paths in habitual use. Gates and stiles in the fence do not necessarily indicate a right of entry — they may be there for the use of farmers and foresters only. Public paths usually display fire-warning notices.

As additional areas are claimed from the fell for afforestation, and fencing is still not completed, this map may become unreliable in detail, but it may be assumed that the popular right of way from Grassguards to Eskdale will be preserved for all time, even though, in due course, it may pass through the plantations instead of skirting them as at present, or be slightly deviated.

MAP

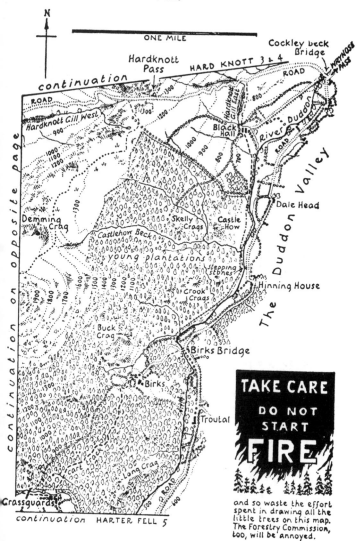

ONE MILE

N

Cockley beck
Bridge

Hardknott
Pass

HARD KNOTT 3 & 4

ROAD

WRYNOSE PASS

continuation

ROAD

Hardknott Gill West

Hardknott Gill East

River Duddon

Black
Hall

Dale Head

Demming
Crag

Skelly
Crags

Castle
How

Castlehow Beck

young plantations

The Duddon Valley

Stepping
stones

Hinning House

Crook
Crags

Buck
Crag

Birks Bridge

Birks

Troutal

cart

ROAD

Long Crag

Grassguards

continuation on opposite page

continuation   HARTER FELL 5

**TAKE CARE
DO NOT
START
FIRE**

and so waste the effort
spent in drawing all the
little trees on this map.
The Forestry Commission,
too, will be annoyed.

MAP

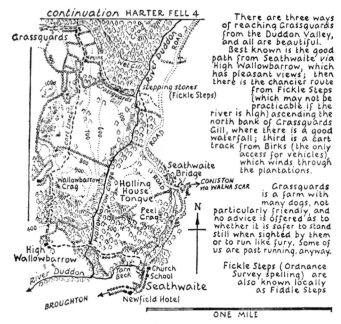

There are three ways of reaching Grassguards from the Duddon Valley, and all are beautiful.

Best known is the good path from Seathwaite via High Wallowbarrow, which has pleasant views; then there is the chancier route from Fickle Steps (which may not be practicable if the river is high) ascending the north bank of Grassguards Gill, where there is a good waterfall; third is a cart track from Birks (the only access for vehicles) which winds through the plantations.

Grassguards is a farm with many dogs, not particularly friendly, and no advice is offered as to whether it is safer to stand still when sighted by them or to run like fury. Some of us are past running, anyway.

Fickle Steps (Ordnance Survey spelling) are also known locally as Fiddle Steps

ONE MILE

Grassguards Gill forms the southern boundary of Harter Fell, but the map has been extended in that direction to include the approaches from Seathwaite.

*Harter Fell
from the Walna Scar path*

ASCENT FROM ESKDALE
2000 feet of ascent : 3½ miles from Boot

HARTER FELL

On the approach via Penny Hill, doubts will arise in the little tangle of rough country in the vicinity of Spothow Gill, above the walls of the enclosures, where footsteps will tend to gravitate in error to the path going across to the Duddon Valley. The correct path is more to the east, coming up from the ford at the foot of Hardknott Pass and reaching the open fell just beyond Spothow Gill.

looking east-south-east

There is not a more charming ascent than this, which is a delight from start to finish. Harter Fell's grand rocky pyramid gives an air of real mountaineering to the climb, the views of Eskdale are glorious and the immediate surroundings richly colourful.

ASCENT FROM HARDKNOTT PASS
900 feet of ascent : 1½ miles

Little can be said in favour of the obvious route along the swampy ridge from the top of Hardknott Pass, which is pathless and lacking in interest. Keep left of the conspicuous Demming Crag and gain the final rocks by a grassy shelf slanting up to the right (north) of the summit.

ASCENT FROM THE DUDDON VALLEY

There is no longer free and open access to the fellside from the Duddon because of the plantations, and the approach is almost exclusively restricted to the time-honoured route to Eskdale from Grassguards, and even here there have been slight deviations, with possibly further deflections to come if planting is extended. Reach Grassguards by any of the three public paths shown on the map, and here (the farm-dogs permitting) go on across the swampy moor until the wide top of the pass is gained beyond the plantation. A broken wall running up Harter Fell may now be followed; or by continuing towards Eskdale for a quarter-mile further a narrow track turning off to the right may be used: in either case the distinct path to the summit from Eskdale will be joined.

THE SUMMIT

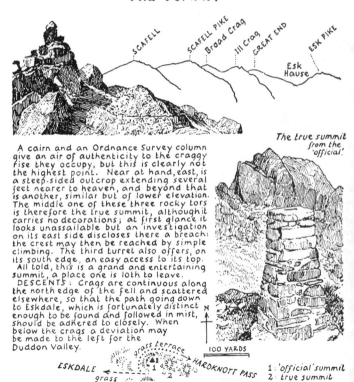

SCAFELL · SCAFELL PIKE · Broad Crag · Ill Crag · GREAT END · ESK PIKE

Esk Hause

The true summit from the 'official'

A cairn and an Ordnance Survey column give an air of authenticity to the craggy rise they occupy, but this is clearly not the highest point. Near at hand, east, is a steep-sided outcrop extending several feet nearer to heaven, and beyond that is another, similar but of lower elevation. The middle one of these three rocky tors is therefore the true summit, although it carries no decorations; at first glance it looks unassailable but an investigation on its east side discloses there a breach: the crest may then be reached by simple climbing. The third turret also offers, on its south edge, an easy access to its top.

All told, this is a grand and entertaining summit, a place one is loth to leave.

DESCENTS: Crags are continuous along the north edge of the fell and scattered elsewhere, so that the path going down to Eskdale, which is fortunately distinct enough to be found and followed in mist, should be adhered to closely. When below the crags a deviation may be made to the left for the Duddon Valley.

ESKDALE ← grass ··· grass terrace ··· → HARDKNOTT PASS

N

100 YARDS

1 : 'official' summit
2 : true summit

THE VIEW

Having exercised himself by scrambling up and down the three summits, the visitor can settle himself on the sharp arete of the highest and enjoy a most excellent view. The Scafell group and Upper Eskdale dominate the scene, appearing not quite in such detail as when surveyed from Hard Knott but in better balance — added distance often adds quality to a picture. Over Wrynose Pass there is an array of faraway fells in the Kirkstone area, which will not surprise walkers familiar with that district, where Harter Fell often pops into the views therefrom. Near at hand, east, the Coniston fells bulk largely but unattractively.
Lower Eskdale and the Duddon Valley
lead the eye to golden sands
and glittering sea.

Principal Fells

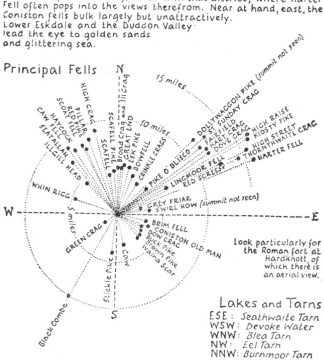

Look particularly for
the Roman fort at
Hardknott, of
which there is
an aerial view.

Lakes and Tarns

ESE: Seathwaite Tarn
WSW: Devoke Water
WNW: Blea Tarn
NW: Eel Tarn
NNW: Burnmoor Tarn

RIDGE ROUTES

There is no defined ridge seawards, although it is possible to keep to the height of land for a dozen miles without (except at one point) descending below 1000! Northeast, a high ridge continues to Hard Knott and at its lowest depression is crossed by a motor road (Hardknott Pass), from whence the route onwards has been described as a separate ascent (see page Hard Knott 5).

Holme Fell

*from Tunnel Quarry
Low Fell*

*from the north ridge
(Ivy Crag on the left)*

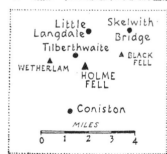

Little
Langdale

Skelwith
Bridge

Tilberthwaite

▲ BLACK
FELL

WETHERLAM ▲

▲

HOLME
FELL

● Coniston

MILES

0   1   2   3   4

*the big cairn of Ivy Crag
(there are two smaller cairns nearby
at a slightly higher elevation)*

MAP

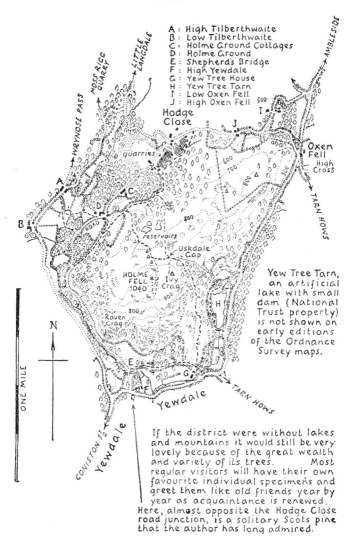

A: High Tilberthwaite
B: Low Tilberthwaite
C: Holme Ground Cottages
D: Holme Ground
E: Shepherd's Bridge
F: High Yewdale
G: Yew Tree House
H: Yew Tree Tarn
I: Low Oxen Fell
J: High Oxen Fell

Yew Tree Tarn, an artificial lake with small dam (National Trust property) is not shown on early editions of the Ordnance Survey maps.

If the district were without lakes and mountains it would still be very lovely because of the great wealth and variety of its trees.   Most regular visitors will have their own favourite individual specimens and greet them like old friends year by year as acquaintance is renewed. Here, almost opposite the Hodge Close road junction, is a solitary Scots pine that the author has long admired.

NATURAL FEATURES

It is a characteristic of many of Lakeland's lesser heights that what they lack in elevation they make up in ruggedness. Slopes a thousand feet high can be just as steep and rough as those three times as long, while crags occur at all levels and are by no means the preserve of the highest peaks, so that the climbing of a small hill, what there is of it, can call for as much effort, over a shorter time, as a big one; moreover, the lower tops have the further defence of a tangle of tough vegetation, usually heather and bracken, through which progress is a far more laborious task than on the grassy slopes of higher zones. Such a one is Holme Fell, at the head of Yewdale, isolated by valleys yet very much under the dominance of Wetherlam. A craggy southern front, a switchback ridge, a cluster of small but very beautiful tree-girt tarns (old reservoirs), and a great quarry that reveals the core of colourful slate lying beneath the glorious jungle of juniper and birch, heather and bracken, make this one of the most attractive of Lakeland's fells.

ASCENTS

The worst roughnesses may be avoided, fortunately, by using a charming path that crosses the fell north of the summit. From the east, the path starts at Yew Tree Farm and slants upwards, mostly amongst trees, to Uskdale Gap on the ridge, where the cairn on Ivy Crag is in sight and quickly reached. From the west, the path may be joined above Holme Ground (see map), in which case it is not necessary to continue quite as far as the Gap, the main summit being gained by a scramble on the right.

THE SUMMIT

The highest point is a platform of naked rock, set at the top of slabs and curiously weathered into pockets of small pebbles, in the middle of a summit-ridge with a continuous escarpment on the east side. 200 yards away, across a heathery plateau, is the subsidiary summit of Ivy Crag, identified by a big cairn.
DESCENTS: Uskdale Gap is the key to easy descent. Avoid the steep southern declivities, which are much too rough for comfort.

THE VIEW

Outstanding in a moderate view is the striking full length of Coniston Water; this is the best place for viewing the lake.

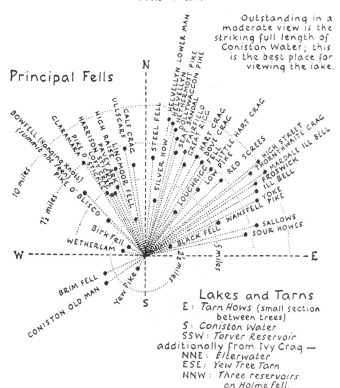

Principal Fells

N

BOWFELL (Hanging Knott)
(summit not seen)
10 miles
CLARAMARA O S (HEAD)
PIKE O' SLICCRAG
HARRISON STICKLE
HIGH RAISE
LINCMOOR FELL
PAVEY ARK
LOFT CRAG
ULLSCARF
CALF CRAG
STEEL FELL
SILVER HOW
HELVELLYN LOWER MAN
HELVELLYN
NETHERMOST PIKE
SEAT SANDAL
DOLLYWAGGON PIKE
FAIRFIELD
GREAT RIGG
HART CRAG
DOVE CRAG
LITTLE HART CRAG
LOUGHRICC FELL
LOW PIKE
HART CRAG
RED SCREES
HIGH STREET
THORNTHWAITE CRAC
MARDALE ILL BELL
FROSWICK
ILL BELL
YOKE
ILL BELL
WANSFELL PIKE
SALLOWS
SOUR HOWES
BLACK FELL
Birk Fell
WETHERLAM
1½ miles
7½ miles
W
E
2½ miles
5 miles
BRIM FELL
Yew Pike
CONISTON OLD MAN
S

Lakes and Tarns
E: *Tarn Hows (small section between trees)*
S: *Coniston Water*
SSW: *Torver Reservoir*
additionally from Ivy Crag —
NNE: *Elterwater*
ESE: *Yew Tree Tarn*
NNW: *Three reservoirs on Holme Fell.*

The Hodge Close quarries have many features of interest — a travelling crane, an aqueduct, a mineral railway, tunnels and a great arch, an emerald lake — while the two tremendous holes are extremely impressive.

The arch

Illgill Head

often referred to as
Wastwater Screes

from Green How

Wasdale Head •

SCAFELL ▲

ILLGILL HEAD ▲
• Strands

▲ WHIN RIGG

• Santon Bridge

• Boot

MILES

0   1   2   3   4

from Miterdale

NATURAL FEATURES

Illgill Head is known to most visitors to Lakeland as Wastwater Screes, although this latter title is strictly appropriate only to the stone-strewn flank that falls so spectacularly into the depths of Wast Water. Much of this north-western slope, however, is bracken-covered and grassy, the screes descending only from the actual summit and its southerly continuation to Whin Rigg. It is here that the fellside from top to bottom, down even to the floor of the lake 250' below the surface, is piled deep with stones lying at their maximum angle of rest, 35°-40°, through a vertical height of almost 2000'. The top of the fell is a smooth sheepwalk; these many acres of loose and shifting debris must therefore have resulted from the disintegration of crags that, ages ago, rimmed the top of the fell: some rocks remain still in a state of dangerous decay. The screes, when seen in the light of an evening sun, make a picture of remarkable colour and brilliance : a scene unique in this country.

The opposite flank, descending to Burnmoor and the shy little valley of Miterdale in patches of heather and bracken, has, in contrast, nothing of interest to show.

Wastwater Screes

MAP

The Lakeside Path

From Wasdale Head Hall the lakeside path starts innocuously as a broad avenue in the bracken, and although it soon climbs a little and narrows to a track the way continues quite easy, even when the first screes are reached and for a mile beyond, during which section the path returns almost to the lakeside, crossing successive bands of stony debris which cause no trouble.   Then just as the walker who has been forewarned of the difficulties of the route is beginning to wonder what all the fuss is about, and with the end almost in sight, there comes a vicious quarter-mile compared with which the top of Scafell Pike is like a bowling green — here the screes take the form of big awkward boulders, loosely piled at a steep angle and avoidable only by a swim in the lake; it has been impossible to tread out a path here despite a brave effort by somebody to cairn a route. This section is really trying and progress is slow, laborious and just a little dangerous unless the feet are placed carefully; ladies wearing stiletto heels will be gravely inconvenienced and indeed many a gentle pedestrian must have suffered nightmares in this dreadful place and looked with hopelessness and envy at people striding along the smooth road on the opposite shore.   The boulders end abruptly at a little copse of trees, and here, in between giving thanks for deliverance, the tremendous cliffs and gullies high above may be studied in comfort. A distinct path now leads easily to the foot of the lake.

To get to the Screes from the road, use the field-gate opposite Woodhow (closing it afterwards), go down to the River Irt, cross Lund Bridge and follow the south bank of the river to the outlet of the lake.

GOSFORTH

ROAD TO WASDALE HEAD

Wast Water

continuation on opposite page

ROAD

cattle grid

ROAD TO STRANDS & SANTON BRIDGE 2¾

The Screes

1800

1700

1600

1500

Woodhow (farm)

Wasdale Hall

continuation WHIN RIGG 4

MAP

The submarine contours in the lake are interesting. The 6" Ordnance map shows that the steepness of the fellside is maintained down to the bottom of the lake, 258' below the surface, and Lakeland's deepest. (58' below sea level).

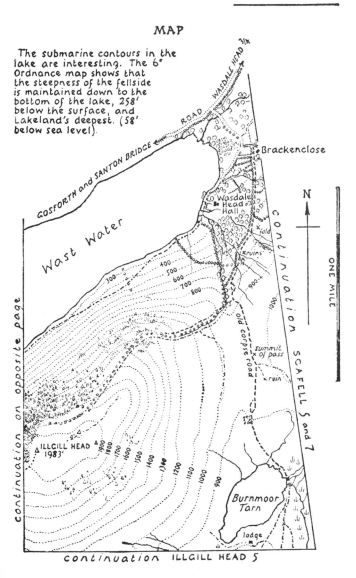

GOSFORTH and SANTON BRIDGE ROAD

WASDALE HEAD

Brackenclose

Wasdale Head Hall

Wast Water

x fold

x ruins

400
500
600
700
800
900
1000

continuation on opposite page

old corpse road

summit of pass

x ruin

ILLGILL HEAD 1983'

1900
1800
1700
1600
1500
1400
1300
1200
1100
1000
900

Burnmoor Tarn

lodge

N

ONE MILE

continuation SCAFELL 5 and 7

continuation ILLGILL HEAD 5

MAP

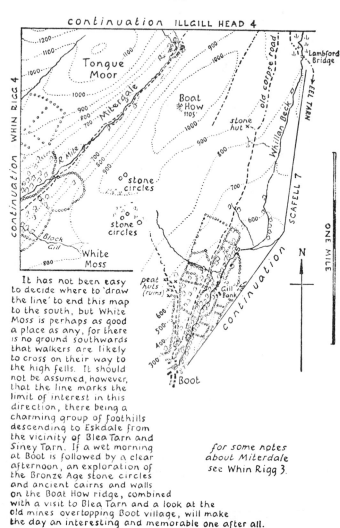

It has not been easy to decide where to 'draw the line' to end this map to the south, but White Moss is perhaps as good a place as any, for there is no ground southwards that walkers are likely to cross on their way to the high fells. It should not be assumed, however, that the line marks the limit of interest in this direction, there being a charming group of foothills descending to Eskdale from the vicinity of Blea Tarn and Siney Tarn. If a wet morning at Boot is followed by a clear afternoon, an exploration of the Bronze Age stone circles and ancient cairns and walls on the Boat How ridge, combined with a visit to Blea Tarn and a look at the old mines overtopping Boot village, will make the day an interesting and memorable one after all.

for some notes about Miterdale see Whin Rigg 3.

ASCENT FROM WASDALE HEAD
1750 feet of ascent : 4 miles (from Wastwater Hotel)

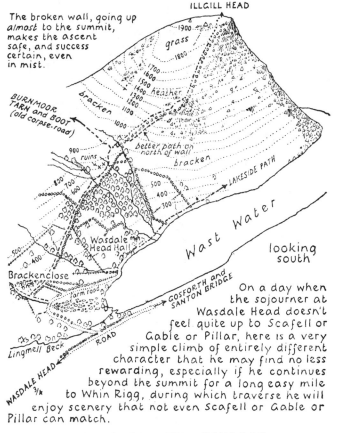

ILLGILL HEAD

The broken wall, going up *almost* to the summit, makes the ascent safe, and success certain, even in mist.

1900

grass

1800

1700
1600
1500
1400
1300
1100

heather

bracken

BURNMOOR TARN and BOOT (old corpse-road)

1000

900

better path on north of wall

bracken

ruins

800
700
600
500

500
400
300

LAKESIDE PATH

Wast Water

looking south

500
400

Wasdale Head Hall

Brackenclose

Tarn road

GOSFORTH and SANTON BRIDGE

Lingmell Beck

ROAD

WASDALE HEAD 3/4

On a day when the sojourner at Wasdale Head doesn't feel quite up to Scafell or Gable or Pillar, here is a very simple climb of entirely different character that he may find no less rewarding, especially if he continues beyond the summit for a long easy mile to Whin Rigg, during which traverse he will enjoy scenery that not even Scafell or Gable or Pillar can match.

ASCENTS FROM ESKDALE

The climb may be made with equal facility from Boot by using the old corpse-road to and beyond Burnmoor Tarn until it begins a gentle descent to Wasdale Head, when the route by the broken wall may be joined. Or a shorter but more tedious ascent direct from the Tarn may be made. But, from Eskdale, a more rewarding plan is to climb Whin Rigg first, then go on to Illgill Head and return via the broken wall and Burnmoor Tarn; a splendid round.

THE SUMMIT

There is nothing at all about the actual summit to give a hint of its dramatic situation almost on the lip of the tremendous plunge to Wast Water. All is grass — dry springy turf that, on a hot day, cries aloud for a siesta; but heavy sleepers should not so position themselves that they can slide down the gradual decline to the rim of the cliffs, 35 yards from the cairn. This remarkable point of vantage, high above the lake, should be visited nevertheless: if it is omitted the whole ascent becomes purposeless. There is a lower cairn in a rash of stones nearer to Wasdale Head: this may be mistaken in mist for the true summit on the northeast approach.

RIDGE ROUTE

To WHIN RIGG, 1755': 1⅓ miles : SW
Depression at 1550': 240 feet of ascent
A magnificent walk

There is no path in the short grass of the summit but one is soon picked up on the long slope to the depression and continues clear to the top of Whin Rigg. In three places on the journey the path skirts the head of big gullies down which are thrilling views; otherwise its course along the grassy ridge is uneventful. But scenery of a very high order may be obtained throughout by following instead a sketchier track that skirts the escarpment closely. Indicated on the diagram are two viewpoints, both at the edge of vertical crags and needing caution in high winds.

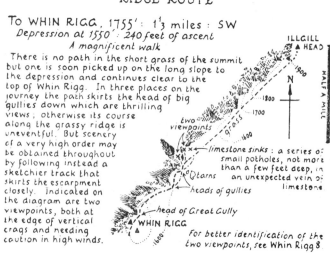

ILLGILL HEAD

HALF A MILE

two viewpoints

limestone sinks: a series of small potholes, not more than a few feet deep, in an unexpected vein of limestone

tarns

heads of gullies

head of Great Gully

WHIN RIGG

For better identification of the two viewpoints, see Whin Rigg 8.

THE VIEW

This summit is the only really satisfactory viewpoint for Wasdale Head — a finely proportioned scene, with gaunt mountains soaring up suddenly from the level strath of this grandest of all daleheads. (It is better seen from the lower cairn). Scafell is disappointing: a vast and featureless mass, showing its dullest side. Visitors will, *of course*, walk across to the rim of the escarpment for the view down the screes into Wast Water far below; an impressive scene indeed.

Principal Fells

N

15 miles

SKIDDAW
LONG SIDE
ROBINSON
SCOAT FELL
RED PIKE
PILLAR
YEWBARROW
KIRK FELL
BRANDRETH
GREAT GABLE
HAYCOCK
MIDDLE FELL
SEATALLAN
LINGMELL
BUCKBARROW
SCAFELL

W — E

SLIGHT SIDE
CRINKLE CRAGS — — — —
5 miles
WHIN RIGG
WETHERLAM
GREAT CARRS
SWIRL HOW
GREY FRIAR
BRIM FELL
DOW CRAG
CONISTON OLD MAN
HARTER FELL
BROWN PIKE
10 miles
COW
GREEN CRAG
STICKLE PIKE

Black Combe

S

Lakes and Tarns

The summit cairn is not the best place for viewing lakes and tarns, the only sheets of water clearly seen (apart from the sea) being those in the depression southwest below Whin Rigg, and an easterly perambulation of the top will be necessary if it is desired to view the Eskdale tarns. But the *piece de resistance* is Wast Water, which comes amazingly into the picture after a walk of only 35 yards west.

looking down on Wast Water from the summit

Lingmell

Seathwaite •

▲ GREAT GABLE
• Wasdale Head
▲ LINGMELL
▲ SCAFELL PIKE
▲ SCAFELL

MILES
0   1   2   3

from the Corridor route,
Great End

NATURAL FEATURES

Following the general pattern of the fells, Lingmell has a smooth outline to the south and west but exhibits crags and steep rough slopes to the north and east. The distinction is very marked, the ground falling away precipitously from the gentle western rise to the watershed as though severed by a great knife and laying naked a decaying confusion of crags and aretes, screes and boulders. On this flank is the huge cleft of Piers Gill, a natural chute for the stones that pour down the thousand-foot declivity, and the finest ravine in the district. Eastwards, a high saddle connects the fell with Scafell Pike, but on other sides steep slopes descend abruptly from the wide top. Lingmell Beck and Lingmell Gill are its streams, both flowing into Wast Water in wide channels and boulder-choked courses, testimony to the fury of the storms and cloudbursts that have riven the fellsides in past years; there is, indeed, a vast area of denudation (Lingmell Scars) on the slope overlooking Brown Tongue, and the devastated lakeside fields below Brackenclose add their witness to the power of the floods that have carried the debris down to the valley.

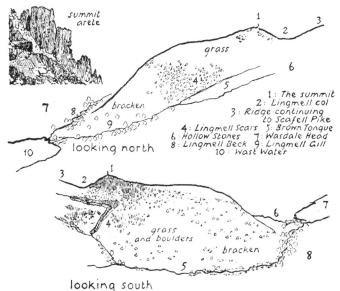

summit
arete

grass

bracken

looking north

1: The summit
2: Lingmell col
3: Ridge continuing to Scafell Pike
4: Lingmell Scars   5: Brown Tongue
6: Hollow Stones   7: Wasdale Head
8: Lingmell Beck   9: Lingmell Gill
10: Wast Water

grass
and boulders

bracken

looking south

1: The summit   2: Lingmell col   3: Ridge continuing to Scafell Pike
4: Piers Gill   5: Lingmell Beck   6: Lingmell Gill   7: Wast Water
8: Wasdale Head

MAP

A rare and remarkable (and almost unbelievable) aberration on the part of a cartographer of the Ordnance Survey has resulted in 'Lingmell Beck' being named CAWFELL BECK (in capitals, too!) on their 2½" map. One prefers to think that this is not an error but an alternative name; it is certainly inconsistent, however, with the 1" and 6" maps, which say Lingmell Beck.

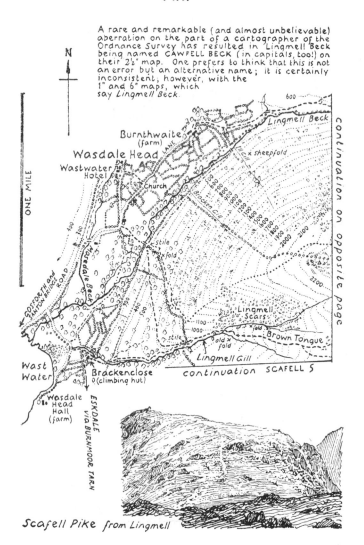

Scafell Pike from Lingmell

MAP

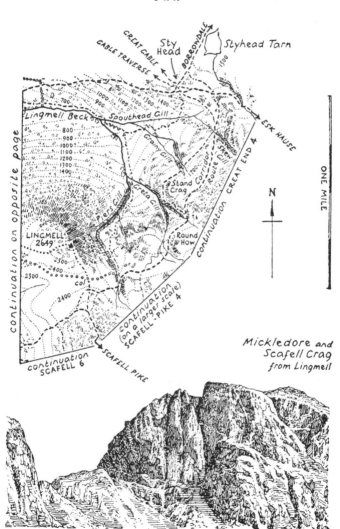

Mickledore and Scafell Crag from Lingmell

ASCENT FROM WASDALE HEAD
via (A) THE SHOULDER or (B) BROWN TONGUE

2450 feet of ascent
(A) 2½ miles
(B) 3 miles
from Wastwater Hotel

looking east

LINGMELL

Lingmell col

SCAFELL PIKE

Pikes Crag

Hollow Stones

SCAFELL OF MICKLEDORE

grass

grass

Goat Crags

grassy plateau

old wall

falls

Lingmell Scars

Brown Tongue

x old sheepfold

bracken

stile

Lingmell Gill

old sheepfolds

stiles

bracken

bracken

Church

old school

bridge

signpost

Lingmell Beck

Wastwater Hotel

Mosedale Beck

Brackenclose

WASDALE HEAD HALL

ROAD

LANE

Wast Water

GOSFORTH and SANTON BRIDGE

The vast wall of Lingmell facing the dining-room of the Wastwater Hotel is unattractive, and it is asking a lot of a man who has eaten well at the breakfast-table to send him forth to tackle its 2000' of unremitting steepness, but the ascent can be made tolerable by using a path above the wall to join the obvious west shoulder above Brackenclose, where fragrant mountain flowers and noble views temper the steepness. At 1900', beyond a few rocks, the slope suddenly eases, and there remains only a gentle walk to the summit.

It is usual to follow the Scafell Pike path as far as the Lingmell col, there going up the short slope to the left. But, instead of adhering closely to the track up Brown Tongue, the stony bed of the gill may be ascended to a subsidiary tongue, which rises easily to the grassy plateau: this variation is pathless, but useful if Brown Tongue is crowded with Pike-bound travellers. The direct route up the shoulder is better still, but should be reserved as a line of descent.

ASCENT FROM WASDALE HEAD
via PIERS GILL
2450 feet of ascent : 3½ miles (from Wastwater Hotel)

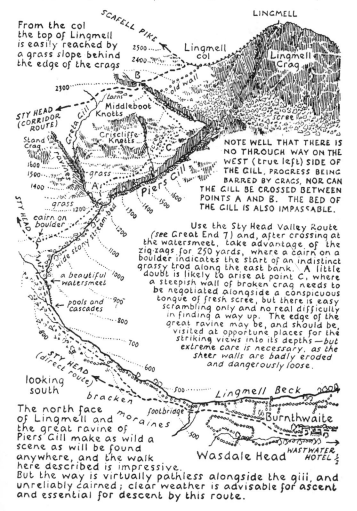

From the col the top of Lingmell is easily reached by a grass slope behind the edge of the crags

SCAFELL PIKE

LINGMELL

Lingmell col

Lingmell Crag

old wall

STY HEAD (CORRIDOR ROUTE)

Greta Gill

tarns

Middleboot Knotts

Criscliffe Knotts

Stand Crag

ravine

grass

Piers Gill

scree

B

A

C

STY HEAD

cairn on boulder

wide stony stream bed

a beautiful watersmeet

pools and cascades

STY HEAD (direct route)

looking south

bracken

moraines

footbridge

Lingmell Beck

Burnthwaite

Wasdale Head

WASTWATER HOTEL ½

NOTE WELL THAT THERE IS NO THROUGH WAY ON THE WEST (true left) SIDE OF THE GILL, PROGRESS BEING BARRED BY CRAGS, NOR CAN THE GILL BE CROSSED BETWEEN POINTS A AND B. THE BED OF THE GILL IS ALSO IMPASSABLE.

Use the Sty Head Valley Route (see Great End 7) and, after crossing at the watersmeet, take advantage of the zig-zags for 250 yards, where a cairn on a boulder indicates the start of an indistinct grassy trod along the east bank. A little doubt is likely to arise at point C, where a steepish wall of broken crag needs to be negotiated alongside a conspicuous tongue of fresh scree, but there is easy scrambling only and no real difficulty in finding a way up. The edge of the great ravine may be, and should be, visited at opportune places for the striking views into its depths — but extreme care is necessary, as the sheer walls are badly eroded and dangerously loose.

The north face of Lingmell and the great ravine of Piers Gill make as wild a scene as will be found anywhere, and the walk here described is impressive. But the way is virtually pathless alongside the gill, and unreliably cairned; clear weather is advisable for ascent and essential for descent by this route.

THE SUMMIT

Summit·cairns are welcome sights, but they are seldom objects of beauty or admiration. Here, however, on the highest point of Lingmell, is one of singular elegance, a graceful ten·foot spire that quite puts to shame the squat and inartistic edifice crowning the neighbouring very superior Scafell Pike. Long may it escape the attentions of the new gallants, the cairn·wreckers.

Its position, on the rim of the tremendous downfall of Lingmell Crag, commanding the length of the Corridor Route, is superb.

The summit area is stony, but not too stony to hamper progress unduly, and a short exploration along the top of the cliff northwards earns a reward of magnificent views.

DESCENTS:

TO WASDALE HEAD: The shoulder route is a quick and easy way down, with excellent views right left and centre, and much better than the longer alternative via Lingmell col and the Brown Tongue path. In mist the latter is to be preferred, as the pathless shoulder at first is too broad to give direction naturally.

TO BORROWDALE: Join the Corridor Route just beyond Lingmell col.

RIDGE ROUTE

To SCAFELL PIKE, 3210':
7/8 mile : SSE
Depression (Lingmell col) at 2370'
850 feet of ascent
A tedious half·hour

With steep ground on the left hand descend the grass slope (not much of a track) to Lingmell col, where cross the broken wall and join the cairned path coming up from Brown Tongue; this is distinct over stones and boulders to the summit.

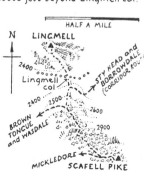

THE VIEW

Scafell Pike dominates the scene, but from this side is the dullest of mountains; Scafell is better, but the grouping of the western fells around Mosedale is best of all. The views of Borrowdale and down Wast Water to the coastal plain and the sea are also good.

Principal Fells

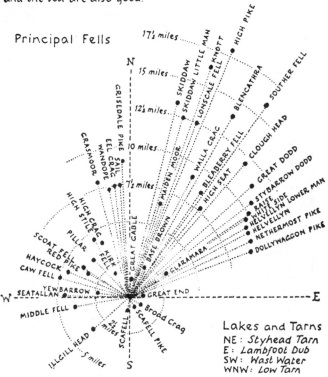

Lakes and Tarns

NE: *Styhead Tarn*
E: *Lambfoot Dub*
SW: *Wast Water*
WNW: *Low Tarn*

Two features of the view deserve special mention. The first is the surprising aspect of Great Gable across the deep gulf of Lingmell Beck (seen more fully from the summit-ridge north of the main cairn), the eye being deceived into seeing its half-mile of height as quite perpendicular: a remarkable picture. The other is the astonishing downward view into the stony depths of Piers Gill, a thousand-foot drop which again is not nearly so vertical as it appears at first sight to the startled beholder.

Piers Gill

above
  the upper section (looking down from the Corridor Route)

right
  the lower section (looking up)

top right
  pinnacles and spires in the gill

Great Gable from Lingmell

Lingmoor Fell

from Elterwater

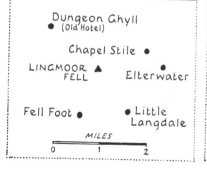

Dungeon Ghyll
(Old Hotel)

Chapel Stile

LINGMOOR ▲
FELL   Elterwater

Fell Foot   Little
              Langdale

MILES

0   1   2

Oak How
Needle

NATURAL FEATURES

A crescent-shaped ridge of high ground rises to the west from Elterwater's pleasant pastures, climbs to a well-defined summit, a fine vantage point, and then curves northwards as it descends to valley-level near Dungeon Ghyll. Within the crescent lies Great Langdale, the longer outside curve sloping down into Little Langdale and the Blea Tarn depression. The mass is Lingmoor Fell, so named because of the extensive zone of heather clothing the northern flanks below the summit. The fell has contributed generously to the prosperity of the surrounding valleys, for not only has it nurtured the sheep but it has also been quarried extensively for many generations, yielding a very beautiful and durable green stone. Bracken and heather, some ragged patches of juniper and well-timbered estate woods, many crags and a delectable little tarn, all combine to make this fell a colourful addition to the varied attractions of the Langdale area.

looking west

1: The summit
2: Side Pike
3: Oak How Crag
4: Oak How Needle
5: Bield Crag
6: Sawrey's Wood
7: Baisbrown Wood
8: Elterwater
9: Little Langdale Tarn
10: Lingmoor Tarn
11: Great Langdale Beck
12: River Brathay
13: Bleamoss Beck
14: Great Langdale
15: Little Langdale

MAP

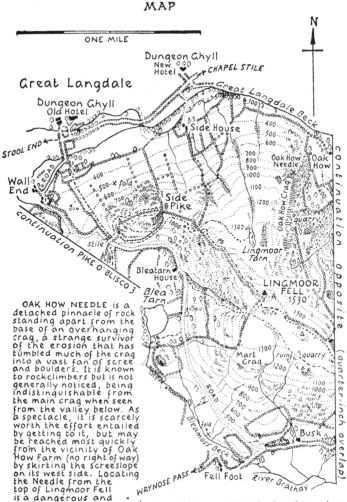

OAK HOW NEEDLE is a detached pinnacle of rock standing apart from the base of an overhanging crag, a strange survivor of the erosion that has tumbled much of the crag into a vast fan of scree and boulders. It is known to rockclimbers but is not generally noticed, being indistinguishable from the main crag when seen from the valley below. As a spectacle, it is scarcely worth the effort entailed by getting to it, but may be reached most quickly from the vicinity of Oak How Farm (no right of way) by skirting the screeslope on its west side. Locating the Needle from the top of Lingmoor Fell is a dangerous and difficult proceeding, for it cannot be seen from the heathery slope above the crag, which breaks away suddenly in a vertical cliff: the safest course is to descend the east bank of the beck issuing from Lingmoor Tarn until a big area of juniper is seen on the right, whence by walking eastwards above it, a small bracken col is reached — and there, directly in front and quite close, is Oak How Needle.

MAP

Great Langdale is probably the most-frequented valley in the district, with a heavy inflow of visitors summer and winter alike, most of them bound for Dungeon Ghyll. It is all the more strange, therefore, that the whole of the traffic, both on foot and awheel, is confined to the one road in the valley, on the north side, while the south side along the base of Lingmoor Fell, although scenically more attractive, seldom sees a soul.   Obviously there should be a public footpath linking Baisbrown, Oak How, Side House and Wall End — and how much pleasanter than the busy road this would be! — but there isn't.   Almost every other inhabited valley in Lakeland has popular rights of way along *both* sides of the main stream.
But not Great Langdale.

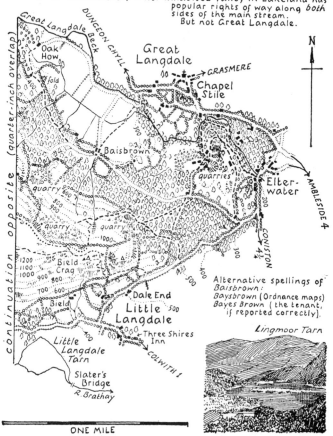

N

Alternative spellings of Baisbrown:
Baysbrown (Ordnance maps)
Bayes Brown (the tenant, if reported correctly).

Lingmoor Tarn

ONE MILE

ASCENT FROM DUNGEON GHYLL
1250 feet of ascent : 2 miles
(Add 250 feet and ½ mile if Side Pike is included)

looking south-east

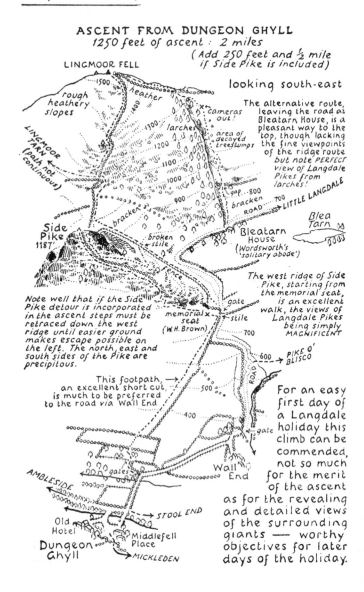

LINGMOOR FELL

1500

rough heathery slopes

heather

1400

LINGMOOR TARN (path not continuous)

x cameras out!

larches

1300

area of decayed treestumps

1200

1100

1000

900 gap...800 bracken

bracken 700 ROAD LITTLE LANGDALE

Blea Tarn

Side Pike 1187'

bracken

broken stile

Bleatarn House *(Wordsworth's 'solitary abode')*

fence

The alternative route, leaving the road at Bleatarn House, is a pleasant way to the top, though lacking the fine viewpoints of the ridge route but note PERFECT view of Langdale Pikes from larches!

gate

memorial seat *(W.H. Brown)* stile

700

The west ridge of Side Pike, starting from the memorial seat, is an excellent walk, the views of Langdale Pikes being simply MAGNIFICENT

600 → PIKE O' BLISCO

Note well that if the Side Pike detour is incorporated in the ascent steps must be retraced down the west ridge until easier ground makes escape possible on the left. The north, east and south sides of the Pike are precipitous.

This footpath, → an excellent short cut, is much to be preferred to the road via Wall End

500

ROAD

400

gate

Wall End

AMBLESIDE

gates

STOOL END

Old Hotel

Middlefell Place

Dungeon Ghyll

MICKLEDEN

For an easy first day of a Langdale holiday this climb can be commended, not so much for the merit of the ascent as for the revealing and detailed views of the surrounding giants — worthy objectives for later days of the holiday.

Side Pike
*from the ridge
running up to
Lingmoor Fell*

Side Pike is accessible to the walker by its west ridge only, and there is no other safe way off. When descending from the cairn do not be tempted by a track going down eastwards: this ends suddenly above a vertical drop, with easy ground tantalisingly close, *but out of reach*. On the drawing above, this dangerous trap is seen directly below the X.

Langdale Pikes
from Side Pike
1: Pike o' Stickle
2: Loft Crag
3: Thorn Crag
4: Harrison
      Stickle
5: Pavey Ark

ASCENTS FROM ELTERWATER AND CHAPEL STILE
1350 feet of ascent : 2½ miles

When the ridge-wall is reached,
cross it at the hurdle and follow
it to the right. The wall is not
continuous to the summit.
The edge of the top quarry
is unprotected and
dangerous.

LINGMOOR
FELL

hurdle

quarries

1500
1400
1300
1200
1100
1000

900 *prominent*
yew — Watch for sharp turn
left when opposite to it

bracken

If the route from
the gate on the road
is taken, watch for
the indistinct
bifurcation left,
passing through
a gap in the wall

juniper

quarries

800
700

LITTLE LANGDALE ⅓

From this section
of the path, Oak How
Needle is clearly in
view (to the right)
standing apart from
the base of a crag.

cave

gate

500

500

500

From Elterwater
it is a simpler plan to
by-pass the lower
quarries by using
one of the two routes
leaving the upper
Little Langdale road

Baisbrown
Wood
400

400

Sawrey's
Wood

BAISBROWN ½

Baisbrown
Estate

store ground
spoil heaps

Great Langdale Beck

DUNGEON GHYLL ½

300

CONISTON 4

quarries

Chapel
Stile

Youth Hostel

200

GRASMERE 3

Langdale Estate

Britannia
Inn

looking
west-south-west

AMBLESIDE 4

Elterwater

AMBLESIDE 4

The lower quarries
are a labyrinth of paths
and cart-tracks, confusing on a
first visit. The extensive spoil-heaps
are not pretty, the many trees being an
ineffective screen; nevertheless, this is an
interesting and attractive approach to the ridge.

ASCENT FROM LITTLE LANGDALE

1100 feet of ascent :
1½ miles (from Dale End)

LINGMOOR FELL

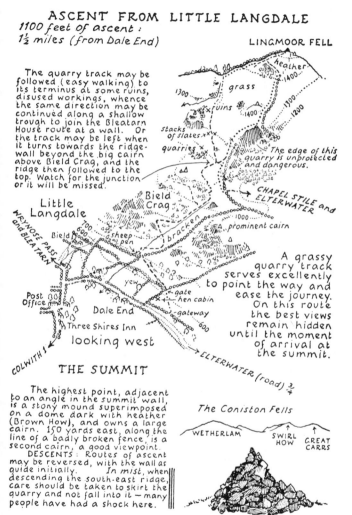

The quarry track may be followed (easy walking) to its terminus at some ruins, disused workings, whence the same direction may be continued along a shallow trough to join the Bleatarn House route at a wall. Or the track may be left when it turns towards the ridge-wall beyond the big cairn above Bield Crag, and the ridge then followed to the top. Watch for the junction or it will be missed.

The edge of this quarry is unprotected and dangerous.

CHAPEL STILE and ELTERWATER

A grassy quarry track serves excellently to point the way and ease the journey. On this route the best views remain hidden until the moment of arrival at the summit.

looking west

THE SUMMIT

The highest point, adjacent to an angle in the summit wall, is a stony mound superimposed on a dome dark with heather (Brown Howl), and owns a large cairn. 150 yards east, along the line of a badly broken fence, is a second cairn, a good viewpoint.

DESCENTS: Routes of ascent may be reversed, with the wall as guide initially.   In mist, when descending the south-east ridge, care should be taken to skirt the quarry and not fall into it — many people have had a shock here.

The Coniston Fells

WETHERLAM   SWIRL HOW   GREAT CARRS

RIDGE ROUTES : Lingmoor Fell is isolated from other fells and therefore has no connecting ridges. Its nearest neighbour is Pike o' Blisco, but the considerable descent to the Bleatarn road makes a climb therefrom virtually a complete ascent.

THE VIEW

looking north-west

1 : Pike o' Stickle	2 : Loft Crag	3 : Thorn Crag
4 : Harrison Stickle	5 : Pavey Ark	6 : High Raise
7 : Sergeant Man	8 : Gimmer Crag	9 : Dungeon Ghyll
10 : Mill Gill	11 : Tarn Crag	12 : Middlefell Buttress
13 : Pike How		

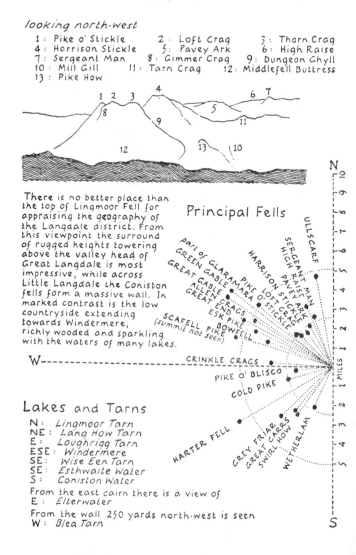

There is no better place than the top of Lingmoor Fell for appraising the geography of the Langdale district. From this viewpoint the surround of rugged heights towering above the valley head of Great Langdale is most impressive, while across Little Langdale the Coniston fells form a massive wall. In marked contrast is the low countryside extending towards Windermere, richly wooded and sparkling with the waters of many lakes.

Principal Fells

Lakes and Tarns

N : *Lingmoor Tarn*
NE : *Lang How Tarn*
E : *Loughrigg Tarn*
ESE : *Windermere*
SE : *Wise Een Tarn*
SE : *Esthwaite Water*
S : *Coniston Water*

From the east cairn there is a view of
E : *Elterwater*

From the wall 250 yards north-west is seen
W : *Blea Tarn*

THE VIEW

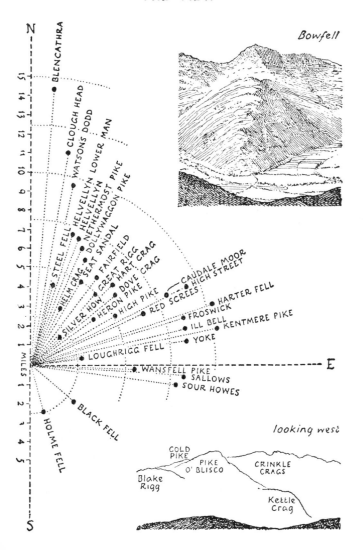

Bowfell

N
15
14
13
12
11
10
9
8
7
6
5
4
3
2
1
MILES

BLENCATHRA
CLOUGH HEAD
WATSONS DODD
HELVELLYN LOWER MAN
HELVELLYN
NETHERMOST PIKE
DOLLYWAGGON PIKE
STEEL FELL
HELM CRAG
SEAT SANDAL
SILVER HOW
FAIRFIELD
GREAT RIGG
HART CRAG
HERON PIKE
DOVE CRAG
HIGH PIKE
CAUDALE MOOR
HIGH STREET
RED SCREES
HARTER FELL
FROSWICK
ILL BELL
KENTMERE PIKE
LOUGHRIGG FELL
YOKE

— E

1
2
3
4
5

WANSFELL PIKE
SALLOWS
SOUR HOWES

BLACK FELL
HOLME FELL

S

looking west

COLD PIKE
PIKE O' BLISCO
CRINKLE CRAGS
Blake Rigg
Kettle Crag

Pike o' Blisco

Sunday name: Pike OF Blisco

BOWFELL ▲

Dungeon
● Ghyll

CRINKLE
CRAGS ▲

LINGMOOR
▲ FELL

▲ PIKE O'
BLISCO

COLD PIKE ▲

Little ●
Langdale

● Cockley Beck

MILES

0   1   2   3

from Side Pike

NATURAL FEATURES

A mountain has added merit if its highest point can be seen from the valley below, instead of being hidden beyond receding upper slopes as is often the case, for then the objective is clear to the climber, there is no deception about height or steepness, and the full stature from base to summit can readily be comprehended. Such a mountain is Pike o' Blisco, with a tall columnar cairn plainly in view from the floor of Great Langdale and perched high above the steep and rugged flank that forms a massive south wall to the side valley of Oxendale. This peak has great character, for shapeliness and a sturdy strength combine well in its appearance, and that splendid cairn etched against the sky is at once an invitation and a challenge — while the man has no blood in his veins who does not respond eagerly to its fine-sounding swashbuckling name, savouring so much of buccaneers and the Spanish Main. There are higher summits all around, some of far greater altitude; but height alone counts for nothing, and Pike o' Blisco would hold its own in any company.

Easy routes to the top can be worked out between the crags, which are in abundance. Kettle Crag above Wall End, and Blake Rigg towering over Blea Tarn, are notable. Except for minor runnels near the top of Wrynose Pass, all streams from the fell join ultimately in the River Brathay.

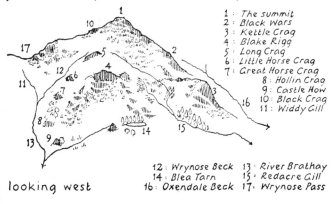

1 : The summit
2 : Black Wars
3 : Kettle Crag
4 : Blake Rigg
5 : Long Crag
6 : Little Horse Crag
7 : Great Horse Crag
8 : Hollin Crag
9 : Castle How
10 : Black Crag
11 : Widdy Gill
12 : Wrynose Beck
13 : River Brathay
14 : Blea Tarn
15 : Redacre Gill
16 : Oxendale Beck
17 : Wrynose Pass

looking west

MAP

The route shown from Kettle Crag to Black Wars should be adopted with caution. After crossing the top of two deep ravines the path fades below a wall of cliffs. Reach the summit by a rough scramble immediately *beyond* the prominent overhanging crag up on the left.

Browney Gill (popularly so called) is named 'Brown Gill' on Ordnance Survey 2½" maps. As the name probably derives from Brown How, it seems that 'Browney' is a corruption.

ONE MILE

Blea Tarn's once well-wooded western shore is now denuded of many of its trees, although a fringe has been left by the water's edge (including the pines that have graced many a thousand photographs).

Rhododendron thickets, spreading unchecked in the vicinity, are choking paths and the whole place bears the appearance of a garden that has long been neglected

MAP

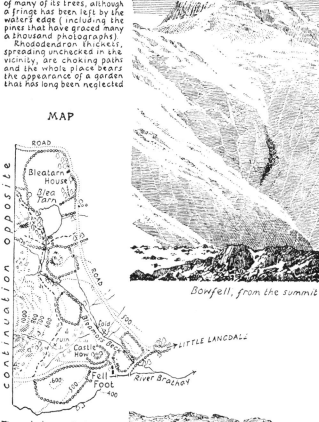

Bowfell, from the summit

Kettle Crag

The omission on Ordnance maps (even on the 6" scale) of the well-defined stream that issues from a tarn (also omitted) west of Long Crag may cause confusion in bad weather. This is the stream (an important landmark) crossed just above the top of Redacre Gill on the Wall End route.

ASCENT FROM DUNGEON GHYLL (via WALL END)
2100 feet of ascent : 2¼ miles

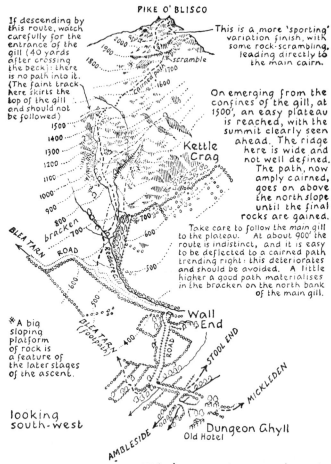

PIKE O' BLISCO

If descending by this route, watch carefully for the entrance of the gill (40 yards after crossing the beck): there is no path into it. (The faint track here skirts the top of the gill and should not be followed)

This is a more 'sporting' variation finish, with some rock-scrambling, leading directly to the main cairn.

On emerging from the confines of the gill, at 1500', an easy plateau is reached, with the summit clearly seen ahead. The ridge here is wide and not well defined. The path, now amply cairned, goes on above the north slope until the final rocks are gained.

Kettle Crag

Take care to follow the main gill to the plateau. At about 900' the route is indistinct, and it is easy to be deflected to a cairned path trending right: this deteriorates and should be avoided. A little higher a good path materialises in the bracken on the north bank of the main gill.

BLEA TARN ROAD

bracken

Redacre Gill

Wall End

*A big sloping platform of rock is a feature of the later stages of the ascent.

BLEA TARN (footpath)

ROAD

STOOL END

MICKLEDEN

looking south-west

AMBLESIDE

Dungeon Ghyll
Old Hotel

This is a good natural route, much easier than is suggested by the formidable appearance of the objective. The path, although occasionally intermittent, is generally good.

ASCENT FROM DUNGEON GHYLL (via STOOL END)
2100 feet of ascent : 2½ miles

Leave the Red Tarn path (which goes on to Wrynose Pass) 100 yards short of the tarn, (opposite the branch to Crinkle Crags). A cairned track, indistinct at first, becomes clearer.

In mist note that the turn left is 50 yards beyond a well alongside the path.

The usual route passes through the farmyard of Stool End, fords Oxendale Beck at the sheepfold (no bridge) and climbs a cairned track (not distinct at the start). Normally the crossing of the beck is simple, but if there is much water in it the north bank may be continued to the footbridge, whence it is quicker to ascend the west bank of Browney Gill (scramblers may climb the bed of the gill). OR to avoid the crossing of Oxendale Beck, keep to its south bank all the way from Stool End Bridge.

The wide, bouldery course of Oxendale Beck testifies to its power in flood. Note that some tributaries are also choked by stones upon reaching the valley.

The subsoil, brown on the climb up from the valley, becomes a rich red as height is gained

PIKE O' BLISCO

Black Wars

well

falls

2000
1900
1800

to WRYNOSE PASS

Red Tarn

CRINKLE CRAGS

1700
1600

Browney Gill

grass

Isaac Gill

Crinkle Gill

CRINKLE CRAGS

Brown How

footbridge

tor

Oxendale Beck

Oxendale

sheepfold

stile

stile

BOWFELL

awkward stile

WALL END

bridge

farm road

gate

Great Langdale Beck

MICKLEDEN

Stool End

looking south-west

Dungeon Ghyll
Old Hotel

An interesting climb, with good rock- and ravine scenery. The section between the beck and Brown How is bumpy and rough (not good for descent).

ASCENT FROM LITTLE LANGDALE
1800 feet of ascent : 2½ miles from Fell Foot

looking
west·north·west

PIKE O' BLISCO

Black
Crag

grass

2100
2000
1900
1800

WALL END

small
tarn

1700

Wrynose
Pass

1600

Long
Crag

Blake
Rigg

1500

sheepfold
cairn

1400

1300

Little
Horse
Crag

Identify the
gully by its
holly trees
and the
ruin
below it

ROAD

1200

1100

1000

Great
Horse
Crag

Wrynose
Bridge

900

1400

1300

holly trees

Widdy Gill

Hollin
Crag

bracken

BLEA
TARN

800

700

600

× ruin

fold

The route from
Wrynose Bridge
takes advantage of
the easiest contours
and affords a simple
passage, avoiding all
contact with crags. There
is no path, however, and the
climbing is tedious until the
final rocks are reached and
the cairned track from Wall
End joined.

ROAD

500

600

500

Castle
How

fold

River Brathay

Fell
Foot

BLEA
TARN

More exciting (and exacting)
is a gully running straight down
from the skyline just to the right
of the craggy shoulder above Hollin
Crag: this gives access to Blake Rigg,
a good viewpoint, whence the flat top
is crossed to join the cairned track from
Wall End. The gully is for scramblers only
and should not be used for descent, being
difficult to locate from above. There is no
path in the gully or on the ridge at the top of it, nor is there
any evidence that human beings have passed this way before.
Bracken on the lower slopes is a hindrance in late summer.

small
arched bridge

gate

ROAD

LITTLE
LANGDALE

An obvious alternative (not shown on the diagram above —
see next page) is by the broken ridge going up to the summit from
Wrynose Pass, or, more easily, by the Red Tarn path from the Pass,
either of which adds half a mile in distance.

; Pike o' Blisco is well worth climbing from any
direction, and, indeed, from all directions. The
approach from Little Langdale by the usual way
leaving Wrynose Bridge, however, is rather dull
in comparison with those from Great Langdale.

ASCENT FROM WRYNOSE PASS
1100 feet of ascent : 1¼ miles

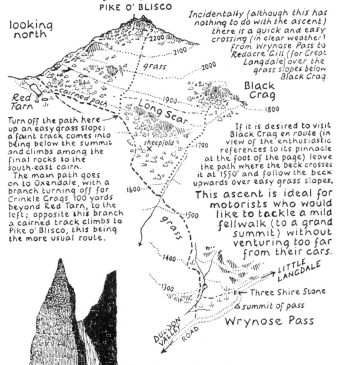

PIKE O' BLISCO

looking north

Incidentally (although this has nothing to do with the ascent) there is a quick and easy crossing (in clear weather) from Wrynose Pass to Redacre Gill (for Great Langdale) over the grass slopes below Black Crag.

2200
2100
2000
grass
1900
1800
Black Crag

Red Tarn

cairned path

Long Scar

Turn off the path here — up an easy grass slope; a faint track comes into being below the summit and climbs among the final rocks to the south-east cairn.

The main path goes on to Oxendale, with a branch turning off for Crinkle Crags 100 yards beyond Red Tarn, to the left; opposite this branch a cairned track climbs to Pike o' Blisco, this being the more usual route.

sheepfold
1700

1600

If it is desired to visit Black Crag en route (in view of the enthusiastic references to its pinnacle at the foot of the page) leave the path where the beck crosses it at 1550' and follow the beck upwards over easy grass slopes.

This ascent is ideal for motorists who would like to tackle a mild fellwalk (to a grand summit) without venturing too far from their cars.

1500
grass
1400
1300
LITTLE LANGDALE
Three Shire Stone
△ summit of pass
Wrynose Pass
DUDDON VALLEY ROAD

The Needle, Black Crag

This smooth and slender pinnacle, detached from the face of Black Crag, is precariously balanced on a massive plinth of rock, 12 ft. high, the total height to the tip being 35 ft. Well off the beaten track (although only a long half-mile from Wrynose Pass) it may have escaped the notice of cragsmen, there being no evidence of ascent on the pinnacle or in the rock-climbing literature at present available for the area. It seems (to a novice who hasn't tried) that the tip may be gained by 'bridging' the gap with the main crag. He will be a good man who can stand erect on the point of the needle.

The author feels rather proud of this 'discovery' and hopes people will not write to claim (i) a knowledge of the pinnacle (since they were children), (ii) that they have climbed it (blindfolded), and (iii) stood for hours on its point (on their heads).

THE SUMMIT

see 'Some Personal Notes in conclusion'

This is a beautiful 'top', and a colourful one, with pinky-grey rocks outcropping everywhere from dark heather and green mosses. The main cairn is a shapely edifice, gloriously situated on a platform of naked rock at the north-western terminus of a summit-ridge 100 yards long. At the south-east extremity is another cairn, less imposing; this too crowns a craggy pyramid.

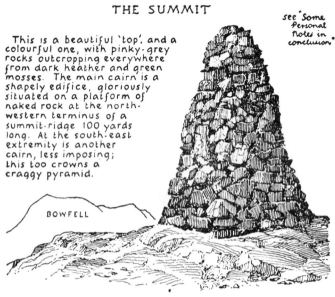

BOWFELL

PLAN OF SUMMIT

N

2100

2100

100 yards

GREAT
LANGDALE
(follow cairns)
WRYNOSE BRIDGE
(bear right below
top rocks)

RED TARN
(cairned
path)

WRYNOSE PASS
(path fades;
keep to grass)

DESCENTS : Use the paths when leaving the summit, in fair weather or foul. The north face is terraced with crags, making a direct descent to Oxendale impracticable, nor should streams be followed, many of them plunging into rough and deep ravines.

RIDGE ROUTE

TO COLD PIKE, 2259', 1¼ miles :
SW, then W, NW, W, S and SE
    Depression at 1650'
    650 feet of ascent
    An easy, interesting walk

Follow the line of cairns down to Red Tarn and then make use of the path to Crinkle Crags, turning left at the first stream on the plateau and crossing the bouldery slope to the prominent cairn of Cold Pike

N

PIKE O'
BLISCO

1700

2100

2000

1900

1800

1800

Red
Tarn

2000

COLD
PIKE

2200

HALF A MILE

THE VIEW

Principal Fells

As the diagram suggests, most of the detail in the panorama is concentrated between north and east, and here the distant views, from Skiddaw round to the Kentmere fells, are certainly good. At close quarters, however, are Bowfell and Crinkle Crags, displaying their features to such effect that they will win most attention. Wander a few paces (not too many!) from the cairn, in the direction of Great Langdale, for a splendid prospect of that valley.

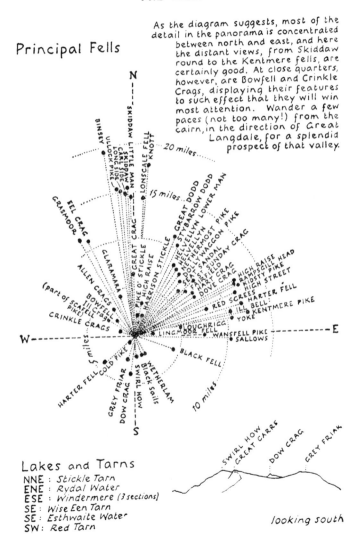

Lakes and Tarns

NNE : Stickle Tarn
ENE : Rydal Water
ESE : Windermere (3 sections)
SE : Wise Een Tarn
SE : Esthwaite Water
SW : Red Tarn

looking south

Rossett Pike

from Mickleden

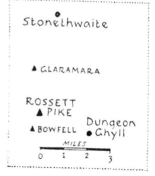

Stonethwaite

▲ GLARAMARA

ROSSETT
▲ PIKE
▲ BOWFELL   Dungeon
● Ghyll

MILES
0   1   2   3

*from the top
of Rossett
Pass*

NATURAL FEATURES

Perhaps, to be strictly correct, Rossett Pike and the fell of which it is part should be regarded as the north-east shoulder of Bowfell continuing from Hanging Knotts to Langstrath, but the sharp rise across the high saddle of Rossett Pass is so pronounced that, for present purposes, Bowfell may be considered to terminate at the Pass. It is especially convenient to regard Rossett Pike as having a separate identity because of its splendid strategical position (independent of and different in function from Bowfell's own and even more splendid position) dominating the deep glacial hollow of Mickleden and rising steeply between the two passes that provide the only routes of exit from that valley. Rossett Pass (south-west) and Stake Pass (north-east), both well-known and much-trodden walkers' routes, define the fell exactly. The east face, between the two diverging passes (which start from the same point at its foot) is excessively rough, but the western slopes are grassy and slope easily to Langstrath with the solitary rocky exception of Lining Crag. The crest of the fell, which carries the county boundary of Cumberland and Westmorland, is undulating and interesting.

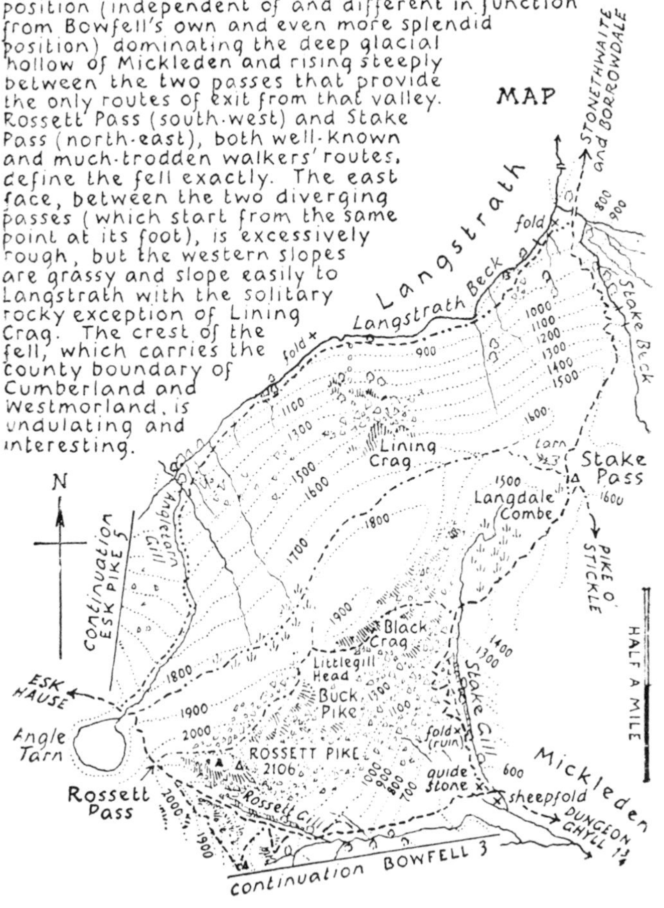

MAP

continuation ESK PIKE 5

continuation BOWFELL 3

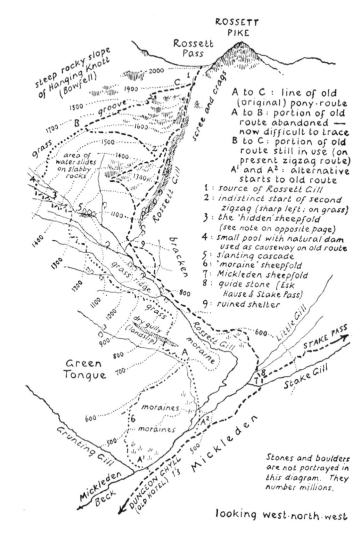

Rossett Gill

ROSSETT PIKE

Rossett Pass

steep rocky slope of Hanging Knott (Bowfell)

2000

1900

1800

1700

groove

grass

1600

1500

1400

area of water slides on slabby rocks

1300

4

3

5

1100

1400

1300

1200

1100

grass ledge

grass

800

dry gully (landslip)

1000

800

700

900

Green Tongue

600

moraines

moraines

500

Grunting Gill

Mickleden Beck

A¹

DUNGEON GHYLL (OLD HOTEL) 1¾

scree and crags

Rossett Gill

bracken

9

600   Little Gill

STAKE PASS

Rossett moraine

A

7 8   Stake Gill

A²

Mickleden

A to C : line of old (original) pony-route
A to B : portion of old route abandoned — now difficult to trace
B to C : portion of old route still in use (on present zigzag route)
A¹ and A² : alternative starts to old route

1 : source of Rossett Gill
2 : indistinct start of second zigzag (sharp left; on grass)
3 : the 'hidden' sheepfold (see note on opposite page)
4 : small pool with natural dam used as causeway on old route
5 : slanting cascade
6 : 'moraine' sheepfold
7 : Mickleden sheepfold
8 : guide stone (Esk Hause & Stake Pass)
9 : ruined shelter

Stones and boulders are not portrayed in this diagram. They number millions.

looking west·north·west

Rossett Gill

Rossett Gill is probably the best-known of Lakeland foot-passes, which is not to say that it is the most popular; indeed it is almost certainly the least-liked, due not so much to its steepness (which is more apparent than real, the gradient being nowhere in excess of 30°) but to its stoniness (a condition worsening year by year as swarming legions of booted pedestrians grind away the scanty vestiges of grass and soil). The two zigzags are an aid to easier progress, but the time has come for discriminating fellwalkers to revive the use of the old pony-route, which makes a leisurely way around the base of Green Tongue and, keeping entirely to the slopes of Bowfell, avoids the gill altogether; its final stage is the 'zag' of the second zigzag. The point where the old route left Mickleden is now obscure, but the streams there may easily be forded almost anywhere in normal weather: the route itself is also obscure for most of the way, although a few ancient cairns remain; curiously it is better discerned from a distance (eg. the Stake Pass path, or Rossett Pike) than when underfoot. The old route is especially useful in descent (keep straight on from the bend in the big zigzag), providing a carpet of soft grass for the feet and a solitude that contrast well with the execrable stones and clatter of boots and tongues on the usual direct route.

Rossett Gill has a history, and a few evidences remain, although now almost forgotten or unknown. A knowledge of them will add some interest to the tedious climb.

The old pony route: From the traces still existing it is obvious that this was originally a skilfully-graded and well-engineered path. It is believed to have been used for the secret transporting of goods smuggled into Ravenglass. Much of the former route seems to have been later abandoned in favour of the present double zigzag, but they coincide in the upper stages.

The hidden sheepfold: Cleverly screened from the sight of people passing along Mickleden and Rossett Gill, and situated within the big curve of the old route, is an old sheepfold, still in good condition, used to hide sheep in the far-off days when raiders often looted the valleys.

The packwoman's grave: Neglected and forgotten, yet within very easy reach of the gill, is the grave of a woman who used to call at Langdale farms carrying a pack of articles for sale — and whose mortal remains were found and buried here 170 years ago. A simple cross of stones laid on the ground, pointing southeast, indicates the grave; it has suffered little disturbance

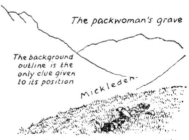

The packwoman's grave

The background outline is the only clue given to its position

Mickleden

down the years, but because so many folk nowadays seem unable to leave things alone its precise location is not divulged here.

(Historical notes on this page kindly supplied by MR. H. MOUNSEY, Skelwith)

Rossett Pike and Rossett Gill
from the old pony-route

From this viewpoint it would appear
that the Pike can be reached from
the top of the pass only by a steep
climb. But in fact the top of the pass
is further back than the illustration
suggests, and a gentle grass slope
there leads up to the rear of the Pike

ASCENT FROM MICKLEDEN
1600 feet of ascent : 1½ miles from the sheepfold

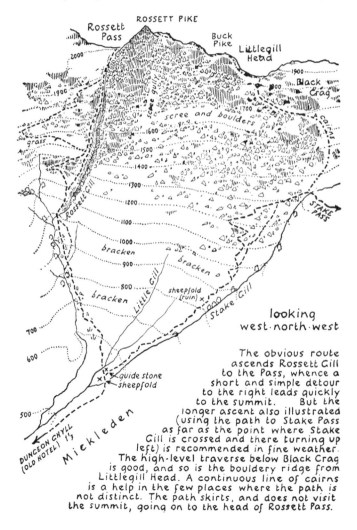

ROSSETT PIKE

Rossett Pass

Buck Pike

Littlegill Head

Black Crag

2000

1900

1900

1800

1700

cairns

scree gully

scree and boulders

1600

1500

1400

1300

1200

1100

1000

900

800

grass

Rossett Gill

bracken

bracken

bracken

Little Gill

sheepfold (ruin) ×

Stake Gill

STAKE PASS

700

600

500

×× guide stone
× sheepfold

DUNGEON GHYLL
(OLD HOTEL) 1½

Mickleden

looking
west·north·west

The obvious route
ascends Rossett Gill
to the Pass, whence a
short and simple detour
to the right leads quickly
to the summit.   But the
longer ascent also illustrated
(using the path to Stake Pass
as far as the point where Stake
Gill is crossed and there turning up
left) is recommended in fine weather.
The high-level traverse below Black Crag
is good, and so is the bouldery ridge from
Littlegill Head. A continuous line of cairns
is a help in the few places where the path is
not distinct. The path skirts, and does not visit
the summit, going on to the head of Rossett Pass.

THE SUMMIT

1: *Harrison Stickle*
2: *Pike o'Stickle*
3: *Loft Crag*
4: *Gimmer Crag*

LANGDALE PIKES

Mickleden cairn

The Mickleden cairn

The summit is in the form of a stony ridge running parallel to Rossett Gill, about 120 yards in length and gently inclined down to the sudden plunge of the Mickleden face; here is the principal cairn. The west end of the ridge is higher; a small cairn here is actually overtopped by outcropping rocks nearby. A continuous escarpment fringes the ridge on the Rossett Gill side, but the west and north slopes below the top are easy.

Mickleden

THE VIEW

The view is naturally inferior to those from the greater fells close by, but it excels in an impressive aerial scene of Mickleden and in the intimate detail of Bowfell's northern cliffs, the great sloping slab of Flat Crags, unique in the district, appearing as a striking feature.

Principal Fells

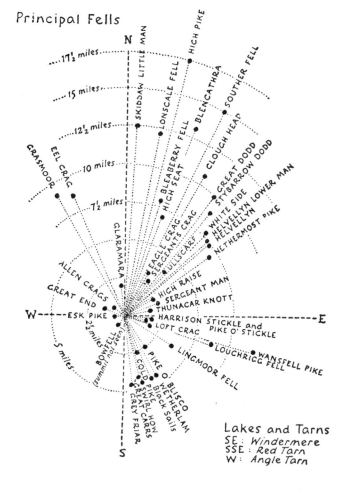

Lakes and Tarns
SE : *Windermere*
SSE : *Red Tarn*
W : *Angle Tarn*

Rosthwaite Fell

from Stonethwaite road end

Rosthwaite Fell, shadowing the level strath of the Stonethwaite valley, is really the northern extremity of the Scafells (although seldom recognised as such) and a strong walker may start from the green pastures here and make a fine high-level walk over the fell and the adjacent Glaramara to the summit of Scafell Pike. Few do this, preferring the more orthodox approaches, and Rosthwaite Fell's pathless and undulating top is rarely visited, understandably so for the rough stony sides yield no easy and attractive routes of ascent and the summit is rather a dreary place when compared with more worth-while objectives all around.

Rosthwaite Fell is flanked by the Langstrath and Seathwaite extensions of Borrowdale, to both of which, and to Stonethwaite, it presents a rim of crags. The top has two sections, distinctly divided by the hollow of Tarn at Leaves; the highest point of the northern half is Bessyboot (*treated in this chapter as the summit of the fell*), the southern rising in greater steps until, at Comb Door, it merges into Glaramara. Of special interest are Comb Gill, the rock summit of Rosthwaite Cam, and Doves Nest Caves. Tarn at Leaves has a lovely name but no other appeal.

- Rosthwaite
- Stonethwaite
- ▲ ROSTHWAITE FELL
- Seathwaite
- ▲ GLARAMARA

MILES
0   1   2   3

MAP

Doves Nest Caves

At some time in the distant past, as the result of a natural convulsion, Doves Nest Crag in Comb Gill gave a great shudder, part of the rockface breaking away and slipping downwards for a few feet before again coming to rest and thus creating a cavity which today gives unusual sport: a subterranean rock climb in darkness.

The interior is out of bounds for walkers, but the place is worth a visit and a gentle exploration. A path leads up scree to the bouldery entrance of South Cave.

To locate the Crag, first find the sheepfold at the head of the Comb: the Crag is plainly in view here — up on the left — and is reached by a stiff climb of ten minutes.

A good idea for a wet day!

South Chimney and Cave

1 : South Chimney and Cave (usual entrance)
2 : Attic Cave (the place of emergence)
3 : North Cave
4 : The Pinnacle
5 : Central Chimney
6 : North Chimney
7 : North Gully

Caves in Lakeland

Some readers have written to ask whether there are caves in the Lake District. If they have in mind natural caves eroded by water, as in the Craven underworld of Yorkshire, the answer is NO; for the rocks of Lakeland are hard volcanic ash, granite and slate, resistant to the action of water. The softer limestone occurs in the neighbouring fringes only, chiefly to the south-east.

The natural Lakeland caves, hardly worth the name, are formed by the wedging of fallen rocks (chockstones) in gullies and clefts, or by the piling-up of boulders below crags, or, infrequently, by a slip of a rock-face, as at Doves Nest. The first variety are beloved of climbers, the second of foxes, but neither will appeal to cavers.

Artificial man-made caves are plentiful, particularly in areas of copper and lead-mining operations, where tunnels, adits, levels and shafts are all to be found; more generally distributed are similar engineering devices to facilitate the shifting of stone in quarries on steep fellsides. Many of them are objects of great interest, and, if it is remembered that they were constructed manually long before the age of modern machines, of admiration too; but the strongest warning must be given to intending explorers that, except in a few cases, the mines and quarries have been unworked and abandoned for many years and their subterranean passages are derelict, often blocked by roof-falls, often flooded, and supporting timbers may be rotted and ready to collapse at a whisper. In other words, these ugly black holes and pits are not merely dangerous but damned dangerous. Sons should think of their mothers, and turn away. Husbands should think of their wives, after which gloomy contemplation many no doubt will march cheerfully in to a possible doom.

No, there is nothing in Lakeland for speleologists and cavers, unless they care to try fellwalking, i.e. crawling about on the surface.

ASCENT FROM STONETHWAITE
1500 feet of ascent : 1½ miles

Note the strange array of rock spurs

BESSYBOOT

perched boulder

COMB GILL

Cairn indicates a viewpoint for the meeting of the Greenup valley and Langstrath below

1500

1400

fall

wall to climb

1300

Follow the stream to its source in a marsh, then turn left up an easy ridge to the summit. (Take care not to by-pass Bessyboot and aim in error for the distinctive Rosthwaite Cam, half a mile further)

Bull Crag

Hanging Haystack

very awkward stile

1100

1000

bracken

900

indistinct section

800

700

600

500

Bessyboot may also be reached by a straightforward climb from Comb Gill, keeping between Rottenstone Gill and Dry Gill up a grassy slope with some boulders, but this route becomes tedious and should be reserved for a simple way down after ascent by the route shown in the diagram, which is much more attractive but less suitable as a route of descent

looking south-south-west

400

LANGSTRATH

LANE

Stonethwaite

ROAD

field path

ROSTHWAITE

Watch for the path leading into the wood, just after crossing the second of two streams close together (¼ mile from Stonethwaite)

Stonethwaite Beck

This route takes advantage of the one obvious breach in the rim of cliffs overlooking Stonethwaite, where a great notch in the skyline is formed by the deep cleft of Stanger Gill. The steep climb up the gill, amongst trees, is charming, with lovely views of Borrowdale in retrospect, and the ravine itself is scenically good: a fair path here is a help over rough ground

THE SUMMIT

Bessyboot is the most distinctive height in the northern half of the fell, and its small, neat top, easily reached through breaches in a surround of low crags, is pleasant enough, but somewhat disappointing in the matter of views.

Rosthwaite Cam
(from the south)

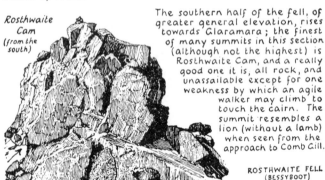

The southern half of the fell, of greater general elevation, rises towards Glaramara; the finest of many summits in this section (although not the highest) is Rosthwaite Cam, and a really good one it is, all rock, and unassailable except for one weakness by which an agile walker may climb to touch the cairn. The summit resembles a lion (without a lamb) when seen from the approach to Comb Gill.

Arrow indicates start of easy way up.

RIDGE ROUTE

To GLARAMARA, 2560': 1¾ miles
S, then SW and finally WNW
1000 feet of ascent
A path would improve matters

Much marshy, trackless and confusing ground detracts from this unfrequented walk; nevertheless it is better done in this direction than in the reverse. Keep generally to the Langstrath side of the ridge, where there is a little help from occasional traces of a path. Interest may be added to the walk, if time is available, by visits to Rosthwaite Cam, Comb Door and Comb Head. *This is dangerous country in mist.*

THE VIEW

This is the view from the summit of Bessyboot. It will disappoint people who expect to look down on the villages of Borrowdale or on Stonethwaite or Langstrath, these valleys being concealed by the wide slopes around the top. The best views are obtained from mid-height during the ascent.

Principal Fells

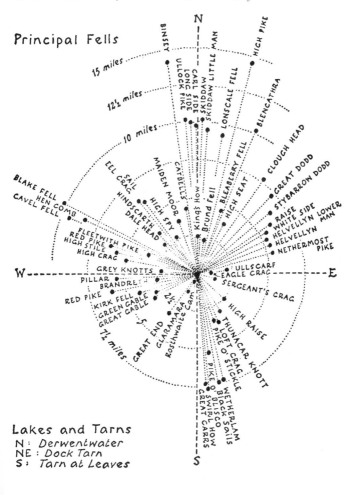

Lakes and Tarns
N: Derwentwater
NE: Dock Tarn
S: Tarn at Leaves

Scafell

3162'

formerly Scawfell or Scaw Fell
(pronounced Scawfle)

from Cam Spout

- Wasdale Head
  - SCAFELL PIKE
    ▲
    SCAFELL   ▲ BOWFELL

  ▲   ▲
  ILLGILL   SLIGHT SIDE
  HEAD

- Boot

MILES

0   1   2   3   4

NATURAL FEATURES

When men first named the mountains, the whole of the high mass south of Sty Head was known as Scaw Fell; later, as the work of the dalesfolk took them more and more onto the heights and closer identification became necessary, they applied the name to the mountain that seemed to them the greatest, the other summits in the range, to them individually inferior, being referred to collectively as the Pikes of Scaw Fell. Many folk today, even with the added knowledge that the main Pike is not only higher but actually the highest land in the country, share the old opinion that Scaw Fell (now Scafell) is the superior mountain of the group.

This respect is inspired not by the huge western flank going down to Wasdale nor by the broad southern slopes ending in the Eskdale foothills but rather by the towering rampart of shadowed crags facing north and east below the summit, the greatest display of natural grandeur in the district, a spectacle of massive strength and savage wildness but without beauty, an awesome and a humbling scene. A man may stand on the lofty ridge of Mickledore, or in the green hollow beneath the precipice amongst the littered debris and boulders fallen from it, and witness the sublime architecture of buttresses and pinnacles soaring into the sky, silhouetted against racing clouds or, often, tormented by writhing mists, and, as in a great cathedral, lose all his conceit. It does a man good to realise his own insignificance in the general scheme of things, and that is his experience here.

Fuller notes on the topography are contained in the Scafell Pike chapter

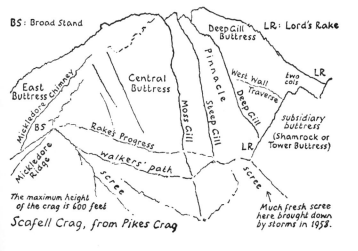

The maximum height of the crag is 600 feet

Much fresh scree here brought down by storms in 1958.

Scafell Crag, from Pikes Crag

Scafell 3

Broad Stand

Broad Stand and Mickledore

   The greatest single obstacle confronting ridge-walkers on the hills of Lakeland is the notorious Broad Stand, with which every traveller from Scafell Pike to Scafell comes face to face at the far end of the Mickledore traverse. Obstacles met on other ridges can be overcome or easily by-passed; not so Broad Stand. It is an infuriating place, making a man angry with himself for his inability to climb the thirty feet of rock that bar his way to the simple rising slope beyond. From a distance it looks nothing; close at hand it still looks not much to worry about; but with the first platform underfoot, while still not seeming impossible, the next awkward movement to the left plus an uneasy fear of worse hazards above and as yet unseen, influences sensible walkers to retreat from the scene and gain access to Scafells top by using one or the other of the two orthodox pedestrian routes (via Lord's Rake or Foxes Tarn), each of which entails a long detour and, unfortunately, a considerable descent.

   Nevertheless, Broad Stand has a long history and a lot of stories to its name, and it should at least be visited. Where the Mickledore ridge abuts against the broken crags of Scafell turn down the scree on the Eskdale side (east) and in no more than a dozen yards a deep vertical cleft, paved with stones, can be entered and passed through to a small platform. This cleft is a tight squeeze, well named as "Fat Man's Agony," and ladies, too, whose statistics are too vital, will have an uncomfortable time in it. The platform is shut in by smooth walls, the route of exit (for experts only) being up the scratched corner on the left. But for mere pedestrians the platform is the limit of their exploration and they should return through the cleft, resolving, as is customary, to do the climb next time. The author first made this resolve in 1930 and has repeated it a score of times since then; his continuing disappointment is amply compensated by the pleasure of going on living.

YOU HAVE BEEN WARNED!

Lord's Rake

Lord's Rake is a classic route, uncomfortable underfoot but magnificent all around. It is used on the ascent of Scafell from Wasdale Head via Brown Tongue and on the traverse of the main ridge. The Rake is unique, and one's fellwalking education is not complete until its peculiar delights and horrors have been experienced.

Strangers to Scafell may have some difficulty in locating the Rake, small-scale maps being unable to supply the details, but users of this book will have no such worries, of course.

the first section

The Rake starts (in ascent) as a steep, wide scree-gully or channel rising *not into the mountain* but obliquely *across* it and between the main crag and a subsidiary buttress, the top edge of which forms a parapet to the Rake. This first section is almost 100 yards in length, and ends at a perfect little col, so narrow that it can be straddled. A descent of 10 feet and a rise of 20 feet in 20 yards leads to another col, equally sweet, and the end of the Rake is now in sight 100 yards ahead and at the same elevation, although a steep descent to a stony amphitheatre is necessary before the exit can be reached. Here, now, is the open fell, and a rough track (left) leads to the top of Scafell.

subsidiary buttress

main crag

foot of Scafell Pinnacle

HOLLOW STONES

The great thing to remember (important in mist) is that Lord's Rake has 3 ups and 2 downs, and maintains a dead-straight course throughout.

The first section calls for strenuous effort, as the assortment of buttons, boot soles, dentures, broken pipes and other domestic articles scattered en route testifies. The best footing higher up is at the right side. In a place like this, where boots cannot gain a purchase on the sliding stones and polished rocks, other methods of locomotion may usefully be adopted, especially when descending. It is no disgrace even for stalwart men to come down here on their bottoms, while ladies may certainly use their feminine equivalents without any feeling of shame. The yellow flower growing in crevices of the rock walls is the starry saxifrage.

Lord's Rake is not dangerous, and is a safe route in mist. In standard of difficulty it is *much easier* than Jack's Rake on Pavey Ark, much harder than Rossett Gill.

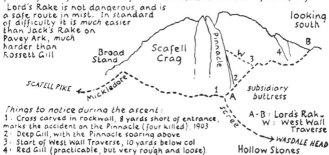

looking south

Broad Stand

Scafell Crag

Pinnacle

SCAFELL PIKE

Mickledore

subsidiary buttress

scree

A–B : Lord's Rake
W : West Wall Traverse

WASDALE HEAD

Hollow Stones

Things to notice during the ascent:
1 : Cross carved in rockwall, 8 yards short of entrance, marks the accident on the Pinnacle (four killed), 1903
2 : Deep Gill, with the Pinnacle soaring above
3 : Start of West Wall Traverse, 10 yards below col
4 : Red Gill (practicable, but very rough and loose).

These paths are shown as good (---) but trodden ways here are constantly obliterated by sliding stones: the routes, however, are much-used and obvious.

MAP

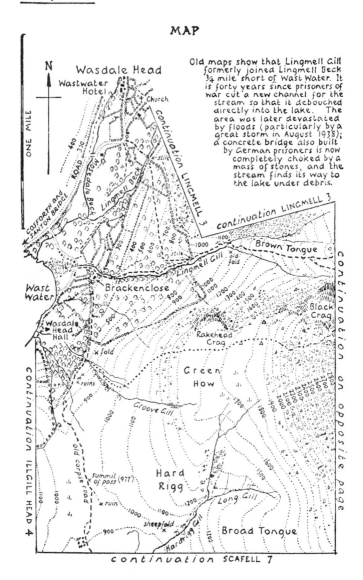

Old maps show that Lingmell Gill formerly joined Lingmell Beck ¼ mile short of Wast Water. It is forty years since prisoners of war cut a new channel for the stream so that it debouched directly into the lake. The area was later devastated by floods (particularly by a great storm in August 1938); a concrete bridge also built by German prisoners is now completely choked by a mass of stones, and the stream finds its way to the lake under debris.

MAP

The inadequacy of maps to serve as a guide over rough
and complicated ground, more especially where there are
vertical elevations, is nowhere better illustrated than in
the small area between Scafell and Scafell Pike. A lost
and hapless wanderer standing on Mickledore ridge, trying
to fit the tremendous scene around him into a half-inch
space on his map, is deserving of every sympathy. So is
the map-maker, furnished with many details and festooned
with merging contours — and nowhere to put them; but this
does not really excuse the rather nonchalant hachuring of
crags on both the Ordnance Survey and Bartholomews maps,
nor the omission of important paths. The map on this page
is itself little better than useless. But never mind: there is
a large-scale plan of this
particular area on page 14
which, while not aspiring
to portray the character of
the terrain, should at least
be informative enough to
get the afore-mentioned
hapless wanderer off
Mickledore and on
his way safely. It
is a tribute to
the place that
it cannot be
recorded
properly
on a map.

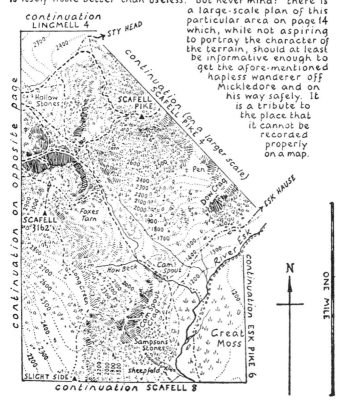

Scafell 7

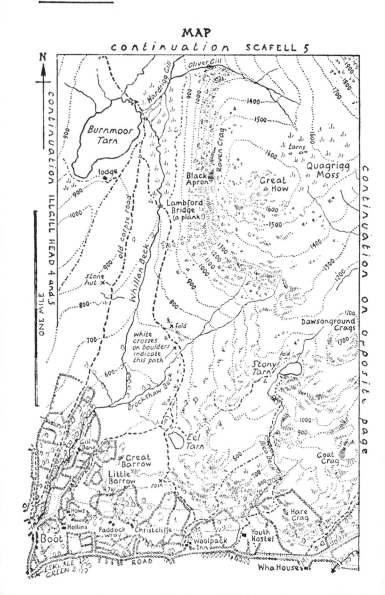

MAP

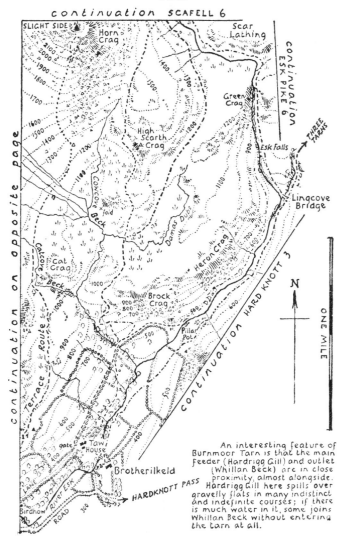

SLIGHT SIDE

Horn Crag

Scar Lathing

continuation on opposite page

2100
2000
1900
1800
1700
1600
1500
1400
1300
1200
1100

continuation ESK PIKE 6

1400
1300
1500

Green Crag

High Scarth Crag

1200

900

Esk Falls

THREE TARNS

Concove Beck

fold

Damas Dubs

1100

Lingcove Bridge

Calcove Beck

Cat Crag

Heron Crag

1000

continuation HARD KNOTT 3

Brock Crag

900
800
700

N

ONE MILE

600
500

Pillar Pot

900

Terrace Route

800

700

600
500
400

gate

Taw House

Brotherilkeld

LANE

Birdhow

ROAD

RIVER ESK

HARDKNOTT PASS

300

An interesting feature of Burnmoor Tarn is that the main feeder (Hardrigg Gill) and outlet (Whillan Beck) are in close proximity, almost alongside. Hardrigg Gill here spills over gravelly flats in many indistinct and indefinite courses; if there is much water in it, some joins Whillan Beck without entering the tarn at all.

The head of Deep Gill
(the top of the descent to
the West Wall Traverse)
with the Pinnacle
(left-centre)
and the Oracle
(bottom right)

The West Wall Traverse

The massive crags of Scafell are split asunder by the tremendous chasm of Deep Gill, which has two vertical pitches in its lower part that put the through route out of bounds for walkers. The upper half, however, although excessively stony, can be used by all and sundry without difficulty, and is linked with Lord's Rake by a simple path across a grassy shelf. This is the West Wall Traverse. The rock scenery is awe-inspiring.

ASCENT: Go up the first section of Lord's Rake. On the left, 10 yards short of the col, a distinct path goes up to the grassy shelf, along which it rises to enter Deep Gill, the two pitches now being below. Steep scree then follows to the open fell at the top of the Gill. The exit used to be a desperate scramble up a loose and earthy wall, but clutching hands over the years have torn down the cornice and escape is now easy, especially on the left.

DESCENT: Go down into Deep Gill (easier on the right), a descent not as bad as may be thought from its appearance, but made unpleasant by sliding stones. Watch for the path turning left out of the Gill 80 yards down, where the crag on this side eases off: this path slants easily across a shelf into Lord's Rake. It is vital that this path be taken; the Gill itself, further down, drops vertically over chockstones and is entirely impracticable for walkers.

SCAFELL PIKE
col

The start of Lord's Rake
(in descent)

ASCENT FROM WASDALE HEAD

via BROWN TONGUE: 3,000 feet of ascent : 3 miles
via GREEN HOW:
2,950 feet : 3¾ miles
(from Wastwater Hotel)

SCAFELL

The Brown Tongue
— Lord's Rake route
is becoming
increasingly
popular, although
very rough above
2000', and is much
the finest way to
the summit. The
Green How route is
as much out of
fashion as the
Victorians who
favoured it.

Mickledore

exit of Lord's Rake

Lords
Rake

3100
3000
2900
2800
2700
2600
2500
2400
2300
2200
2100
2000

big
boulder
spring

2400

2500

Hollow
Stones

Green
How

1800

Black
Crag

Groove Gill

watch for junction
of paths (cairn)

1600
1500

Rakehead
Crag

1600

1500

Brown Tongue

grass

1500
1400
1300

1200
1100

grass

1000

bracken

900

old
fold

fold

Upon arrival at
the scree-slope
debouching from
Lord's Rake refer
to page 4 for
greater detail of
the remainder
of the climb.

800

700

600

500

1000

900

800

300

ESKDALE
VIA
BURNMOOR
TARN

700

Brackenclose

WASDALE
HEAD HALL

FARM ROAD

600

Wast
Water

500

400

300

ROAD

GOSFORTH &
SANTON BRIDGE

Wasdale
Head

Lingmell Beck

Mosedale Beck

signpost

Wastwater Hotel

Whatever the demerits
of the Green How route as
an ascent (and admittedly it
is a dull and tiring climb) there
is no denying that as a quick way
down it is first-class.

looking south-east

ASCENT FROM ESKDALE
3100 feet of ascent : 6 miles from Boot

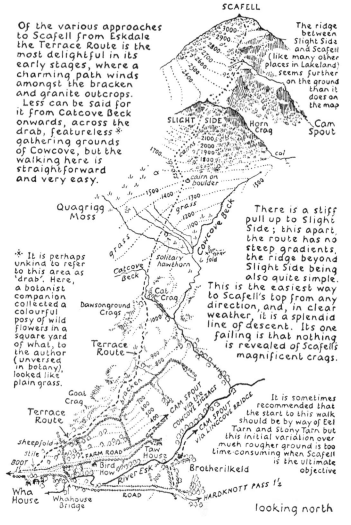

SCAFELL

SLIGHT SIDE

Horn Crag

Cam Spout

Quagrigg Moss

cairn on boulder

grass

Cowcove Beck

col

solitary hawthorn

sheepfold

Catcove Beck

Cat Crag

Dawsonground Crags

Terrace Route →

Goat Crag

Terrace Route

bracken

CAM SPOUT via the COWCOVE ZIGZAGS

CAM SPOUT via LINGCOVE BRIDGE

sheepfold
stile
BOOT 1½

FARM ROAD

Taw House

Bird How

River Esk

Brotherilkeld

Wha House

Whahouse Bridge

ROAD

HARDKNOTT PASS 1½

Of the various approaches to Scafell from Eskdale the Terrace Route is the most delightful in its early stages, where a charming path winds amongst the bracken and granite outcrops.
Less can be said for it from Catcove Beck onwards, across the drab, featureless * gathering grounds of Cowcove, but the walking here is straightforward and very easy.

The ridge between Slight Side and Scafell (like many other places in Lakeland) seems further on the ground than it does on the map

There is a stiff pull up to Slight Side; this apart, the route has no steep gradients, the ridge beyond Slight Side being also quite simple. This is the easiest way to Scafell's top from any direction, and, in clear weather, it is a splendid line of descent. Its one failing is that nothing is revealed of Scafell's magnificent crags.

* It is perhaps unkind to refer to this area as 'drab'. Here, a botanist companion collected a colourful posy of wild flowers in a square yard of what, to the author (unversed in botany), looked like plain grass.

It is sometimes recommended that the start to this walk should be by way of Eel Tarn and Stony Tarn but this initial variation over much rougher ground is too time-consuming when Scafell is the ultimate objective

looking north

ASCENT FROM ESKDALE
via CAM SPOUT
3050 feet of ascent : 7¼ miles from Boot

For a diagram and notes
of the alternative routes
to Cam Spout, see pages
Scafell Pike 21 and 22.

If the
Cam Spout
path is used
for descent
care is needed
on the rock slab
alongside the
waterfalls,
where loose
pebbles and
stones could
cause a slip.
Keep away
from the edge
of the ravine.

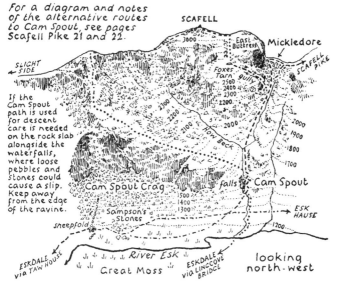

looking
north-west

Take the scrambling route alongside the waterfalls, above which
a good path goes up towards Mickledore, but before reaching the
level of East Buttress and 100 yards below its nearest crags enter
a stony gully going up squarely to the left; a small stream emerges
from it. The gully, rough but not difficult, leads directly to Foxes
Tarn (which is no more than a tiny pond with a large boulder in it),
whence a long scree-slope is climbed to the saddle above, the top
then being 250 easy yards distant. This is the quickest route to
the summit from Cam Spout, and avoids the worst sections of the
Mickledore screes.

Gluttons for punishment may, instead, continue up loose scree
to the Mickledore ridge, descend the other side, and finish the
climb by way of Lord's Rake, taking half an hour longer and
making personal acquaintance with a few thousand more stones,
but being rewarded by the finest scenery Scafell has to offer.

The pathless route along the curving ridge of Cam Spout Crag is
very roundabout and the ridge itself is too broad to be exciting,
although it narrows and becomes quite attractive near the end.
The one advantage of this route, of importance to people with
bunions, is that it is possible to walk on grass throughout, and in
fact it is the only way to the main ridge of Scafell from Cam Spout
that avoids scree entirely.

THE SUMMIT

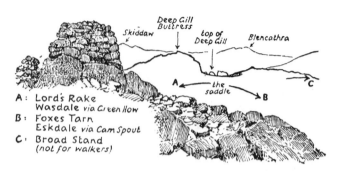

A: Lord's Rake
   Wasdale *via Green How*
B: Foxes Tarn
   Eskdale *via Cam Spout*
C: Broad Stand
   (not for walkers)

The face of Scafell Crag is the grandest sight in the district, and if only the highest point of the fell were situated on the top of Deep Gill Buttress, perched above the tremendous precipices of stone, it would be the best summit of all. As nature has arranged things, however, it lies back, away and remote from the excitement, the cairn being on a simple rise where there is little of interest at close quarters although the view southwards is enough to transfix the visitor's attention for some minutes. On the south side of the cairn is a ruinous shelter, not now more serviceable as a protection against wind and rain than the cairn itself. The top is everywhere stony.

DESCENTS

More than ordinary care is needed in choosing a route of descent. The western slope is stony, the eastern craggy, the northern precipitous. Except for Eskdale via Slight Side, recommended routes leave the saddle: turn left for Wasdale, right for Eskdale; go straight ahead for Deep Gill and the West Wall Traverse if Borrowdale is the objective *but only if the Traverse is already known; otherwise use Lord's Rake.*

In mist, the Slight Side route may be tried, but if lost turn right down to Hardrigg Gill and the Burnmoor path. For other destinations aim for the saddle (big cairn) to which the path is clear but there is indistinct, and follow, cautiously, the fine-weather routes; see also map, page 14

RIDGE ROUTE

To SLIGHT SIDE, 2499': 1¼ miles: S
Depression at 2400'
100 feet of ascent

An easy walk, becoming pathless on grass. In clear weather there is no difficulty. *In mist,* when the path fades, remember to keep the escarpment on the left hand throughout.

RIDGE ROUTE

To SCAFELL PIKE, 3210': 1¼ miles : compass useless.
750' of ascent via Lord's Rake, 900' via Foxes Tarn.
Loins should be girded up for an hour's hard labour.

There is no bigger trap for the unwary and uninformed walker than this. Scafell Pike is clearly in view but the intervening crags cannot be seen. The natural inclination will be to make a beeline for the Pike and to be deflected by the edge of the precipice down the easy slope to the right, encouraged by a good path that now appears.   But this is the climbers' way to Broad Stand, which walkers cannot safely attempt. A desperate situation now arises. Just beyond the drop of Broad Stand, and tantalisingly near, is Mickledore Ridge, the easy connecting link between Scafell and the Pike. The choice is to risk a serious accident or toil all the way back and start again : not an easy decision for a walker already tired and pressed for time.   The advice is to go back and start again.

From the grassy saddle (cairn) three routes are available:

1 : via LORD'S RAKE: This is the usual way, and it is arduous. Turn *left* down a slope that steepens and becomes all stones. The start of the Rake is further down the fellside than will generally be expected, and it should be identified exactly (see illustration, page 9). Avoid the gaping entrance to Red Gill midway. For details of the Rake, see page 4, where it is described in ascent — it will occur to the mentally alert that if there are 3 ups and 2 downs in the ascent there must be 3 downs and 2 ups in the descent. From the foot of the Rake continue ahead below the crags and scramble up to Mickledore Ridge, where turn *left* along a good path to the Pike.

2 : via FOXES TARN: This is easier, but involves a greater descent and re-ascent. Turn *right* down a steepening slope to the Tarn, then *left* by the issuing stream (rough gully) to join the stony path coming up from Cam Spout for Mickledore and the Pike (right).

3 : via THE WEST WALL TRAVERSE: This is something special. Consult the notes on page 9.

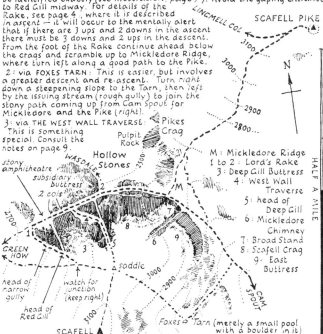

M : Mickledore Ridge
1 to 2 : Lord's Rake
3 : Deep Gill Buttress
4 : West Wall Traverse
5 : head of Deep Gill
6 : Mickledore Chimney
7 : Broad Stand
8 : Scafell Crag
9 : East Buttress

Foxes Tarn (merely a small pool with a boulder in it)

Note that this map is on the scale of six inches to one mile.   To assist clarity, areas of stones and boulders are omitted, but nobody should assume there aren't any : they occur all over the place.

THE VIEW

The bulky mass of Scafell Pike, north-east, obstructs the view of a considerable slice of Lakeland, but nevertheless Scafell's top is a most excellent viewpoint and, additionally, a place for reverie, especially when reached from the north, for here there is awareness that one has come at last to the outer edge of the mountains and that, beyond, lie only declining foothills to the sea. Vaguely, in the mind of a fellwalker long past his youth, there arises a feeling of sadness, as though at this point the mountains are behind, in the past, and ahead is a commonplace world, a future in which mountains have no part, his own future. Yet this vision of low hills and green valleys, of distant sands and wide expanses of sea, is very beautiful. From Morecambe Bay to Furness and across the Duddon Estuary and Black Combe to the sand dunes of Ravenglass, and along the glorious length of Eskdale, all is smiling and serene, often when the high mountains are frowning. The bright pastures of Eskdale, won from the rough fells, have a happy quality of seeming to be in sunlight even under cloud. The view in this direction, unmarred by any scars of industry, is superb.

The western fells, and the Bowfell and Coniston groups, all show to advantage. Look in particular for the little hidden valley of Miterdale, rarely seen but from this viewpoint, and no other, disclosed in its full length. On a clear day the Isle of Man may be seen above and to the left of Calder Hall atomic power station—which is too conspicuous — and the Solway Firth, backed by the Scottish hills, overtops Kirk Fell. Beyond Bowfell and Crinkle Crags the Pennines are visible. Most visitors look for Helvellyn in every view, but from Scafell's summit it is exactly covered by the south peak of Scafell Pike across Mickledore.

N

CRISEDALE PIKE
ROBINSON
HOPEGILL HEAD
DEAD CRAG
WANDOPE
GRASMOOR
HIGH CRAG
RED PIKE
HIGH STILE
KIRK FELL
PILLAR
SCOAT FELL
RED PIKE
STARLING DODD
HAYCOCK
YEWBARROW
Long Barrow
LANK RIGG
CAW FELL
SEATALLAN
MIDDLE FELL
W
BUCKBARROW
ILLGILL HEAD
WHIN RIGG
S

THE VIEW

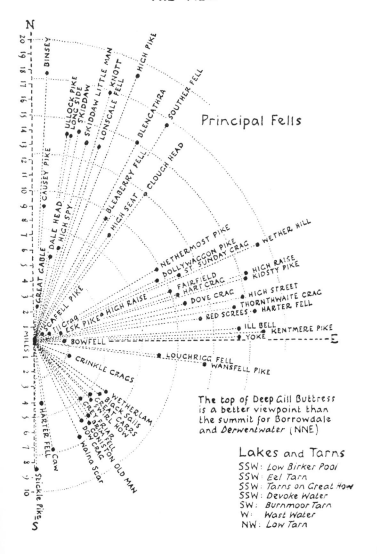

Principal Fells

N

20 19 18 17 16 15 14 13 12 11 10 9 8 7 6 5 4 3 2 1 MILES 1 2 3 4 5 6 7 8 9 10

• BINSEY
ULLOCK PIKE
LONG SIDE
SKIDDAW
SKIDDAW LITTLE MAN
KNOTT
LONSCALE FELL
• HIGH PIKE
SOUTHER FELL
• CAUSEY PIKE
BLENCATHRA
DALE HEAD
HIGH SPY
BLEABERRY FELL
HIGH SEAT
CLOUGH HEAD
NETHERMOST PIKE
DOLLYWACCON PIKE
ST. SUNDAY CRAG
• WETHER HILL
GREAT GABLE
FAIRFIELD
HART CRAG
HIGH RAISE
KIDSTY PIKE
DOVE CRAG
HIGH STREET
THORNTHWAITE CRAG
RED SCREES • HARTER FELL
SCAFELL PIKE
ILL CRAG
ESK PIKE • HIGH RAISE
• ILL BELL   KENTMERE PIKE
BOWFELL
YOKE
E
LOUGHRIGG FELL
WANSFELL PIKE
CRINKLE CRAGS
WETHERLAM
BLACK SAILS
GREY FRIAR
SWIRL HOW
BRIM FELL
DOW CRAG
CONISTON OLD MAN
HARTER FELL
Wana Scar
• Caw
• Stickle Pikes
S

The top of Deep Gill Buttress
is a better viewpoint than
the summit for Borrowdale
and *Derwentwater* (NNE)

Lakes and Tarns

SSW: *Low Birker Pool*
SSW: *Eel Tarn*
SSW: *Tarns on Great How*
SSW: *Devoke Water*
SW: *Burnmoor Tarn*
W: *Wast Water*
NW: *Low Tarn*

Scafell Pike

the highest mountain in England

formerly 'The Pikes' or 'The Pikes of Scawfell';
'Scafell Pikes' on Ordnance Survey maps.

from Great Moss,
Upper Eskdale

Scafell Pike

Ill Crag

*from the gorge
of the Esk*

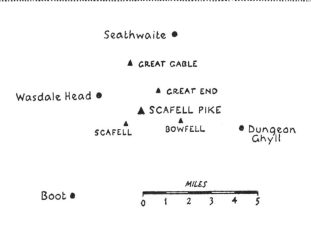

Seathwaite ●

▲ GREAT GABLE

Wasdale Head ●   ▲ GREAT END

▲ SCAFELL PIKE

SCAFELL ▲   ▲ BOWFELL   ● Dungeon
Ghyll

Boot ●

MILES

0   1   2   3   4   5

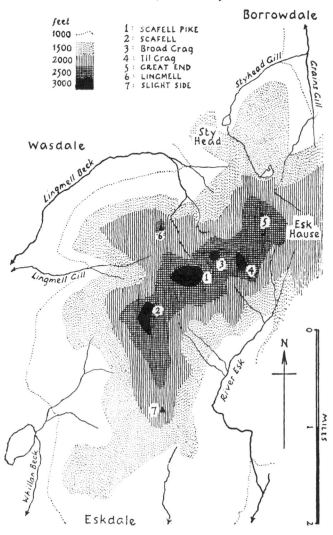

The Scafell Range

Borrowdale

feet	
1000	
1500	
2000	
2500	
3000	

1 : SCAFELL PIKE
2 : SCAFELL
3 : Broad Crag
4 : Ill Crag
5 : GREAT END
6 : LINGMELL
7 : SLIGHT SIDE

Sty Head

Styhead Gill

Grains Gill

Wasdale

Lingmell Beck

Esk Hause

Lingmell Gill

River Esk

N

Whillan Beck

Eskdale

MILES

Scafell Pike's grandest crag:
Dow Crag

Known to climbers as Esk Buttress, this 400-foot near-vertical crag rises from the fellside low down on the mountain's east flank, overlooking the River Esk.

Scafell Pike's best-known crag:
Pulpit Rock

This fine pinnacle (seen here from Mickledore) is the best feature of Pikes Crag, above Hollow Stones. Its top (easily reached from the summit-to-Mickledore path) is the best of all viewpoints for Scafell Crag

NATURAL FEATURES

The difference between a hill and a mountain depends on *appearance*, not on *altitude* (whatever learned authorities may say to the contrary) and is thus arbitrary and a matter of personal opinion. Grass predominates on a hill, rock on a mountain. A hill is smooth, a mountain rough. In the case of Scafell Pike, opinions must agree that here is a mountain without doubt, and a mountain that is, moreover, every inch a mountain. Roughness and ruggedness are the necessary attributes, and the Pike has these in greater measure than other high ground in the country —— which is just as it should be, for there is no higher ground than this.

Strictly, the name 'Scafell Pike' should be in the plural, there being three principal summits above 3000 feet, the two lesser having the distinguishing titles of Broad Crag and Ill Crag. The main Pike is, however, pre-eminent, towering over the others seemingly to a greater extent than the mere 160 feet or so by which it has superiority in altitude, and in general being a bulkier mass altogether.

The three summits rise from the main spine of an elevated ridge which keeps above 2800 feet to its abrupt termination in the cliffs of Great End, facing north to Borrowdale; lower spurs then run down to that valley. In the opposite direction, southwest, across the deep gulf of Mickledore, is the tremendous rock-wall of the neighbouring and separate mountain of Scafell, which also exceeds 3000 feet: this is the parent mountain in the one sense that its name has been passed on to the Pikes. Scafell's summit-ridge runs south and broadens into foothills, descending ultimately to mid-Eskdale.

continued

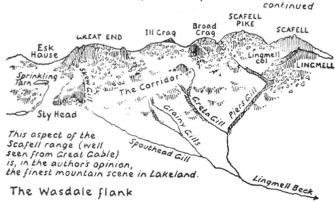

This aspect of the Scafell range (well seen from Great Gable) is, in the author's opinion, the finest mountain scene in Lakeland.

The Wasdale flank

NATURAL FEATURES

The flanks of the range are bounded on the west by Wasdale, and by the upper reaches of Eskdale, east. All the waters from the Pikes (and from Scafell) flow into one or other of these two valleys, ultimately to merge in the Ravenglass estuary. Thus it will be seen that Scafell Pike, despite a commanding presence, has not the same importance, geographically, as many other fells in the district. It does not stand at the head of any valley, but between valleys: it is not the hub of a wheel from which watercourses radiate; it is one of the spokes. It is inferior, in this respect, to Great Gable or Bowfell nearby, or even its own Great End.

Another interesting feature of Scafell Pike is that although it towers so mightily above Wasdale it can claim no footing in that valley, its territory tapering quickly to Brown Tongue, at the base of which it is nipped off by the widening lower slopes of Lingmell and Scafell.

Tarns are noticeably absent on the arid, stony surface of the mountain, but there is one sheet of water below the summit to the south, Broadcrag Tarn, which is small and unattractive, but, at 2725 feet, can at least boast the highest standing water in Lakeland.

Crags are in evidence on all sides, and big areas of the upper slopes lie devastated by a covering of piled-up boulders, a result not of disintegration but of the volcanic upheavals that laid waste to the mountain during its formation. The landscape is harsh, even savage, and has attracted to itself nothing of romance or historical legend. There is no sentiment about Scafell Pike.

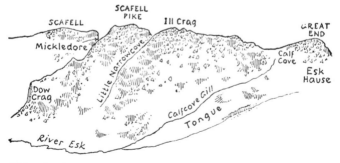

This view is as seen from the south ridge of Esk Pike

The Eskdale flank

MAP

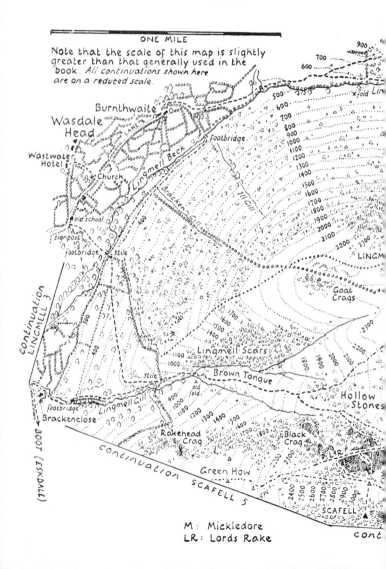

ONE MILE

Note that the scale of this map is slightly greater than that generally used in the book. All continuations shown here are on a reduced scale.

Burnthwaite

Wasdale Head

Wastwater Hotel

Lingmell Beck

Footbridge

Church

old school

signpost

footbridge stile

Bracken Gill

Till Gill

fold Lin

LINGM

Goat Crags

Lingmell Scars

Brown Tongue

old fold

stile

continuation LINGMELL 3

BOOT (ESKDALE)

footbridge

Lingmell Gill

Brackenclose

Rakehead Crag

Black Crag

Hollow Stones

continuation SCAFELL 5

Green How

SCAFELL

cont

M : Mickledore
LR : Lords Rake

MAP

A : to BORROWDALE
B : to GREAT LANGDALE

C : to ESKDALE (via CAMSPOUT)

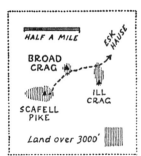

Broad Crag. 3054'

Broad Crag is the second of the Scafell Pikes, and a worthy mountain in itself — but it has little fame, is not commonly regarded as a separate fell, and its summit is rarely visited. This latter circumstance appears strange, because the blazed highway between Esk Hause and the main Pike not only climbs over the shoulder of Broad Crag but actually passes within a hundred yards of its summit, which is not greatly elevated above the path. Yet not one person in a thousand passing along here (and thousands do!) turns aside to visit the cairn. The reason for this neglect is more obvious when on the site than it is from a mere study of the map, for the whole of the top is littered deep with piled boulders across which it is quite impossible to walk with any semblance of dignity, the detour involving a desperate and inelegant scramble and the risk of breaking a leg at every stride. Most walkers using the path encounter enough trouble underfoot without seeking more in the virgin jungle of tumbled rock all around. Broad Crag is, in fact, the roughest summit in Lakeland.

The eastern slope descends into Little Narrowcove, and is of small consequence, but the western flank is imposing. On this side the top breaks away in a semi-circle of crags, below which is a shelf traversed by the Corridor Route and bounded lower down a steepening declivity by the great gash of Piers Gill.

Only the proximity of the main Scafell Pike, overtopping the scene, robs Broad Crag of its rightful place as one of the finest of fells.

Broad Crag, and Broad Crag col (right) from the Corridor Route

Ill Crag, 3040'

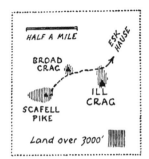

HALF A MILE

ESK HAUSE

BROAD CRAG

ILL CRAG

SCAFELL PIKE

Land over 3000'

Ill Crag is the third of the Scafell Pikes, and the most shapely, appearing as a graceful peak when viewed from upper Eskdale, which it dominates. Like Broad Crag, the summit lies off the path from Esk Hause to the main Pike but is more distant, although in this case too the shoulder of the fell is crossed at a height exceeding 3000, so that the summit is raised but little above it. The detour to the top is simple, only the final short rise being really rougher than the boulder-crossings on the path itself. Ill Crag is prominently seen from the vicinity of Esk Hause, and many wishful (and subsequently disappointed) walkers hereabouts, engaged on their first ascent of Scafell Pike will wrongly assume it to be their objective.

The western slope goes down uneventfully between Broad Crag and Great End to the Corridor Route, and the glory of the fell is its excessively steep and rough fall directly from the cairn eastwards into the wilderness of upper Eskdale: a chaotic and desolate scene set at a precipitous gradient, a frozen avalanche of crags and stones, much of it unexplored and uncharted, wild in the extreme, and offering a safe refuge for escaped convicts or an ideal depository for murdered corpses. Someday, when the regular paths become overcrowded, it may be feasible to track out an exciting and alternative route of ascent for scramblers here, but the author prefers to leave the job to someone with more energy and a lesser love of life.

Ill Crag, from the path above Esk Hause

Scafell Pike 11

Pikes Crag

Pulpit Rock

Mickledore Buttress

Mickledore

Scafell Crag

from Hollow Stones

Once in a while every keen fellwalker should have a *pre-arranged* night out amongst the mountains. Time drags and the hours of darkness can be bitterly cold, but to be on the tops at dawn is a wonderful experience and much more than recompense for the temporary discomfort.

Hollow Stones is an excellent place for a bivouac, with a wide choice of overhanging boulders for shelter, many of which have been walled-up and made draught-proof by previous occupants. Watch the rising sun flush Scafell Crag and change a black silhouette into a rosy-pink castle! (This doesn't always happen. Sometimes it never stops raining).

Not many readers, not even those who are frequent visitors to Scafell Pike, could give a caption to this picture. It is, in fact, a scene in the unfrequented hollow of Little Narrowcove, looking up towards the summit of the Pike (the top cairn is out of sight). The crags, unsuspected on the usual routes, are a great surprise. Little Narrowcove (reached from Broad Crag col) is a grassy basin sheltered or encircled by cliffs: a good site for a mountain camp.

ASCENTS

The ascent of Scafell Pike is the toughest proposition the 'collector' of summits is called upon to attempt, and it is the one above all others that, as a patriot, he cannot omit. The difficulties are due more to roughness of the ground than to altitude, and to the remoteness of the summit from frequented valleys. From all bases except Wasdale Head the climb is long and arduous, and progress is slow: this is a full-day expedition, and the appropriate preparations should be made. Paths are good, but only in the sense that they are distinct; they are abominably stony, even bouldery — which is no great impediment when ascending but mitigates against quick descent. Ample time should be allowed for getting off the mountain.

In winter especially, when conditions can be Arctic, it is important to select a fine clear day, to start early, and keep moving; reserve three hours of daylight for the return journey. If under deep snow the mountain is better left alone altogether, for progress would then be laborious, and even dangerous across the concealed boulders, with a greater chance of death from exposure than of early rescue if an accident were to occur.

Scafell Pike may be ascended most easily from Wasdale Head, less conveniently from Borrowdale or Great Langdale or Eskdale. But all routes are alike in grandeur of scenery.

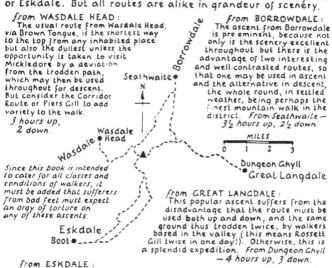

from WASDALE HEAD:
The usual route from Wasdale Head, via Brown Tongue, is the shortest way to the top from any inhabited place but also the dullest unless the opportunity is taken to visit Mickledore by a deviation from the trodden path, which may then be used throughout for descent. But consider the Corridor Route or Piers Gill to add variety to the walk.

3 hours up,
2 down.

Since this book is intended to cater for all classes and conditions of walkers, it must be added that sufferers from bad feet must expect an orgy of torture on any of these ascents.

from BORROWDALE:
The ascent from Borrowdale is pre-eminent, because not only is the scenery excellent throughout but there is the advantage of two interesting and well-contrasted routes, so that one may be used in ascent and the alternative in descent, the whole round, in settled weather, being perhaps the finest mountain-walk in the district. From Seathwaite —
3½ hours up, 2½ down

from GREAT LANGDALE:
This popular ascent suffers from the disadvantage that the route must be used both up and down, and the same ground thus trodden twice, by walkers based in the valley (this means Rossett Gill twice in one day!). Otherwise, this is a splendid expedition. From Dungeon Ghyll — 4 hours up, 3 down.

from ESKDALE:
This is the best line of approach to the mountain: from the south its grandest and most rugged aspect is seen. Variations of route may be adopted, but time is a great enemy: the walk is lengthy (a feature most noticed when returning). From Boot — 4½ hours up, 3½ down.

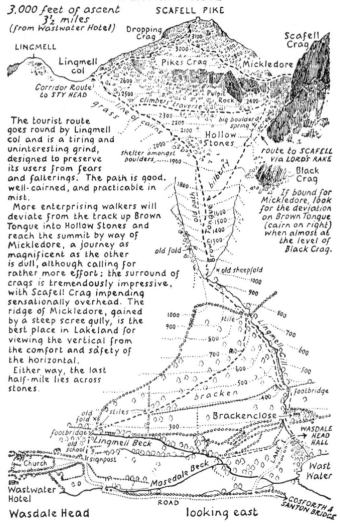

ASCENT FROM WASDALE HEAD
via BROWN TONGUE

3,000 feet of ascent
3½ miles
(from Wastwater Hotel)

SCAFELL PIKE

Dropping Crag

Scafell Crag

LINGMELL

Lingmell col

Pikes Crag

Mickledore

Corridor Route to STY HEAD

grass line of cairns

climbers traverse

Pulpit Rock

2600
2500
2300
2200
2100
2000
1900

big boulder & spring

Hollow Stones

route to SCAFELL via LORD'S RAKE

Black Crag

shelter amongst boulders

The tourist route goes round by Lingmell col and is a tiring and uninteresting grind, designed to preserve its users from fears and falterings. The path is good, well-cairned, and practicable in mist.

More enterprising walkers will deviate from the track up Brown Tongue into Hollow Stones and reach the summit by way of Mickledore, a journey as magnificent as the other is dull, although calling for rather more effort: the surround of crags is tremendously impressive, with Scafell Crag impending sensationally overhead. The ridge of Mickledore, gained by a steep scree gully, is the best place in Lakeland for viewing the vertical from the comfort and safety of the horizontal.

Either way, the last half-mile lies across stones.

If bound for Mickledore, look for the deviation on Brown Tongue (cairn on right) when almost at the level of Black Crag.

bilberry

old path

1800
1700
1600
1500
1400
1300

old fold

x old sheepfold

1000
900
800

stile

700

Lingmell Gill

600
500

1000
900
800
700
600

500

400

footbridge

bracken

old fold x

stiles

300

Brackenclose

WASDALE HEAD HALL

footbridge

Lingmell Beck

old school

signpost

Church

Mosedale Beck

LANE L.

Wast Water

Wastwater Hotel

ROAD

COSFORTH & SANTON BRIDGE

Wasdale Head

looking east

ASCENT FROM WASDALE HEAD
via PIERS GILL

3,000 feet of ascent
3¾ miles
(from Wastwater Hotel)

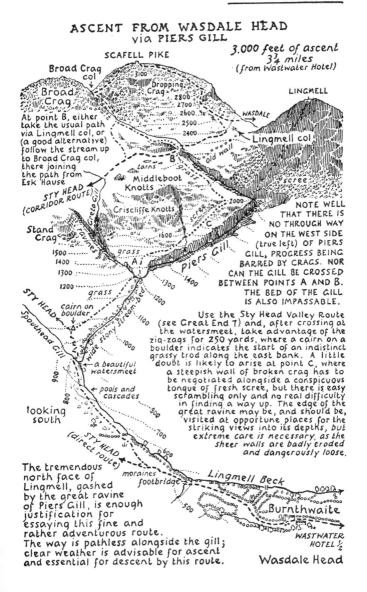

SCAFELL PIKE

Broad Crag col

Broad Crag

3100

Dropping Crag
2800
2700
2600
2500
2400

LINGMELL

WASDALE

Lingmell col

At point B, either take the usual path via Lingmell col, or (a good alternative) follow the stream up to Broad Crag col, there joining the path from Esk Hause.

B

tarns

grass

scree

STY HEAD (CORRIDOR ROUTE)

old wall

Middleboot Knotts

Criscliffe Knotts

1600

2000

scree

C

Stand Crag

ravines

grass

Piers Gill

1500
1400
1300

1200

A

grass

1300

1400

NOTE WELL THAT THERE IS NO THROUGH WAY ON THE WEST SIDE (true left) OF PIERS GILL, PROGRESS BEING BARRED BY CRAGS. NOR CAN THE GILL BE CROSSED BETWEEN POINTS A AND B. THE BED OF THE GILL IS ALSO IMPASSABLE.

STY HEAD

Spouthead Gill

cairn on boulder

wide stony stream-bed

1200

1100

1000

a beautiful watersmeet

pools and cascades

looking south

900

800

700

Use the Sty Head Valley Route (see Great End 7) and, after crossing at the watersmeet, take advantage of the zig-zags for 250 yards, where a cairn on a boulder indicates the start of an indistinct grassy trod along the east bank. A little doubt is likely to arise at point C, where a steepish wall of broken crag has to be negotiated alongside a conspicuous tongue of fresh scree, but there is easy scrambling only and no real difficulty in finding a way up. The edge of the great ravine may be, and should be, visited at opportune places for the striking views into its depths, but extreme care is necessary, as the sheer walls are badly eroded and dangerously loose.

STY HEAD (direct route)

600

moraines
footbridge

Lingmell Beck

500

Burnthwaite

WASTWATER HOTEL ½

The tremendous north face of Lingmell, gashed by the great ravine of Piers Gill, is enough justification for essaying this fine and rather adventurous route. The way is pathless alongside the gill; clear weather is advisable for ascent and essential for descent by this route.

Wasdale Head

ASCENT FROM BORROWDALE
via STY HEAD
3,000 feet of ascent
6 miles from Seatoller

Sty Head — 1600

Having duly arrived at Styhead Tarn (so proving the reliability of the diagram thus far) refer now (with confidence) to the foot of the next page for the continuation of the route.

Styhead Tarn

boulder

Patterson's Fold (sheepfold)

The footbridge was originally sited 150 yards downstream, where the buttresses of the former bridge can still be seen.

By keeping to the left of the many variations, a section of the original grooved and paved path will be found, and how superior it is to the modern 'short-cuts'!

Don't panic if unable to ford the stream here (normally easy); keep on along the west bank

1300 1400 1500
1100 1200
cascades
700 600

ESK HAUSE

Taylorgill Force

The steep fell here is BASE BROWN

Stockley Bridge

Styhead Gill old folds

The crag high on the left is Hind Crag

River Derwent

GREAT GABLE via GREEN GABLE

gates

Seathwaite Slabs

Sourmilk Gill

Seathwaite
one of the friendliest of farms. No need to fear the dogs or other animals here: visitors merely bore them.
The lane to the footbridge here passes under the arch of the farm buildings

LANE

sheepfold

disused plumbago mines

The Borrowdale Yews ('the fraternal four')

ROAD 500

Seathwaite Bridge

Few readers will need to refer to this page, as the walk to Sty Head is amongst the best known in the district, this being evidenced by the severe wear and tear of the path.

It is remarkable that the splendid variation route passing up through the gorge of Taylorgill Force has never found popular favour and is ignored by map-makers although it has been used by discerning walkers for many decades. This, compared with the usual Stockley Bridge path, is often rather wet in the lower intakes, a small disadvantage to set against its merits of quietness, quickness, sustained interest and waterfall and ravine scenery of high quality. A certain amount of delectable clambering on rocky sections of the path is likely to prohibit its use generally by all and sundry (including the many Sunday afternoon picnic parties), which is a good thing for the genuine fellwalker.

gate

River Derwent

ROAD

Taylorgill Force

ROSTHWAITE
14 ←

Seatoller

bus terminus → HONISTER PASS

looking south-south-west

ASCENT FROM BORROWDALE
via STY HEAD

continued

SCAFELL PIKE

Broad Crag col

looking south

Broad Crag

Dropping Crag

LINGMELL

Lingmell col

Lingmell

ESK HAUSE

3100

2700
2600
2500
2400

old wall

2300

striking view down Piers Gill

2200

tarns

Piers Gill

This new and recently-cairned variation (joining the path from Esk Hause at the Broad Crag col) is well worth trying. When *descending* from the Pike, it is preferable to the usual route *via* the Lingmell col, especially in mist, and certainly quicker.

Round How

2100

2000

easy access to GREAT END (see page Great End 8)

The point of bifurcation of the lower path is not apparent when descending the Corridor (fortunately, because the loose slope above the ravine can be dangerous in descent)

1900

falls

The one redeeming feature of the lower path (which was, incidentally, the *original* route) is its superb view of the Greta Gill ravine; this is not seen effectively from the upper path

Stand Crag

grass

1800

awkward exit

Greta Gill

Piers Gill

SKEW GILL

upper (direct) path

700

1600

lower path

1500

1400

1400

NOTE

slight descent

Many good men have gone wrong here. TWO paths leave the far bank of the gill: the direct route slants upwards across the wide and stony bed and climbs a short red gully, while the other goes straight across the gill, after which it maintains a horizontal course until forced upwards by the magnificent Greta Gill ravine, a loose and unpleasant scramble being then necessary to join the direct path.

ESK HAUSE

Sty Head

GREAT GABLE

short cut

not clear

path goes on to Wasdale Head

The Corridor starts from the path to Esk Hause and crosses the ruins of a wall below a crag. The short cut leads to it exactly.

Styhead Tarn

BORROWDALE

Carry on here from top of page opposite

The Corridor Route (formerly known as the Guides Route) links grassy shelves on the very rough western slope of Great End and Broad Crag and is, in fact, the one and only easy passage possible along this flank, which is deeply cut by ravines. It provides an excellent way to the Lingmell col (for Scafell Pike and Scafell) from Sty Head, interesting throughout and is the easiest of all routes to the Pike. In recent years the Corridor has become very popular and is now a well-blazoned track, but its start, at the Sty Head end, is indistinct and a newcomer here, not equipped with Book 4, may have trouble in locating it. (ADVT)

ASCENT FROM BORROWDALE
via ESK HAUSE
3,200 feet of ascent : 5½ miles from Seatoller

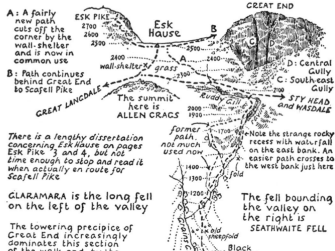

A: A fairly new path cuts off the corner by the wall-shelter and is now in common use

B: Path continues behind Great End to Scafell Pike

GREAT END

ESK PIKE
2700
2600
2500

Esk Hause

B

C

D

wall-shelter

2400
wall-shelter X grass

A

2400

2500

2300

D: Central Gully

C: South-east Gully

2100

STY HEAD and WASDALE

GREAT LANGDALE

The summit here is ALLEN CRAGS

Ruddy Gill

2000
1900

There is a lengthy dissertation concerning Esk Hause on pages Esk Pike 3 and 4, but not time enough to stop and read it when actually en route for Scafell Pike

former path, not much used now

1700

Note the strange rocky recess with waterfall on the east bank. An easier path crosses to the west bank just here

GLARAMARA is the long fell on the left of the valley

1400

1300

fold

1200

The fell bounding the valley on the right is SEATHWAITE FELL

The towering precipice of Great End increasingly dominates this section of the walk and, by the time Ruddy Gill (named from its red subsoil) is reached, assumes awe-inspiring proportions.

Great Gable comes into view at this point, but the gem of the scene hereabouts is the glorious vista of Derwentwater and Skiddaw, looking back over the line of approach.

x old sheepfold

Grains Gill

Black Waugh

signpost

STY HEAD

Stockley Bridge

Cliff high on the left is Hind Crag

Conspicuous waterfall (Taylorgill Force)

Styhead Gill

River Derwent

The fell on the right is BASE BROWN

Is it Grain Gill or Grains Gill? The signpost at Stockley Bridge omits the 's' (it also puts a 'w' in Scafell) but Grains is thought to be correct. At any rate, the floor of the valley here is named Grains, according to Ordnance maps.

gates

Seathwaite

400

ROAD

The Borrowdale Yews (Wordsworth's 'fraternal four')

Seathwaite Bridge

River Derwent

ROAD

ROAD

This diagram continues on the opposite page

ROSTHWAITE 1¼

Seatoller

HONISTER PASS

looking south

ASCENT FROM BORROWDALE
via ESK HAUSE

continued

This diagram is on a larger scale than that on the opposite page.

SCAFELL PIKE

Dropping Crag

Broad Crag

3100

3000

Broad Crag col (2900)

3000

Ill Crag

3000

Ill Crag col (2900)

2800

gravelly plateau

2900

2900

summit now in view for the first time

Ill Crag is prominently in view from the section of path between Esk Hause and Calf Cove. It is the highest thing in sight, and wishful thinkers will assume it to be the summit — until the Pike itself is finally revealed, indisputably higher and still far distant across a waste of stones.

E

Ill Crag col is wide. Broad Crag col is narrow and steepsided.

watershed reached

D

2800

steep slopes on this side go down to Wasdale

Upper Eskdale

C

2900

grass

GREAT END

Calf Cove

Calfcove Gill

B

old shelter

last running water

Esk Hause

2600

A

2500

prominent old cairn away from the path marks parish boundary

ESK PIKE

grass

ROUTE OF APPROACH FROM GRAINS GILL

2400

wall-shelter ✗

STY HEAD AND WASDALE

GREAT LANGDALE

looking south-west

The path is distinct and well-cairned but in places is formed of nail-scratches on boulders.

A–B : easy; gradient slight.

B–C : stony, rising path.

C–D : easy.

D–E : rough; 150 yards of big stones to cross.

E–F : easy.

F onwards: excessively rough —inescapable boulders, stone. and scree.

Of the many routes of approach to Scafell Pike, this, from Borrowdale via Esk Hause, is the finest. The transition from the quiet beauty of the valley pastures and woods to the rugged wildness of the mountain-top is complete, but comes gradually as height is gained and after passing through varied scenery, both nearby and distant, that sustains interest throughout the long march.

ASCENT FROM GREAT LANGDALE
3,400 feet of ascent : 5½ miles (from Dungeon Chyll, Old Hotel)

From Esk Hause onwards the route coincides with that from Borrowdale. Please see the previous page for a description.

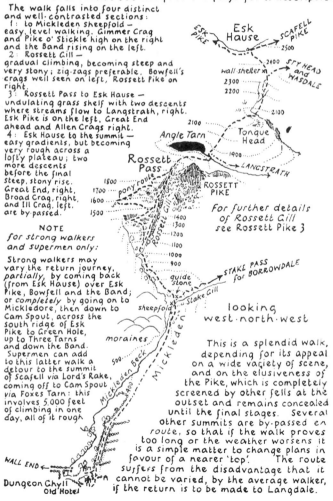

The walk falls into four distinct and well-contrasted sections:

1: to Mickleden sheepfold — easy, level walking. Gimmer Crag and Pike o' Stickle high on the right and the Band rising on the left.

2: Rossett Gill — gradual climbing, becoming steep and very stony; zig-zags preferable. Bowfell's crags well seen on left, Rossett Pike on right.

3: Rossett Pass to Esk Hause — undulating grass shelf with two descents where streams flow to Langstrath, right. Esk Pike is on the left, Great End ahead and Allen Crags right.

4: Esk Hause to the summit — easy gradients, but becoming very rough across a lofty plateau; two more descents before the final steep, stony rise. Great End, right, Broad Crag, right, and Ill Crag, left, are by-passed.

NOTE
for strong walkers
and supermen only:

Strong walkers may vary the return journey, *partially*, by coming back (from Esk Hause) over Esk Pike, Bowfell and the Band; or *completely* by going on to Mickledore, then down to Cam Spout, across the south ridge of Esk Pike to Green Hole, up to Three Tarns and down the Band.
Supermen can add to this latter walk a detour to the summit of Scafell via Lord's Rake, coming off to Cam Spout via Foxes Tarn: this involves 5,000 feet of climbing in one day, all of it rough

Esk Hause
ESK PIKE   SCAFELL PIKE
2500
2400   STY HEAD
wall shelter   and WASDALE
2300
2200
2100   2100
Angle Tarn   Tonque Head
1900
LANGSTRATH
Rossett Pass
ROSSETT PIKE
1800
1700   pony route
1600
1500
For further details
of Rossett Gill
see Rossett Pike 3
1400
1300
1200
1100
1000
900
STAKE PASS
for BORROWDALE
guide stone
Stake Gill
sheepfold
looking
west·north·west

moraines

500.

This is a splendid walk, depending for its appeal on a wide variety of scene, and on the elusiveness of the Pike, which is completely screened by other fells at the outset and remains concealed until the final stages. Several other summits are by-passed en route, so that if the walk proves too long or the weather worsens it is a simple matter to change plans in favour of a nearer 'top'. The route suffers from the disadvantage that it cannot be varied, by the average walker, if the return is to be made to Langdale.

WALL END ←
Dungeon Chyll
Old Hotel

Mickleden Beck
Mickleden
400

Two views on the walk from Esk Hause to the summit

Many hearts have sunk into many boots as this scene unfolds. Here, on the shoulder of Ill Crag, the summit comes into sight, at last; not almost within reach as confidently expected by walkers who feel they have already done quite enough to deserve success, but still a rough half-mile distant, with two considerable descents (Ill Crag col and Broad Crag col) and much climbing yet to be faced before the goal is reached.

Bowfell

Crinkle Crags

Looking down into Little Narrowcove and Eskdale, with Ill Crag on the left, from Broad Crag col

ASCENT FROM ESKDALE
3100 feet of ascent : 7½ miles from Boot

continued on following page

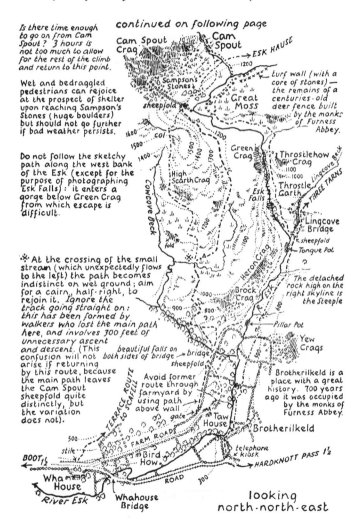

Is there time enough to go on from Cam Spout? 3 hours is not too much to allow for the rest of the climb and return to this point.

Wet and bedraggled pedestrians can rejoice at the prospect of shelter upon reaching Sampson's Stones (huge boulders) but should not go further if bad weather persists.

Do not follow the sketchy path along the west bank of the Esk (except for the purpose of photographing Esk Falls): it enters a gorge below Green Crag from which escape is difficult.

✳ At the crossing of the small stream (which unexpectedly flows to the left) the path becomes indistinct on wet ground; aim for a cairn, half-right, to rejoin it. Ignore the track going straight on: this has been formed by walkers who lost the main path here, and involves 300 feet of unnecessary ascent and descent. (This confusion will not arise if returning by this route, because the main path leaves the Cam Spout sheepfold quite distinctly, but the variation does not).

Cam Spout Crag

Cam Spout

→ ESK HAUSE

turf wall (with a core of stones) — the remains of a centuries-old deer fence built by the monks of Furness Abbey.

Sampson's Stones

sheepfold

Great Moss

col

Green Crag

Throstlehow Crag

High Scarth Crag

Throstle Garth

THREE TARNS

Lingcove Beck

Esk Falls

Concove Beck

Lingcove Bridge

sheepfold

Tongue Pot

fold

Heron Crag

The detached rock high on the right skyline is the Steeple

Brock Crag

Pillar Pot

Yew Crags

beautiful falls on both sides of bridge

bridge

sheepfold

Avoid former route through farmyard by using path above wall

Brotherilkeld is a place with a great history. 700 years ago it was occupied by the monks of Furness Abbey.

TERRACE ROUTE TO SCAFELL

gate

Taw House

Brotherilkeld

FARM ROAD

stile

Bird How

telephone kiosk

→ HARDKNOTT PASS 1½

BOOT 1½ ←

Wha House

River Esk

Whahouse Bridge

ROAD

looking north-north-east

ASCENT FROM ESKDALE

continued

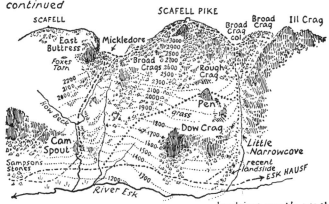

looking north-west

TO CAM SPOUT:

There is no time for dawdling when bound for Scafell Pike, and the fine high-level approach by way of Taw House and the Cowcove zigzags (avoiding the new variation *via* High Scarth Crag) is recommended as the quickest route to Cam Spout. The path from Brotherilkeld *via* Lingcove Bridge has too many distractions and temptations to halt and provides a final problem in crossing Great Moss dryshod.

FROM CAM SPOUT ONWARDS:

The usual route from Cam Spout goes up steeply by the waterfalls and proceeds thereafter on a good path, becoming a river of stones, to the ridge of Mickledore, where a well-blazed track climbs across boulders to the summit. The rock-scenery on the last stages of the struggle to Mickledore is good, Scafell East Buttress being extremely impressive, but conditions underfoot are abominable. The variation just below Mickledore that cuts off a corner and gains the ridge at its lowest point is rather easier. This route can be done in mist.

A secluded but circuitous and no less rough alternative is offered by Little Narrowcove, reached by passing below the imposing buttress of Dow Crag and completely dominated by the tremendous cliff of Ill Crag. Note the dotted line on the diagram indicating a shorter way that skirts the left edge of Dow Crag, crosses a col near the rocky peak of Pen and enters Little Narrowcove at mid-height; by careful observation it is possible, on this variation, to keep to grass all the way across the breast of the Pike. Clear weather is needed here.

It seems remarkable that England's highest mountain has no direct path to its summit on this, its finest side. It is not merely steepness that has kept walkers away from it, but rather the unavoidable, inescapable shawl of boulders covering the final 500 feet, where progress is not only painfully slow but carries a risk of displacing stones that have never before been trodden and may be balanced precariously and easily disturbed. There is no fun in pioneering routes over such rough terrain, which is safest left in virgin state.

THE SUMMIT

This is it: the Mecca of all weary pilgrims in Lakeland; the place of many ceremonies and celebrations, of bonfires and birthday parties; the ultimate; the supreme; the one objective above all others; the highest ground in England; the top of Scafell Pike.

It is a magnet, not because of its beauty for this is not a place of beauty, not because of the exhilaration of the climb for there is no exhilaration in toiling upwards over endless stones, not because of its view for although this is good there are others better. It is a magnet simply because it is the highest ground in England.

There is a huge cairn that from afar looks like a hotel: a well-built circular edifice now crumbling on its east side, with steps leading up to its flat top. Set into the vertical nine-foot north wall of the cairn is a tablet commemorating the gift of the summit to the nation. A few yards distant, west, is a triangulation column of the Ordnance Survey; a visitor in doubt and seeking confirmation of his whereabouts should consult the number on the front plate of the column: if it is anything other than S.1537 he has good cause for doubt — heaven knows where his erring steps have led him, but it is certainly not to the summit of Scafell Pike.

The surrounding area is barren, a tumbled wilderness of stones of all shapes and sizes, but it is not true, as has oft been written and may be thought, that the top is entirely devoid of vegetation: there is, indeed, a patch of grass on the south side of the cairn sufficient to provide a couch for a few hundredweights of exhausted flesh.

Yet this rough and desolate summit is, after all, just as it should be, and none of us would really want it different. A smooth green promenade here would be wrong. This is the summit of England, and it is fitting that it should be sturdy and rugged and strong.

THE SUMMIT

DESCENTS: It is an exaggeration to describe walkers' routes across the top of Scafell Pike as *paths*, because they make an uneasy pavement of angular boulders that are too unyielding ever to be trodden into subjection; nevertheless the routes are quite distinct, the particular boulders selected for their feet by the pioneers having, in the past century or so, become so extensively scratched by bootnails that they now appear as white ribbons across the grey waste of stones. Thus there is no difficulty in following them, even in mist.

The only place in descent where a walker might go astray is in going down by the Wasdale Head path to join the Corridor Route for Sty Head, the bifurcation above Lingmell col being surprisingly vague: in mist a walker might find himself well down Brown Tongue before discovering his error. It is actually safer for a stranger seeking the Corridor Route, particularly in mist, to use the Esk Hause path as far as the first col, at this point turning off *left* down into a hollow; a stream rises here and is a certain guide to the Corridor, which is reached exactly and unmistakably at the head of Piers Gill.

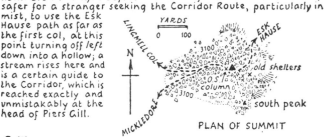

PLAN OF SUMMIT

Soliloquy.........

In summertime the cairn often becomes over-run with tourists, and a seeker after solitary contemplation may then be recommended to go across to the south peak, where, after enjoying the splendid view of Eskdale, he can observe the visitors to the summit from this distance. He may find himself wondering what impulse had driven these good folk to leave the comforts of the valley and make the weary ascent to this inhospitable place.

Why *does* a man climb mountains? Why has he forced his tired and sweating body up here when he might instead have been sitting at his ease in a deckchair at the seaside, looking at girls in bikinis, or fast asleep, or sucking ice-cream, according to his fancy. On the face of it the thing doesn't make sense.

Yet more and more people are turning to the hills; they find something in these wild places that can be found nowhere else. It may be solace for some, satisfaction for others: the joy of exercising muscles that modern ways of living have cramped, perhaps; or a balm for jangled nerves in the solitude and silence of the peaks; or escape from the clamour and tumult of everyday existence. It may have something to do with a man's subconscious search for beauty, growing keener as so much in the world grows uglier. It may be a need to readjust his sights, to get out of his own narrow groove and climb above it to see wider horizons and truer perspectives. In a few cases, it may even be a curiosity inspired by Wainwright's Pictorial Guides. Or it may be, and for most walkers it will be, quite simply, a deep love of the hills, a love that has grown over the years, whatever motive first took them there: a feeling that these hills are friends, tried and trusted friends, always there when needed.

It is a question every man must answer for himself.

THE VIEW

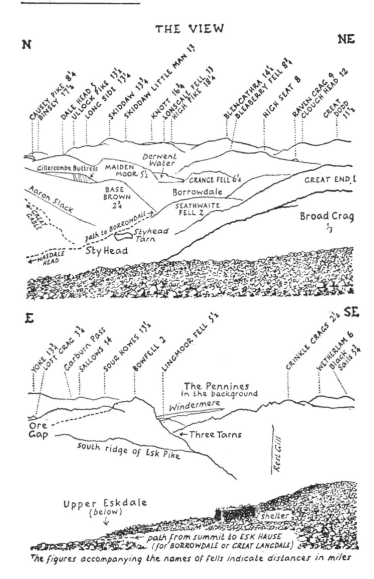

The figures accompanying the names of fells indicate distances in miles

THE VIEW

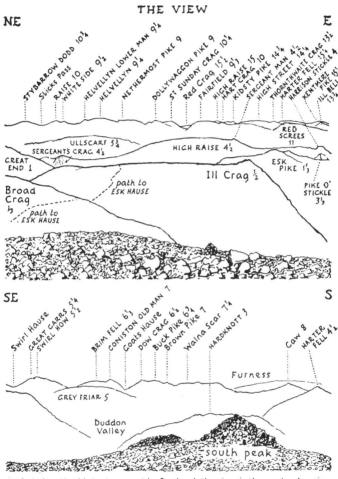

This being the highest ground in England the view is the most extensive, although not appreciably more so than those seen from many nearby fells. There is much interesting detail in every direction, and no denying the superiority of altitude, for all else is below eye-level, with old favourites like Great Gable and Bowfell seeming, if not humbled, less proud than they usually do (Scafell, across Mickledore, often *looks* of equal or greater height). Despite the wide variety of landscape, however, this is not the most pleasing of summit views, none of the valleys or lakes in view being seen really well.

THE VIEW

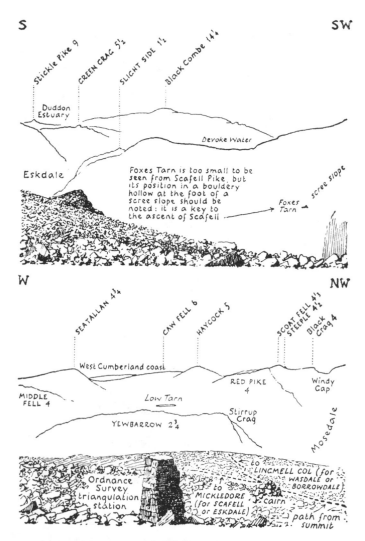

S

SW

Stickle Pike 9
GREEN CRAG 5½
SLIGHT SIDE 1½
Black Combe 14¼

Duddon
Estuary

Devoke Water

Eskdale

Foxes Tarn is too small to be
seen from Scafell Pike, but
its position in a bouldery
hollow at the foot of a
scree slope should be
noted: it is a key to
the ascent of Scafell

Foxes
Tarn

scree slope

W

NW

SEATALLAN 4¾
CAW FELL 6
HAYCOCK 5
SCOAT FELL 4½
STEEPLE 4½
Black Craig 4

West Cumberland coast

RED PIKE
4

Windy
Gap

MIDDLE
FELL 4

Low Tarn

Stirrup
Crag

YEWBARROW 2¾

Mosedale

Ordnance
Survey
triangulation
station

to LINGMELL COL (for
WASDALE or
BORROWDALE)

to
MICKLEDORE
(for SCAFELL
or ESKDALE)

cairn

path from
summit

THE VIEW

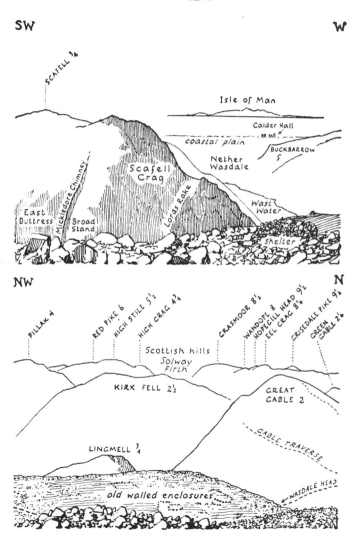

RIDGE ROUTES

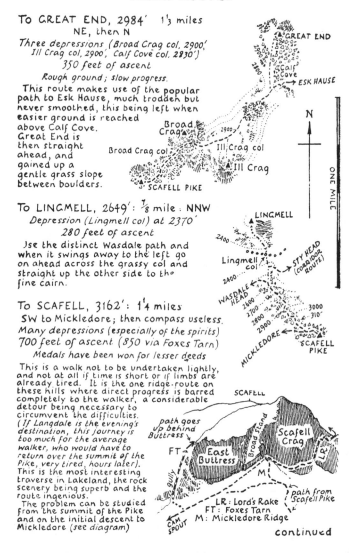

To GREAT END, 2984' 1⅓ miles
NE, then N

*Three depressions (Broad Crag col, 2900',
Ill Crag col, 2900', Calf Cove col. 2830')
350 feet of ascent
Rough ground; slow progress.*

This route makes use of the popular
path to Esk Hause, much trodden but
never smoothed, this being left when
easier ground is reached
above Calf Cove.
Great End is
then straight
ahead, and
gained up a
gentle grass slope
between boulders.

To LINGMELL, 2649': ⅞ mile : NNW
*Depression (Lingmell col) at 2370'
280 feet of ascent*

Use the distinct Wasdale path and
when it swings away to the left go
on ahead across the grassy col and
straight up the other side to the
fine cairn.

To SCAFELL, 3162': 1¼ miles
SW to Mickledore; then compass useless.
*Many depressions (especially of the spirits)
700 feet of ascent (850 via Foxes Tarn)
Medals have been won for lesser deeds*

This is a walk not to be undertaken lightly,
and not at all if time is short or if limbs are
already tired. It is the one ridge-route on
these hills where direct progress is barred
completely to the walker, a considerable
detour being necessary to
circumvent the difficulties.
(If Langdale is the evening's
destination, this journey is
too much for the average
walker, who would have to
return over the summit of the
Pike, very tired, hours later).
This is the most interesting
traverse in Lakeland, the rock
scenery being superb and the
route ingenious.
   The problem can be studied
from the summit of the Pike
and on the initial descent to
Mickledore *(see diagram)*

Map labels: GREAT END · Calf Cove · ESK HAUSE · Broad Crag · Broad Crag col · Ill Crag col · Ill Crag · SCAFELL PIKE · N · ONE MILE

Map labels: LINGMELL · Lingmell col · STY HEAD (CORRIDOR ROUTE) · WASDALE HEAD · MICKLEDORE · SCAFELL PIKE · 3000 · 310

Diagram labels: SCAFELL · path goes up behind Buttress · FT · East Buttress · Broad Stand · Scafell Crag · LR · M · gully · CAM SPOUT · path from Scafell Pike · LR: Lord's Rake · FT: Foxes Tarn · M: Mickledore Ridge

continued

RIDGE ROUTES

To SCAFELL (continued)

Lord's Rake
(top of first section)

Lord's Rake
as seen from
Mickledore

On the way down to Mickledore it appears that the route must continue up the narrow slope directly beyond it, *but this is Broad Stand: no way here.* A choice must be made between the two pedestrian routes *via* Lord's Rake or Foxes Tarn. For Lord's Rake, which is recommended, go to the far end of Mickledore Ridge and (after agreeing that Broad Stand is impossible) slither to the right down scree to a path that runs below the crags to the foot of Lord's Rake *(now see Scafell 4 and 9 for details).* For Foxes Tarn, descend *left* (path) from the near end of Mickledore Ridge to join the main path for Cam Spout but leave this 150 yards lower and enter and ascend a gully on the right to a small pond: this is Foxes Tarn. Steep scree, right, leads up to the top.

And the best of luck...

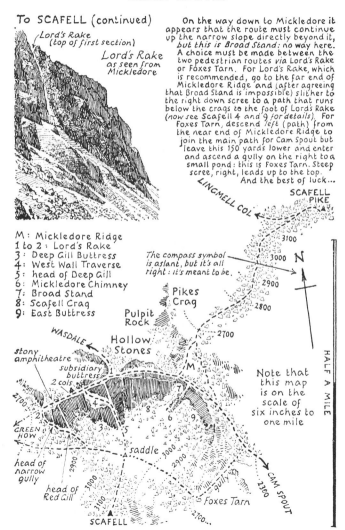

M : Mickledore Ridge
1 to 2 : Lord's Rake
3 : Deep Gill Buttress
4 : West Wall Traverse
5 : head of Deep Gill
6 : Mickledore Chimney
7 : Broad Stand
8 : Scafell Crag
9 : East Buttress

The compass symbol is aslant, but it's all right: it's meant to be.

Note that this map is on the scale of six inches to one mile

Seathwaite Fell

from Seathwaite

Seathwaite Fell, after the fashion of Rossett Pike, rises from, and causes, the bifurcation of two well-known mountain paths, Grains Gill and Sty Head, but additionally is crossed at the neck joining it to the parent fell of Great End by a third, the popular Esk Hause track. Thus it is completely surrounded by much-used pedestrian highways, but the fell itself, with few attractions to compare with those of the greater mountains around, is rarely visited — except, of course, by the custodian of the infamous rain-gauges which record, to its shame, that the fell and its vicinity has much the heaviest rainfall in the country.

Steep, rough slopes and a rim of crags on three sides offer no encouragement to stray from the beaten paths, but the top is easily gained from Sprinkling Tarn, which, with lesser sheets of water, provide the interest of a wide, undulating plateau. Sprinkling Tarn is commonly accredited as the source of the River Derwent.

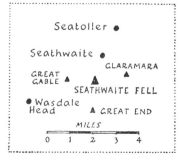

Seatoller •

Seathwaite •

GREAT GABLE ▲   CLARAMARA ▲

▲ SEATHWAITE FELL

• Wasdale Head   ▲ GREAT END

MILES

0   1   2   3   4

MAP

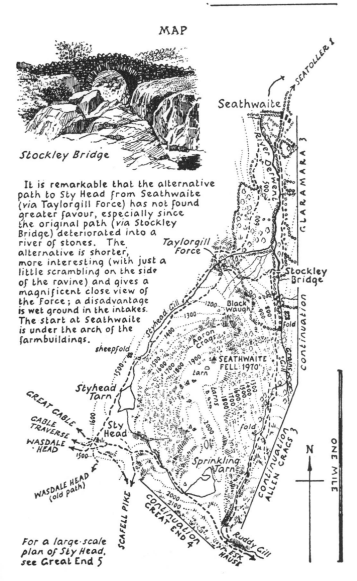

Stockley Bridge

It is remarkable that the alternative path to Sty Head from Seathwaite (via Taylorgill Force) has not found greater favour, especially since the original path (via Stockley Bridge) deteriorated into a river of stones. The alternative is shorter, more interesting (with just a little scrambling on the side of the ravine) and gives a magnificent close view of the Force; a disadvantage is wet ground in the intakes. The start at Seathwaite is under the arch of the farmbuildings.

Seathwaite

SEATOLLER 1

River Derwent

GLARAMARA 3

Taylorgill Force

Stockley Bridge

Black Waugh

fold

Styhead Gill

sheepfold

Aaron Crags

SEATHWAITE FELL 1970'

tarn

Grains Gill

continuation

GREAT GABLE

CABLE TRAVERSE

WASDALE HEAD

Styhead Tarn

Sty Head

Tarns

fold

CONTINUATION ALLEN CRAGS 3

WASDALE HEAD (old path)

Sprinkling Tarn

N

ONE MILE

SCAFELL PIKE

CONTINUATION GREAT END 4

Ruddy Gill

ESK HAUSE

For a large-scale plan of Sty Head, see Great End 5

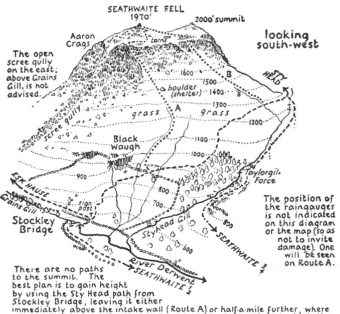

ASCENT FROM BORROWDALE
1550 feet of ascent · 1¼ miles from Seathwaite

SEATHWAITE FELL
1970'

2000' summit

looking south-west

Aaron Crags

tarns

The open scree gully on the east, above Grains Gill, is not advised.

1600

B

1500

boulder (shelter)

1400

1300

grass

grass

1200

A

1100

Black Waugh

1000

Taylorgill Force

900

800

ESK HAUSE

700

sign post

The position of the raingauges is not indicated on this diagram or the map (so as not to invite damage). One will be seen on Route A.

Grains Gill

Stockley Bridge

Styhead Gill

600

800

SEATHWAITE 3

River Derwent

SEATHWAITE 2

SEATHWAITE 1

There are no paths to the summit. The best plan is to gain height by using the Sty Head path from Stockley Bridge, leaving it either immediately above the intake wall (Route A) or half-a-mile further, where a streamlet crosses the path 150 yards short of the point at which the path comes alongside Styhead Gill (Route B). In each case aim for a grassy gully ahead. The top of the rock tower on the left of Route A affords a startling view of Grains Gill. Route A becomes very steep in the gully; Route B is easier.

THE SUMMIT

The 2000' contour occurs in a few places on the map of Seathwaite Fell, but the small areas of ground so enclosed are not nearly as prominent or distinctive as the shapelier pyramid at the north end of the top plateau, where a cairn at 1970', buttressed by blistered rocks, is generally regarded as the summit of the fell although obviously it isn't.

DESCENTS: Use Route B for getting down to Borrowdale most easily. Route A is tricky to find from above and, in mist, should not be sought.

THE VIEW

The diagram indicates the view from the distinctive summit at 1970', the usually-accepted 'top' but not quite the highest point of the fell. Northwards the scene is excellent: there is no better place for viewing the Seathwaite valley. Less beautiful, but more impressive, is the close surround of much higher mountains. Seathwaite Fell is such a lowly member of this group that it is a surprise to see a considerable mileage of the ridge of the Helvellyn Dodds occupying the skyline.

From the next and higher cairn, 300 yards south-west, a vista of Wasdale Head is seen. Additional summits in the view are YEWBARROW, BOWFELL and ULLOCK PIKE. A portion of *Styhead Tarn* is also visible.

From the highest part of the fell, 500 yards to the north of Sprinkling Tarn, the view includes SEATALLAN, RED PIKE in Mosedale, CARL SIDE and LONG SIDE. A corner of *Sprinkling Tarn* can be seen, but Styhead Tarn is now concealed from sight.

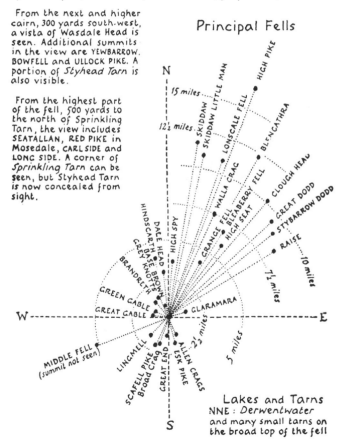

Principal Fells

Lakes and Tarns
NNE: Derwentwater
and many small tarns on
the broad top of the fell

Slight Side

2499'

from Catcove Beck

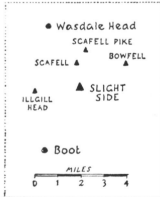

The mile-long south ridge of Scafell descends loftily to an abrupt terminus at a barrier of rock, which rises to a neat peak, Slight Side, and, to the east, falls sharply to Eskdale from the steep cliff of Horn Crag (a name sometimes given to the fell itself). The southern slope widens into a strange plateau, Quagrigg Moss, beyond which is a charming tangle of foothills, where pink granite, ling and bracken colour the environs of Stony Tarn and Eel Tarn.

The official altitude of Slight Side is a tribute to the meticulous care of the Ordnance Survey. But if Nelson had been in charge of the surveying party, and been a mountaineer too, surely he would have recorded 2500!

MAP

At this late stage in the book's preparation, space is becoming terribly short and cannot be spared for repetition of information already given. As the map of Scafell includes the whole area of Slight Side, would readers mind referring to pages Scafell 5-8?

ASCENT FROM ESKDALE
2350 feet of ascent : 4¾ miles from Boot

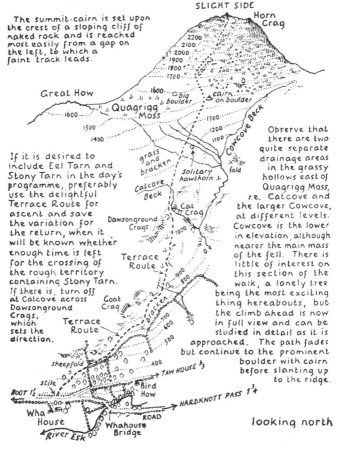

The summit-cairn is set upon the crest of a sloping cliff of naked rock and is reached most easily from a gap on the left, to which a faint track leads.

SLIGHT SIDE

Horn Crag

Great How

Quagrigg Moss

'big boulder

cairn on boulder

Concove Beck

If it is desired to include Eel Tarn and Stony Tarn in the day's programme, preferably use the delightful Terrace Route for ascent and save the variation for the return, when it will be known whether enough time is left for the crossing of the rough territory containing Stony Tarn. If there is, turn off at Calcove across Dawsonground Crags, which sets the direction.

grass and bracken

solitary hawthorn

Calcove Beck

Cat Crag

Dawsonground Crags

Terrace Route

Goat Crag

Terrace Route

bracken

sheepfold

stile

BOOT 1½

Bird How

TAW HOUSE ⅓

HARDKNOTT PASS 1¼

Wha House

Whahouse Bridge

ROAD

River Esk

Observe that there are two quite separate drainage areas in the grassy hollows east of Quagrigg Moss, i.e. Calcove and the larger Cowcove, at different levels. Cowcove is the lower in elevation, although nearer the main mass of the fell. There is little of interest on this section of the walk, a lonely tree being the most exciting thing hereabouts, but the climb ahead is now in full view and can be studied in detail as it is approached. The path fades but continue to the prominent boulder with cairn before slanting up to the ridge.

looking north

THE SUMMIT

Fellwalkers, having climbed their mountain, prefer to find that the summit is rocky, shapely and well-defined; and if, in addition, it can be attained only by a rough final scramble, so much the better. Slight Side has all these qualifications, and the further merit of an excellent view. A defect in its architecture is that the lofty ridge continuing to Scafell behind it is but little lower than the summit itself, so that when seen from this direction it has less significance. Still, this is a grand airy perch, the cairn being poised on the crest of a sweep of slabs of good clean rock, and many must be the walkers who have set out from Eskdale to climb Scafell and given up here.

Considered only as a summit, and not as a fell, Slight Side is the neatest and best of the Scafell group's many tops.

DESCENTS:

TO ESKDALE: The usual route of ascent should be reversed, and no other way from the top is worth considering. *In mist* find the sketchy track among the upper crags.

TO WASDALE: From the plateau north of the summit turn left (west) down a grassy slope, Broad Tongue, to Hardrigg Gill and the Burnmoor path.

RIDGE ROUTE

To SCAFELL, 3162' : 1¼ miles : N
Depression at 2400'
750 feet of ascent
An easy climb with little of interest

There is no path worthy of the name until the scree of the final slopes is reached, beyond Long Green. Keep to the edge of the continuous escarpment on the right for good views to relieve the dull ascent.

HALF A MILE.

THE VIEW

Slight Side's unique situation, at the point where the high mountains of the Scafell range sweep majestically down in foothills to green valleys and the silver sea, gives it a rare distinction as a viewpoint for the coastal area of Lakeland. The prospect seawards is in fact even better than it is from the parent Scafell although much inferior in other directions — but it must be stated in Slight Side's favour that the unlovely cooling towers of Calder Hall are concealed by Illgill Head. As a geography lesson in mountain structure, on the formation and flow of rivers and valleys and the winning of land by man from nature, the picture here simply presented is excellent. There is historical significance in the scene, too, for this is the land the Romans knew, and, before them, the primitive Britons of the Bronze Age.

Principal Fells

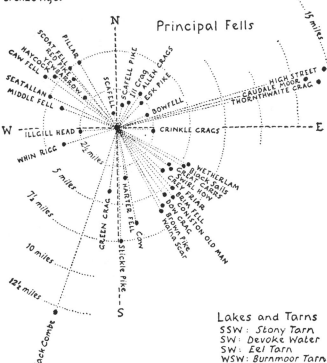

Lakes and Tarns
SSW : Stony Tarn
SW: Devoke Water
SW: Eel Tarn
WSW: Burnmoor Tarn
WNW: Wast Water

Swirl How

from Rough Crags
(Great Carrs on the right)

• Dungeon
Ghyll
▲ PIKE O' BLISCO

Cockley   Little •
Beck   GREAT   Langdale
      ●   CARRS
                    ▲ WETHERLAM
GREY ▲   ▲
FRIAR   SWIRL HOW

        ▲ BRIM FELL

CONISTON ▲ Coniston
  OLD MAN

Seathwaite
  ●

MILES
0   1   2   3   4

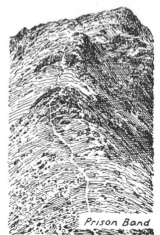

Prison Band

NATURAL FEATURES

Swirl How, although not quite the highest of the Coniston Fells, is the geographical centre of the group, radiating splendid ridges from a peaked summit to the four points of the compass. It is never seen really conspicuously in distant views, being crowded by surrounding fells; nevertheless its appearance is good, especially in profile, for the long southern plateau breaks sharply at the actual summit into a steep and craggy declivity. The area of Swirl How is not extensive, the ridges quickly merging into other fells on all four sides, but worthy of mention is the subsidiary height of Great How Crags on the southern plateau, a pillar of rock rising from the deep hollow of Levers Water and seeming from some viewpoints to be a separate summit.

The geographical supremacy of Swirl How is well illustrated by the direction of flow of its streams, which join the Duddon and the Brathay and Coniston Water (a distinction not shared by any other fell in the group) whereas those of the Old Man, which is slightly higher and popularly but wrongly regarded as the principal fell in the area, feed Coniston Water only. If only Swirl How asserted itself a little more and overtopped its satellites by a few hundred feet it would rank with the noblest fells in Lakeland, its "build-up" being topographically excellent.

Q.E.D. In fact the Old Man and Grey Friar are the only fells with a single drainage system

1: SWIRL HOW 2: GREY FRIAR
3: GREAT CARRS 4: Little Carrs
5: Black Sails 6: WETHERLAM
7: Great How Crags
8: BRIM FELL 9: DOW CRAG
10: CONISTON OLD MAN

The main ridges, and direction of flow of waters

Swirl How 3

MAP

Swirl Hause......

Swirl Hause is a true mountain pass, a neat and narrow defile with a small summit marked by a big cairn. But there are two unusual features about it. The first is that there is no stream descending from it into Greenburn, the beck there coming down from the much higher depression of Broad Slack. The second, which must cause endless confusion, is that the good path leading from it southwards does not descend direct to Levers Water, as may be expected, but wanders away to join the rough Black Sails ridge of Wetherlam. The probable explanation of this path is that originally it was a miners' track that has since been followed unwittingly by walkers under the impression that it would take them to Levers Water. There is no reason why a beeline to the tarn from Swirl Hause should not be made: there is no path, but none is necessary on the easy grass slope.

ONE MILE

looking north-west from Swirl How

N

ASCENT FROM CONISTON
2450 feet of ascent : 3½ miles

SWIRL HOW

Great How Crags

Little How Crags

Prison Band

Levers Hause

BRIM FELL

Gill Cove

Raven Tor

Swirl Hause

WETHERLAM

The Prison

Hause Beck

south ridge of Black Sails

Levers Water

dam

RED DELL (old Copper Works)

Kennel Crag

BOULDER VALLEY

area of caves and mine-shafts (DANGEROUS)

Simons Nick

fall

mill race

cave

BOULDER VALLEY

caves ruin

indistinct turn right uphill near ruin with chimney but no roof.

stream choked

spoil heaps

mill race

site of Paddy End Copper Works

ROAD

site of Coniston Copper Mines

Youth Hostel

Red Dell Beck

From Levers Water two routes of ascent are available: via Swirl Hause or Levers Hause, the former being rather the easier

spoil heaps

RED DELL

spoil heaps

CONISTON OLD MAN

Levers Water Beck

Miners' Bridge

waterfall — go 50 yards down the road for the best view of it

CONISTON

Church Beck

WALNA SCAR

Railway Station

railway bridge

gate

Sun Hotel

BROUGHTON

Coniston

Simon's Nick is a remarkable cleft — a great vertical slice taken out of a high wall of rock; it is clearly seen on the skyline from the vicinity of Paddy End old Copper Works. Between Simon's Nick and the south shore of Levers Water is a surprising area of deep shafts, caves and potholes. All these frightful rifts and gloomy chasms were excavated in copper-mining operations. They are well worth seeing (except, perhaps, by persons subject to nightmares) but exploration should be limited to looking at them from positions of absolute safety. Children should not be taken here.

looking north-west

There is interest all the way, even though, in places, the interest is in things desolate and derelict. A most excellent expedition.

ASCENT FROM LITTLE LANGDALE
2400 feet of ascent : 4 miles

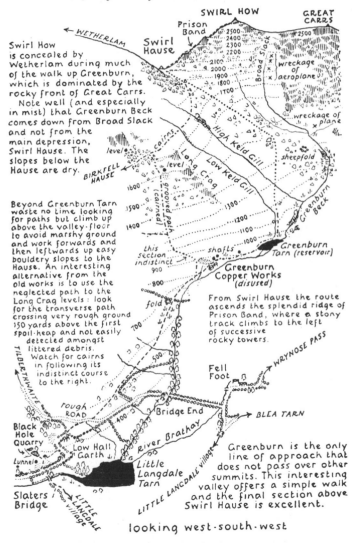

Swirl How is concealed by Wetherlam during much of the walk up Greenburn, which is dominated by the rocky front of Great Carrs.

Note well (and especially in mist) that Greenburn Beck comes down from Broad Slack and not from the main depression, Swirl Hause. The slopes below the Hause are dry.

Beyond Greenburn Tarn waste no time looking for paths but climb up above the valley floor to avoid marshy ground and work forwards and then leftwards up easy bouldery slopes to the Hause. An interesting alternative from the old works is to use the neglected path to the Long Crag levels: look for the transverse path crossing very rough ground 150 yards above the first spoil-heap and not easily detected amongst littered debris.

Watch for cairns in following its indistinct course to the right.

From Swirl Hause the route ascends the splendid ridge of Prison Band, where a stony track climbs to the left of successive rocky towers.

Greenburn is the only line of approach that does not pass over other summits. This interesting valley offers a simple walk and the final section above Swirl Hause is excellent.

looking west-south-west

THE SUMMIT

The cairn is splendidly sited at the extreme end of the long and level summit-plateau, just at the point where the northern slope falls away abruptly; perhaps it is not quite on the highest ground, which appears to be a few yards west. The turf on the top is interspersed with many small outcrops of grey rock.

DESCENTS: TO CONISTON: Swirl Hause is a better way off the fell than Levers Hause, but, especially in mist, go straight down to Levers Water from the Hause, ignoring the good path bearing away to the left. TO LITTLE LANGDALE: The finest route of descent lies over Great Carrs and Wet Side Edge, but if Greenburn is preferred descend thereto by the easy slope from Swirl Hause, not via Broad Slack. No trouble need be expected on either route in mist.

RIDGE ROUTES

To BRIM FELL, 2611': 1½ miles : S, SW and S
Depression (Levers Hause) at 2240'
380 feet of ascent

Aim south across the plateau, joining a path at Great How Crags that goes down to Levers Hause; beyond, it fades on the easy slopes of Brim Fell. In mist, keep to the right of the escarpment.

To WETHERLAM, 2502': 1¼ miles
ENE, NE, ENE and E
Depression (Swirl Hause) at 2020'
500 feet of ascent

Go down Prison Band by the track, cross the Hause, and bear left up the opposite slope. A sketchy path on the Greenburn edge loses itself short of Red Dell Head but sets the direction for the top. The first summit on the right is Black Sails, not to be mistaken for Wetherlam.

To GREAT CARRS, 2575': ⅓ mile : W, NW and N
Depression at 2500'
75 feet of ascent
A simple seven-minute stroll

To GREY FRIAR, 2536'
1 mile : WNW, W and SW.
Depression at 2275'
270 feet of ascent
Steeper climbing follows an easy descent. Not recommended in mist.

THE VIEW

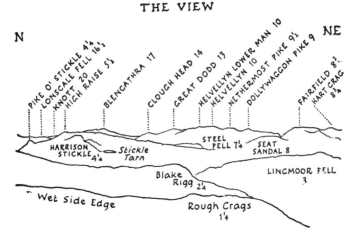

N   NE

PIKE O' STICKLE 4¼
LONSCALE FELL 16½
KNOTT 20
HIGH RAISE 5½
BLENCATHRA 17
CLOUGH HEAD 14
GREAT DODD 13
HELVELLYN LOWER MAN 10
HELVELLYN 10
NETHERMOST PIKE 9½
DOLLYWAGGON PIKE 9
FAIRFIELD 8¾
HART CRAG 8¾

HARRISON STICKLE 4¼ — Stickle Tarn
STEEL FELL 7¼   SEAT SANDAL 8
Blake Rigg 2¼
LINGMOOR FELL 3
Wet Side Edge
Rough Crags 1¼

Greenburn Valley   Greenburn Tarn

E   SE

The Pennines in the background

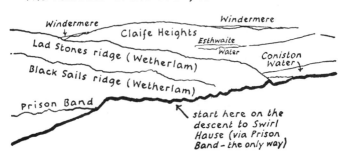

Windermere   Windermere
Claife Heights
Lad Stones ridge (Wetherlam)
Esthwaite Water
Coniston Water
Black Sails ridge (Wetherlam)
Prison Band
start here on the descent to Swirl Hause (via Prison Band – the only way)

THE VIEW

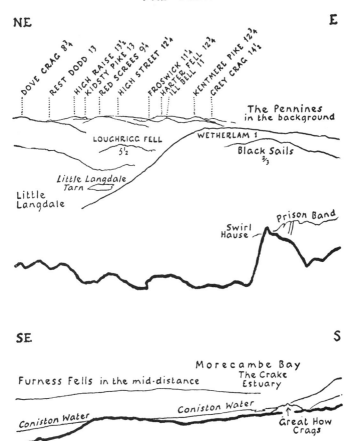

NE   E

DOVE CRAG 8¾
REST DODD 13
HIGH RAISE 13½
KIDSTY PIKE 13
RED SCREES 9½
HIGH STREET 12½
FROSWICK 11¼
HARTER FELL 11
ILL BELL 11½
KENTMERE PIKE 12¾
GREY CRAG 14½

The Pennines
in the background

LOUGHRIGG FELL
5½

WETHERLAM 1

Black Sails
⅔

Little Langdale
Tarn

Little
Langdale

Swirl
Hause

Prison Band

SE   S

Morecambe Bay
The Crake
Estuary

Furness Fells in the mid-distance

Coniston Water

Coniston Water

Great How
Crags

Coniston Water

*The figures accompanying the names of fells
indicate distances in miles*

**The thick line marks the visible boundaries
of the summit from the cairn**

THE VIEW

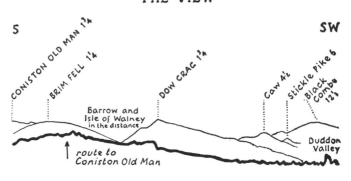

S   SW

CONISTON OLD MAN 1¾

BRIM FELL 1¼

Barrow and
Isle of Walney
in the distance

DOW CRAG 1¾

Caw 4½

Stickle Pike 6

Black Combe 12⅛

Duddon
Valley

route to
Coniston Old Man

W   NW

WHIN RIGG 7¾

ILLGILL HEAD 7

SEATALLAN 9½

SLIGHT SIDE 4⅞

SCAFELL 5⅛

Calder
Hall

HARD KNOTT 2¾

Mickledore

This small
protuberance
appears to be
slightly higher
than the rocks
bearing the cairn,
but it can be a
matter of inches only.

These rocks are above the steep and rough
Greenburn face. Descents here should be eschewed
(*Eschewed means don't do it!*)

THE VIEW

SW   W

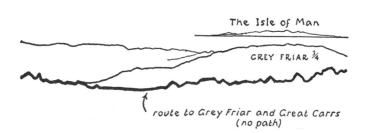

The Isle of Man

GREY FRIAR ¾

↰ route to Grey Friar and Great Carrs
(no path)

NW   N

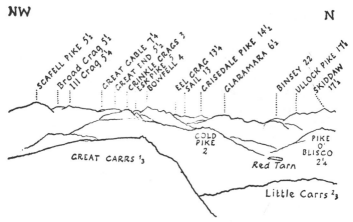

SCAFELL PIKE 5½
Broad Crag 5½
Ill Crag 5¼
GREAT GABLE 7¼
GREAT END 5½
CRINKLE CRAGS 3
ESK PIKE 5¼
BOWFELL 4
EEL CRAG 13¼
SAIL 13
CRISEDALE PIKE 14½
GLARAMARA 6½
BINSEY 22
ULLOCK PIKE 17½
SKIDDAW 17½

COLD PIKE 2

GREAT CARRS ¹₃

Red Tarn

PIKE O'
BLISCO
2¼

Little Carrs ²₃

Some walkers seem to experience a fierce joy in the sight of the Isle of Man in a view; others find greater pleasure in the sight of a first primrose in springtime. For the benefit of the former, the Isle of Man is shown in this diagram: it is visible from many Lakeland tops in good conditions, but from Swirl How its location can be determined particularly quickly for it appears exactly above the long flat top of Grey Friar nearby. The odds against seeing it on any given day are 50 to 1. At dusk or during night-bivouacs on the tops its position can be fixed in clear weather by the regular beams of its shore lighthouses. But oh! the delights of that first primrose...........

Wetherlam

from Little Langdale

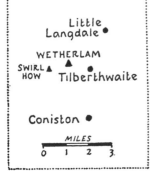

Little
Langdale ●

WETHERLAM ▲

SWIRL ▲
HOW   Tilberthwaite ●

Coniston ●

MILES

0   1   2   3.

from Great Carrs

NATURAL FEATURES

Wetherlam features prominently in Brathay views like a giant whale surfacing above waves of lesser hills: the long rising line of the back springs from the fields of Coniston to a maximum height at the tip of the head, from which the blunt nose curves steeply down into Little Langdale. The outline is simple, but deceptive, for the rising ridge coming up from the south is one only (and not the best) of three parallel ridges that give this fell a strong individuality. Quite apart from an unusual shape of structure, however, and in addition to its merit both as a climb and as a viewpoint, Wetherlam has one great claim deserving of close attention.

Ingleborough, which is in view thirty miles away, is often and with much justification considered to be the most interesting mountain in England because of its potentialities to the explorer on, in and under the ground. But Wetherlam, too, is pierced and pitted with holes — caves, tunnels, shafts and excavations— in not less profusion, although, unlike Ingleborough's, all are man-made. These are the levels and shafts and workings of a dead industry — copper-mining— and of a living industry — quarrying — that between them, over the centuries, have made Wetherlam the most-industrialised of Lakeland mountains. This fine hill, however, is too vast and sturdy to be disfigured and weakened by man's feeble scratchings of its surface, and remains today, as of old, a compelling presence to which walkers in Brathay will oft turn their eager steps.

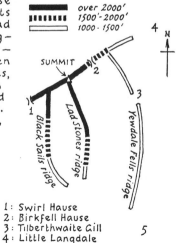

over 2000'
1500'-2000'
1000-1500'

SUMMIT

4 N

2

3

1

Black Sails ridge

Lad Stones ridge

Yewdale Fells ridge

1: Swirl Hause
2: Birkfell Hause
3: Tilberthwaite Gill
4: Little Langdale
5: Coniston

5

The Plan of the Main Ridges

MAP

On this and the next three pages, levels and shafts of old mine and quarry workings are indicated only in locations where they may be noticed on usual walking routes, in order to relieve the maps of overmuch detail. A simplified diagram on page 7 gives the positions of the various workings.

The square mile of territory between Tilberthwaite Gill and the Brathay (see map on opposite page) is scenically one of the loveliest in Lakeland (in spite of the quarries) and surely one of the most interesting (because of the quarries). The valley-road is a favourite of visitors, but they generally have little knowledge of the many fascinating places concealed by the screen of trees. Here, in the quarries, it can be seen that Lakeland's beauty is not merely skin deep, that it goes down below the surface in veins of rich and colourful stone. Here, too, can be admired (indeed, cannot but be admired) the ingenious devices and engineering feats of the old quarrymen of pre-machine days in their efforts to win from the craggy fellside this further precious bounty of an over-generous Nature.

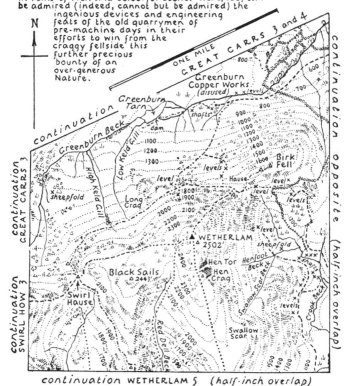

MAP

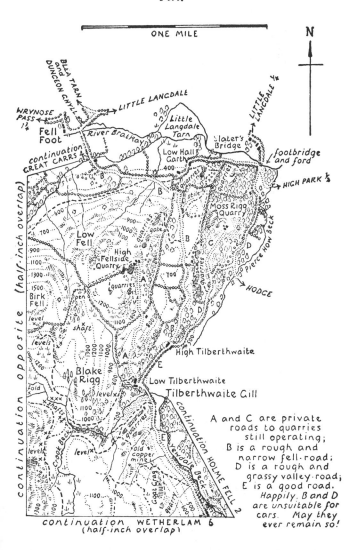

N

ONE MILE

A and C are private
roads to quarries
still operating;
B is a rough and
narrow fell-road;
D is a rough and
grassy valley-road;
E is a good road.
Happily, B and D
are unsuitable for
cars. May they
ever remain so!

MAP

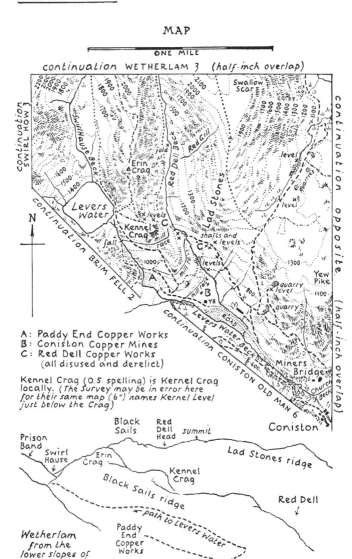

ONE MILE

continuation WETHERLAM 3 (half-inch overlap)

A: Paddy End Copper Works
B: Coniston Copper Mines
C: Red Dell Copper Works
   (all disused and derelict)

Kennel Crag (O.S. spelling) is Kernel Crag
locally. (The Survey may be in error here
for their same map (6") names Kernel Level
just below the Crag.)

Wetherlam
from the
lower slopes of
Coniston Old Man

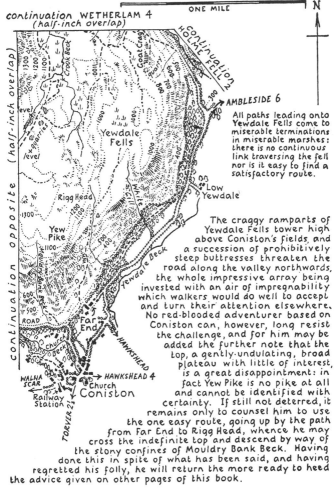

ONE MILE

N

continuation WETHERLAM 4
(half-inch overlap)

continuation HOLME FELL

➤ AMBLESIDE 6

All paths leading onto
Yewdale Fells come to
miserable terminations
in miserable marshes:
there is no continuous
link traversing the fell
nor is it easy to find a
satisfactory route.

Low
Yewdale

The craggy ramparts of
Yewdale Fells tower high
above Coniston's fields, and
a succession of prohibitively
steep buttresses threaten the
road along the valley northwards,
the whole impressive array being
invested with an air of impregnability
which walkers would do well to accept
and turn their attention elsewhere.
No red-blooded adventurer based on
Coniston can, however, long resist
the challenge, and for him may be
added the further note that the
top, a gently-undulating, broad
plateau with little of interest,
is a great disappointment: in
fact Yew Pike is no pike at all
and cannot be identified with
certainty. If still not deterred, it
remains only to counsel him to use
the one easy route, going up by the path
from Far End to Rigg Head, whence he may
cross the indefinite top and descend by way of
the stony confines of Mouldry Bank Beck. Having
done this in spite of what has been said, and having
regretted his folly, he will return the more ready to heed
the advice given on other pages of this book.

A miners' path not well known but strongly recommended for
its unusual appeal is that rising by the old quarries above the
cottages in Coppermines Valley and continuing to the head of
Tilberthwaite Gill; a good alternative to the usual walk by road.

Wetherlam 7

Wetherlam's Hundred Holes —

The sole object of this map is to indicate the locations of the various caves, shafts and quarries, and detail has been omitted other than that helpful in the fascinating pastime of finding them.

o : CAVES, TUNNELS. and LEVELS
● : SHAFTS
🐚 : OPEN QUARRIES

Caves and shafts within open quarries are omitted

('Open' means 'open to the sky,' not 'open for business')

Caves and shafts often occur in clusters. Where for this reason space is insufficient to indicate them separately on this map, they are shown thus :—
🐚 CAVES   ♠ SHAFTS
and such a symbol may represent any number from three to six.

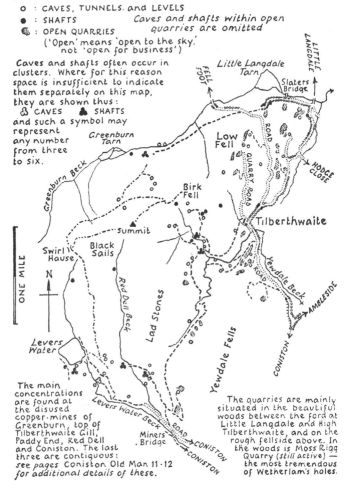

ONE MILE

N

The main concentrations are found at the disused copper-mines of Greenburn, top of Tilberthwaite Gill, Paddy End, Red Dell and Coniston. The last three are contiguous: see pages Coniston Old Man 11·12 for additional details of these.

The quarries are mainly situated in the beautiful woods between the ford at Little Langdale and High Tilberthwaite, and on the rough fellside above. In the woods is Moss Rigg Quarry (still active) — the most tremendous of Wetherlam's holes.

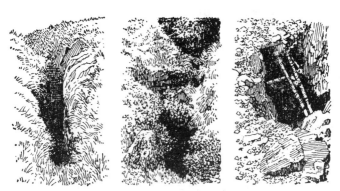

Typical copper·mine shafts

A quarry cave

A copper level

Be content to find the openings, and do not be tempted to enter them. *Roof·falls, flooded passages and rotted timber supports make them DANGEROUS.* The unprotected, unfenced shafts are particularly so. Keep children away, and do not frighten sheep in the vicinity. It really is a matter for surprise that these fearful death·traps are not half·choked with the mingled remains of too·intrepid explorers, sheep, foxes, dogs, and women whose husbands have tired of them.

The Great Arch, Black Hole Quarry
This disused quarry near Slaters Bridge has features common to many hereabouts: the arch, the ravine entrance, the deep shaft from which a tunnel connects with the open fellside.

ASCENT FROM LITTLE LANGDALE
2250 feet of ascent : 3 miles

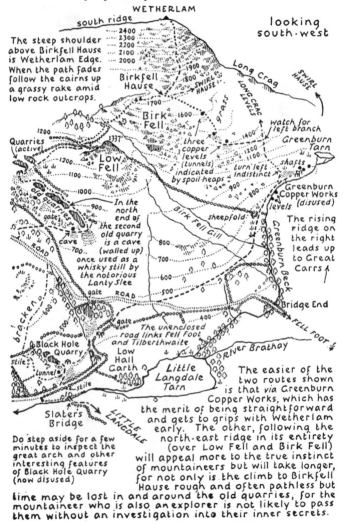

WETHERLAM

looking south-west

south ridge

— 2400
— 2300
— 2200
— 2100
— 2000

The steep shoulder above Birkfell Hause is Wetherlam Edge. When the path fades follow the cairns up a grassy rake amid low rock outcrops.

Birkfell Hause

Long Crag

SWIRL HAUSE

SWIRL HAUSE

LONG CRAG LEVELS

Birk Fell

grass

Quarries (active)

1200

1337

Low Fell

1200

1100

1000

900

In the north end of the second old quarry is a cave (walled up) once used as a whisky still by the notorious Lanty Slee

old quarries

gate

cave

700

ROAD

800

three copper levels (tunnels) indicated by spoil heaps

watch for left branch

Greenburn Tarn

turn left indistinct

shafts

Greenburn Copper Works (disused)

levels

The rising ridge on the right leads up to Great Carrs

Birk Fell Gill

sheepfold

Greenburn Beck

600

500

700

800

ROAD

400

gate

bracken

600

The unenclosed road links Fell Foot and Tilberthwaite

Bridge End

FELL FOOT

Black Hole Quarry

stile

tunnel

Low Hall Garth

River Brathay

Little Langdale Tarn

stile

Slaters Bridge

LITTLE LANGDALE

Do step aside for a few minutes to inspect the great arch and other interesting features of Black Hole Quarry (now disused)

The easier of the two routes shown is that via Greenburn Copper Works, which has the merit of being straightforward and gets to grips with Wetherlam early. The other, following the north-east ridge in its entirety (over Low Fell and Birk Fell) will appeal more to the true instinct of mountaineers but will take longer, for not only is the climb to Birkfell Hause rough and often pathless but time may be lost in and around the old quarries, for the mountaineer who is also an explorer is not likely to pass them without an investigation into their inner secrets.

ASCENT FROM TILBERTHWAITE
2100 feet of ascent : 2 miles

WETHERLAM

Wetherlam Edge

2400
2300
2200
2100
2000
1900
1800
1700

levels: horizontal underground passages with cave entrances. Many are flooded.

shafts: vertical rifts, usually with narrow slit openings. Deep. Frightful places!

This is the easiest way up Wetherlam. Gradients are easy to the Hause (very easy to Hawk Rigg). On the steeper Edge watch for cairns when the path fades.

Birkfell Hause   Birk Fell

1700
1600
1500

shaft

level

wooden steps

Hawk Rigg

1300   level

ruins x   shaft

Dry Cove Moss
- very wet; almost a tarn

1300

1400

levels

1300

1200

Henfoot Beck

fold

1200

Blake Rigg   1300

shafts and levels (old copper mines)

1300

ruins

1000

1200

1100

Tilberthwaite Gill is usually ascended on the south bank but the well-engineered path on the north bank should be used on this occasion to its terminus at the old copper mines at Hawk Rigg.

1000

level

1000

900

800

700

bracken

800

level

ROAD   QUARRIES

900

Tilberthwaite Gill

quarry

800

700   hut

old quarries

600

500

Low Tilberthwaite

500

LITTLE LANGDALE

Don't come this way down in the dark!

CONISTON ←

Yewdale Beck

looking north-west

This splendid climb in attractive and contrasting scenery is given added interest by short detours of inspection to the many old copper workings, which, however, should be approached with caution, the shafts being unfenced and dangerous.

ASCENT FROM CONISTON
2350 feet of ascent : 3½ miles

The secondary ridge from Kennel Crag to Black Sails is a good alternative to the valley of Red Dell Beck as a way up, although entailing more collar-work and being less direct. It is not recommended as a way down in mist.

Black Sails

WETHERLAM

gully

1000

2300
2200
2100
2000
1900

grass terrace

old working (flooded shaft 5 yards from beck)

cascades

Red Gill

tarn

Lad Stones

This depression marks a striking change in the characteristics of the rocks of the ridge

sheepfold

1700
1600
1500

Kennel Crag

caves (old levels)

mill race

DANGEROUS ✕ potholes ✕

Red Dell Copper Works

mill race

site of Coniston Copper Mines

1200

cave (quarry)

× hut

cave in ravine (Cobbler Hole)

tower

water pipe

1300
1200
1100

1000

bracken

900

cable wire

800

tarn

1400

TILBERTHWAITE

If descending by the Lad Stones ridge do not persevere to its craggy extremity but slant down left to join the grass path coming from Tilberthwaite

quarries

quarry

wide grass path

Youth Hostel

Red Dell Beck

Lever's water beck

700

All quarries and mines shown on the diagram are DISUSED, DERELICT, DANGEROUS!

CONISTON OLD MAN

row of ten cottages (ten chimneys, anyway)

spoil heaps

waterfalls in rocky gorge

Miners' Bridge

waterfall – walk 50 yards down the road for the best view of it

ROAD

CONISTON

Preferably, ascend by the deeply-enclosed and bouldery valley of Red Dell, where the old copper works add an interest to dreary surroundings and the gradients are easy, and descend by the pleasant ridge of Lad Stones, which has excellent views.

500

WALNA SCAR

400

Railway Station

railway bridge

gate

Sun Hotel

Church Beck

Black Bull Hotel

BROUGHTON ←

looking north-north-west

Coniston

THE SUMMIT

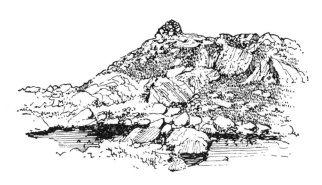

The summit is gently domed on three sides, with steepening curves to north and east, the fourth (south) being a level ridge. There is much rock about, weathered to an ashen-grey colour but, when broken, revealing the tinges of brown characteristic of the spoil-heaps of the copper mines on the lower slopes. The highest point is occupied by a large cairn. Although the summit is much trodden it bears little imprint of paths.

DESCENTS : Considering the popularity of the fell as a climb it is remarkable that there are not good paths linking summit and valley, but there are not, and in fact the selection of a way across the foothills, especially to Little Langdale, is not simple.

TO LITTLE LANGDALE :   Go down Wetherlam Edge, keeping slightly to the left at first, on grass, and looking for the insufficient cairns. A stony track materialises and descends roughly to Birkfell Hause; a turn down the pathless slope to the left here (into Greenburn) is the simplest and quickest route to take.   The direct ridge-route beyond the Hause goes on over Birk Fell and Low Fell, and is interesting (if there is ample time for trial and error), but is unsuitable in mist.

TO TILBERTHWAITE :   From Birkfell Hause slant down to the right, immediately passing an old copper mine, from which a track goes on to the wall ahead, crosses it (not distinctly) and joins the wide grassy mines-path seen in front : this descends easily to the valley.

TO CONISTON :   Go along the gradual south ridge for a full mile until easier ground on the left permits a descent to a path going down to the Coppermines Valley.   The south ridge, if persisted in too far, will lead to difficulties above Red Dell Copper Works.

In mist, the absence of paths make the top confusing. If quite unable to take bearings, it is useful to know that the smaller cairn 20 yards away is south-east of the main cairn, and a tiny rocky pool (which dries in drought) a few paces distant is to the west.   The start of the route down the convex slope to Birkfell Hause is not easy to locate : hunt around for cairns (they are insufficient at first but become profuse). The only difficulty of the south ridge is to decide when to leave it, on the left. The ridge running south from Black Sails is best left alone.

THE VIEW

Wetherlam thrusts well forward, away from the main bulk of the Coniston fells, and thus provides a view free from near obstruction, unlike the others in the group. It rises, moreover, immediately above the deep valley of Little Langdale, so that the mountain scene beyond is given unusual height. The picture is everywhere good, but best of all is the lovely countryside of Brathay, seen in all its glory as from an aeroplane, and revealing a large array of sparkling waters. In the far distance, across Windermere, is the long line of the Pennines. To the south is the estuary of the Kent, and, to the horizon, Morecambe Bay. This is a view that, more than most, benefits by sunlight and dappled shadows.

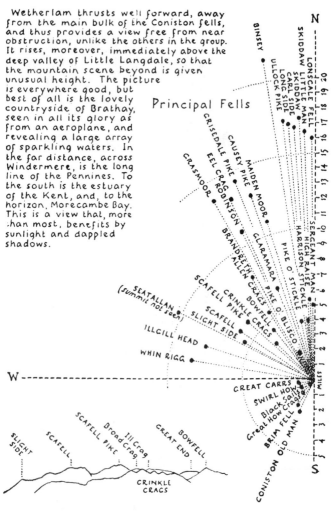

Principal Fells

looking north-west

THE VIEW

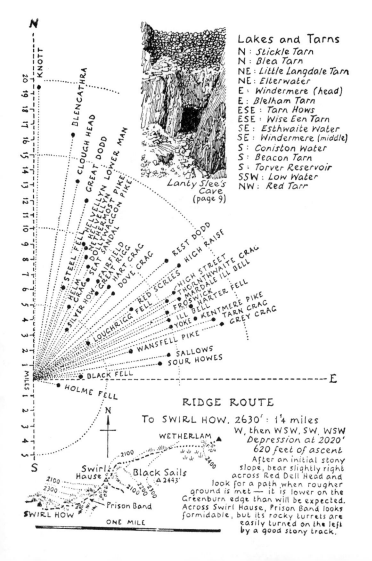

Lanty Slee's Cave
(page 9)

Lakes and Tarns

N : Stickle Tarn
N : Blea Tarn
NE : Little Langdale Tarn
NE : Elterwater
E : Windermere (head)
E : Blelham Tarn
ESE : Tarn Hows
ESE : Wise Een Tarn
SE : Esthwaite Water
SE : Windermere (middle)
S : Coniston Water
S : Beacon Tarn
S : Torver Reservoir
SSW : Low Water
NW : Red Tarn

N

KNOTT
BLENCATHRA
CLOUGH HEAD
GREAT DODD
HELVELLYN LOWER MAN
HELVELLYN
DOLLYWAGGON PIKE
NETHERMOST PIKE
STEEL FELL
HELM CRAG
SEAT SANDAL
SILVER HOW
FAIRFIELD
GREAT RIGG
HART CRAG
DOVE CRAG
REST DODD
HIGH RAISE
RED SCREES
HIGH STREET
THORNTHWAITE CRAG
LOUGHRIGG FELL
MARDALE ILL BELL
FROSWICK
ILL BELL
HARTER FELL
YOKE
KENTMERE PIKE
TARN CRAG
GREY CRAG
WANSFELL PIKE
SALLOWS
SOUR HOWES
BLACK FELL
HOLME FELL
E

S

RIDGE ROUTE

N

WETHERLAM ▲

2100
2400
2100

Swirl Hause
Black Sails ▲ 2443'

2100
2300
2200
2300

Prison Band

SWIRL HOW ▲

2100

ONE MILE

To SWIRL HOW, 2630': 1¼ miles
W, then WSW, SW, WSW
Depression at 2020'
620 feet of ascent

After an initial stony
slope, bear slightly right
across Red Dell Head and
look for a path when rougher
ground is met — it is lower on the
Greenburn edge than will be expected.
Across Swirl Hause, Prison Band looks
formidable, but its rocky turrets are
easily turned on the left
by a good stony track.

Whin Rigg

from Strands

Wasdale Head ●

SCAFELL ▲

ILLGILL HEAD ▲
● Strands
▲ WHIN RIGG

● Santon Bridge
● Eskdale Green

MILES
0   1   2   3   4

from the north-east
(on the approach from Illgill Head)

NATURAL FEATURES

No mountain in Lakeland, not even Great Gable nor Blencathra nor the Langdale Pikes, can show a grander front than Whin Rigg, modest in elevation though the latter is, and so little known that most visitors to the district will not have heard the name.   Wastwater Screes, of course, is a place familiar to many; Whin Rigg is the southern terminus of the shattered ridge above Wast Water, beyond the screes, where the great grey cliffs have resisted erosion and rise in gigantic towers over the foot of the lake to culminate finally in a small shapely summit, a proud eyrie indeed. This savage scene is tempered and given a rare beauty by the blending of dark waters and rich woodlands that form the base of every view of the soaring buttresses — but there is no denying the steepness and severity of its precipices and chasms. This is one fellside that walkers can write off at a glance as having no access for them.

The opposite flank, to the east, is, in a contrast absolute, gently graded and everywhere grassy; it descends dully to the narrow branch-valley of Miterdale, a lovely and almost secret fold of the hills, unspoiled, serene.

The southern ridge of the fell declines to the long grassy shoulder of Irton Fell and the rocky Irton Pike, now largely under timber; beyond is a pleasant countryside watered by the Esk and the Irt, both of them fed by Whin Rigg, and then, to the far horizon, is the sea.

It is along this ridge that walkers may find a simple way to the summit and so look down on the lake from the cairn, and, by going a little further, between the vertical walls of the tremendous gullies. This is dramatic scenery, quite unique, and with an abiding impression of grandeur that makes the ascent of Whin Rigg a walk to be remembered and thought about often.

MAP

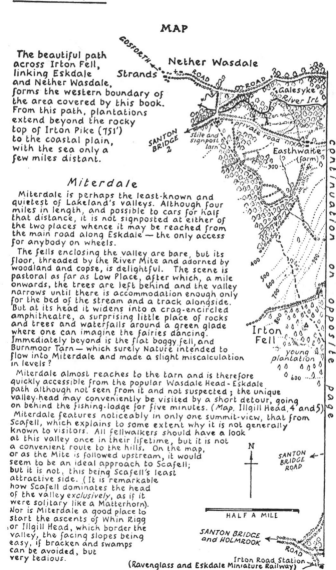

The beautiful path across Irton Fell, linking Eskdale and Nether Wasdale, forms the western boundary of the area covered by this book. From this path, plantations extend beyond the rocky top of Irton Pike (751') to the coastal plain, with the sea only a few miles distant.

Miterdale

Miterdale is perhaps the least-known and quietest of Lakeland's valleys. Although four miles in length, and possible to cars for half that distance, it is not signposted at either of the two places whence it may be reached from the main road along Eskdale — the only access for anybody on wheels.

The fells enclosing the valley are bare, but its floor, threaded by the River Mite and adorned by woodland and copse, is delightful. The scene is pastoral as far as Low Place, after which, a mile onwards, the trees are left behind and the valley narrows until there is accommodation enough only for the bed of the stream and a track alongside. But at its head it widens into a crag-encircled amphitheatre, a surprising little place of rocks and trees and waterfalls around a green glade where one can imagine the fairies dancing. Immediately beyond is the flat boggy fell, and Burnmoor Tarn — which surely Nature intended to flow into Miterdale and made a slight miscalculation in levels?

Miterdale almost reaches to the tarn and is therefore quickly accessible from the popular Wasdale Head – Eskdale path although not seen from it and not suspected; the unique valley-head may conveniently be visited by a short detour, going on behind the fishing-lodge for five minutes. (Map, Illgill Head, 4 and 5.)

Miterdale features noticeably in only one summit-view, that from Scafell, which explains to some extent why it is not generally known to visitors. All fellwalkers should have a look at this valley once in their lifetime, but it is not a convenient route to the hills. On the map, or as the Mite is followed upstream, it would seem to be an ideal approach to Scafell; but it is not, this being Scafell's least attractive side. (It is remarkable how Scafell dominates the head of the valley exclusively, as if it were solitary like a Matterhorn). Nor is Miterdale a good place to start the ascents of Whin Rigg or Illgill Head, which border the valley, the facing slopes being easy, if bracken and swamps can be avoided, but very tedious.

continuation on opposite page

HALF A MILE

(Ravenglass and Eskdale Miniature Railway)

MAP

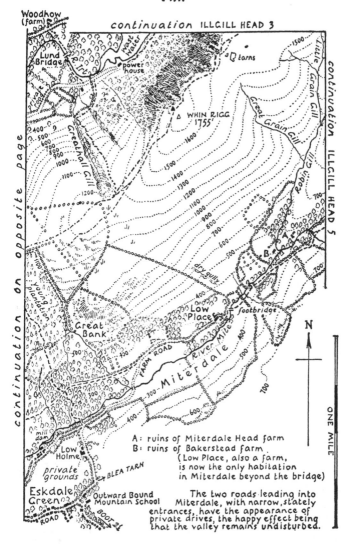

Woodhow (farm)

continuation ILLGILL HEAD 3

Lund Bridge

R. Irt

power house

Q tarns

Little Grain Gill

continuation ILLGILL HEAD 5

Greathall Gill

△ WHIN RIGG 1755

Great Grain Gill

Robin Gill

B.

continuation on opposite page

dry gully

young plantation

Great Bank

Low Place

footbridge

River Mite

N

Miterdale

mill dam

Low Holme

private grounds

BLEA TARN

Eskdale Green

Outward Bound Mountain School

ROAD

BOOT 2½

ONE MILE

A: ruins of Miterdale Head farm
B: ruins of Bakerstead farm.
(Low Place, also a farm,
is now the only habitation
in Miterdale beyond the bridge)

The two roads leading into
Miterdale, with narrow, stately
entrances, have the appearance of
private drives, the happy effect being
that the valley remains undisturbed.

ASCENT FROM NETHER WASDALE
1600 feet of ascent : 2 miles from Woodhow farm

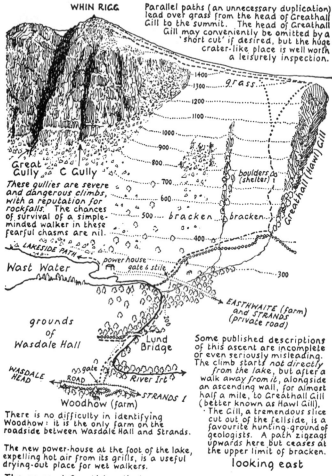

WHIN RIGG

Parallel paths (an unnecessary duplication) lead over grass from the head of Greathall Gill to the summit. The head of Greathall Gill may conveniently be omitted by a 'short cut' if desired, but the huge crater-like place is well worth a leisurely inspection.

grass

1400
1300
1200
1100
1000
900
800
700
600
500
400
300

bracken   bracken

boulders (shelter)

Greathall (Hawl) Gill

Great Gully   C Gully

These gullies are severe and dangerous climbs, with a reputation for rockfalls. The chances of survival of a simple-minded walker in these fearful chasms are nil.

LAKESIDE PATH

power house
gate & stile

Wast Water

EASTHWAITE (farm) and STRANDS (private road)

grounds of Wasdale Hall

Lund Bridge

WASDALE HEAD
ROAD   gate   River Irt   STRANDS 1
Woodhow (farm)

There is no difficulty in identifying Woodhow: it is the only farm on the roadside between Wasdale Hall and Strands.

The new power-house at the foot of the lake, expelling hot air from its grills, is a useful drying-out place for wet walkers.

Some published descriptions of this ascent are incomplete or even seriously misleading. The climb starts *not directly* from the lake, but after a walk away from it, alongside an ascending wall, for almost half a mile, to Greathall Gill (better known as Hawl Gill). The Gill, a tremendous slice cut out of the fellside, is a favourite hunting-ground of geologists. A path zigzags upwards here but ceases at the upper limit of bracken.

looking east

The reward for this climb comes not from the doing of it but from the unique, beautiful and inspiring situation to which it leads: the top of the towering crags and gullies of the Screes, a scene without a counterpart elsewhere.

ASCENT FROM ESKDALE GREEN
1650 feet of ascent · 3½ miles

looking north

Some of the young trees in the new plantation have been planted too near the path and may cause deviations in future.

When the ridge-wall is reached leave the path and turn up the fell by the far side of the wall.

head of Greathall Gill

WHIN RIGG

1600
1500
1400
1300

grass

1200

A unique, ingenious signpost (of wood)

NETHER WASDALE

grass

To ESKDALE

1100

Irton Fell

stile

1000

— artist unknown; probably the work of a forest employee. Congratulations on a bright and original idea!

900

800

Great Bank

young plantation

700

600 — stiles

500

signpost

400

Miterdale

LOW PLACE ½

farm road

River Mite

Note that the path over Irton Fell (which goes on to Nether Wasdale) starts exactly opposite the junction of the two approach roads to Miterdale (go over bridge in wood)

Although a direct ascent may be made from Miterdale up the open fell just beyond Low Place the route is dull and swampy, and the way shown on the diagram, making use of the Irton Fell path to gain the ridge, is much pleasanter, with lovely views seawards across the lower valleys of the Irt and the Esk.

mill dam

Low Holme

private grounds

ROAD

ROAD

Eskdale Green

railway   MAIN ROAD

Outward Bound Mountain School

BOOT 2½

THE SUMMIT

The cairn is so delicately poised above the cliffs that a single stride from one side to the other is sufficient to bring Wast Water into view, and a dramatic moment this is, a highlight indeed. In other directions the summit is simple; there is a second cairn on the Eskdale edge. The ridge path, grassy, passes within a few feet of the main cairn.

DESCENTS: Descend only by the routes of ascent, which are safe in mist. There is positively no way straight down to the lake. Don't be tempted into the wide opening of Great Gully: this fearful chasm has seventeen near-vertical pitches (as well as the remains of an aeroplane).

ILLGILL HEAD

THE VIEW

This is a splendid viewpoint, relying for its charm mainly on the strong contrast between the pastoral softness of the valleys of the Irt and the Esk with the sea beyond, and the sombre hills enclosing Wasdale Head.

As Whin Rigg is the nearest of the Southern Fells to Calder Hall (only seven miles away) the Atomic Power Station is seen in all its glory — if glory is the word.

Principal Fells

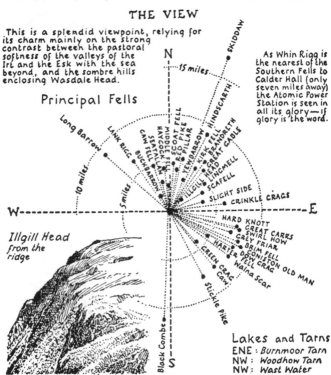

Illgill Head from the ridge

N

15 miles

SKIDDAW

Long Barrow

LANK RIGG

10 miles

5 miles

CAW FELL
SEATALLAN
HAYCOCK
MIDDLE FELL
SCOAT FELL
RED PIKE
PILLAR
YEWBARROW
KIRK FELL
HINDSCARTH
GREAT GABLE
BRANDRETH
ILLGILL HEAD
LINGMELL
SCAFELL

SLIGHT SIDE

CRINKLE CRAGS

W

E

HARD KNOTT
GREAT CARRS
SWIRL HOW
GREY FRIAR
BRIM FELL
CONISTON OLD MAN
HARTER FELL
DOW CRAG
GREEN CRAG
Walna Scar

CAW
Stickle Pike

Black Combe

S

Lakes and Tarns
ENE: Burnmoor Tarn
NW: Woodhow Tarn
NW: Wast Water

RIDGE ROUTE

To ILLGILL HEAD, 1983': 1⅓ miles : NE
Depression at 1550' : 450 feet of ascent
Easy walking ; thrilling views

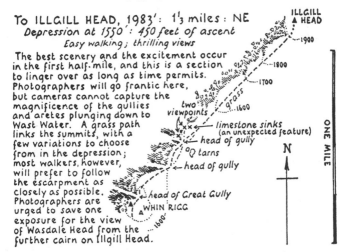

The best scenery and the excitement occur in the first half-mile, and this is a section to linger over as long as time permits. Photographers will go frantic here, but cameras cannot capture the magnificence of the gullies and aretes plunging down to Wast Water. A grass path links the summits, with a few variations to choose from in the depression; most walkers, however, will prefer to follow the escarpment as closely as possible. Photographers are urged to save one exposure for the view of Wasdale Head from the further cairn on Illgill Head.

The two viewpoints indicated on the diagram (as seen from the north-east, i.e. the Illgill Head side)

That on the left forms a small peak on the brink of the escarpment, and is a prominent object on the ridge-walk. The other is a narrow arete (Broken Rib) going down from the ridge. Both places are easily visited.

Wastwater Screes and Gullies

Here is the finest example of the natural ravages of weather, the whole fellside being in a state of decay. The disintegration of the crags has produced many grotesque formations, firm

...ctions of rock remaining like fangs amidst the crumbled debris.   (Note
he dark tower isolated in scree, 2" from the left edge of the drawing).
Climbing on these freak pinnacles and spires is unsafe.
Whin Rigg is the summit on the extreme right.

Some Personal notes
in conclusion

I have said my farewells to Mickledore and Esk Hause and Bowfell and all the other grand places described in this book, with the same 'hollow' feeling one has when taking leave of friends knowing that it may be for the last time. For the next few years I shall be engaged elsewhere, to the north and west, and although I shall be straining my eyes to see these old favourites from afar, I shall not be visiting them during this period; and perhaps never again.

There has been a clamour for Book Four ever since the first in the series appeared, and there is no doubt at all that the region of the Southern Fells has priority in the minds of most lovers of the Lake District, and especially those whose joy it is to walk upon the mountains. I agree, without saying a word to detract from the merits of other areas. All Lakeland is exquisitely beautiful; the Southern Fells just happen to be a bit of heaven fallen upon the earth.

The past two years, spent preparing the book, have been a grand experience — in spite of countless ascents of Rossett Gill (which, incidentally, seems to get easier if you keep on doing it). Fortune smiled on me hugely during the months I had set aside for the Scafells — day after day of magnificent weather, with visibility so amazingly good that one simply got used to seeing the Scottish hills and the Isle of Man permanently on the horizon. I had feared delays on the Scafells by unsuitable conditions or even normal weather, but this never happened. Many glorious mountain days, followed by happy evenings in Wasdale and Eskdale — that was the pattern for the summer of 1959.

It has taken me over 300 pages to describe the fells in this area, and I need say no more about them; but I must emphasise the supreme beauty of the approaches along the valleys — every yard of the way to the tops, and every minute of every day, is utter joy. But a special word for Eskdale: this is walkers' territory par excellence, and as traffic in other valleys increases, it is likely to become the last stronghold for travellers on foot. This lovely valley is quiet and unfrequented. I rarely met anybody when climbing out of Eskdale but, on reaching the watershed, found the ridges alive with folk who had come up from Borrowdale and Langdale.

Great Langdale is a growing problem. This used to be a walkers' valley too, and one of the best. Nowadays walkers are beginning to feel out of place. Coaches, cars, caravans, motor-bikes and tents throng the valley. One cannot complain about people who want to see the scenery but some of the characters infesting the place at weekends have eyes only for mischief. These slovenly layabouts, of both sexes, cause endless damage and trouble, and it behoves all respectable visitors (still in the majority) to help the police and farmers to preserve order. Poor Langdale! How green was my valley!

I finished the Langdale tops in 1958 but had occasion to return in the spring of 1959. Glancing up from the valley to the cairn on Pike o' Blisco (as I always do) I was dismayed to notice that it had been mutilated. I went up to see and found that the tall column of stones had been beheaded, the top part having been demolished, apparently by human agency. Are the wreckers getting up on the tops, too? ..... If all readers who visit this summit will replace one stone firmly, please, the cairn may in time again look as it does in the Pike o' Blisco chapter.

I ought to mention that I am aware that the Duddon Valley is also properly known as Dunnerdale, a name I haven't used in the book, preferring the former; just as I never refer to Blencathra by its better-known modern name of Saddleback. It's a matter of personal choice. I like the Duddon Valley and Blencathra. I don't like Dunnerdale and Saddleback.

Several letters, and even petitions, from Great Gable enthusiasts have been sent in asking me to do Book Seven next after Book Four, and Book Five last. What a frightfully untidy suggestion! It springs from a generally accepted view, of course, that there is nothing "back o' Skidda" worth exploring. I want to go and find out. There is a big tract of lonely fells here, wild and desolate; but this is immortal ground, the John Peel country, and I rely further on a centuries-old saying that "Caldbeck Fells are worth all England else." A land rich with promise, surely!

On this occasion I intend to make an excuse for defects in penmanship. I am going to lay the blame fairly and squarely on the head of Cindy, a Sealyham puppy with roving eyes, introduced to the household some time ago. Cindy has shown absolutely no sympathy whatever with my efforts to write a classic — a fearful waste of time when I might otherwise be tickling her tummy or throwing her ball or having a tug-of-war with an old stocking. Her persistent pokings and tuggings at critical moments of concentration must have resulted in inferior work, for which I am sorry. But it's Cindy's fault, not mine.

AW

Christmas
1959.